Teacher's
Resource Book

Damian Williams

A2 > Business
Partner

FT Publishing
FINANCIAL TIMES

GSE
Global Scale of English

Coursebook contents

UNIT 1 › WORKING DAY p.7
Videos: 1.1 Working day   1.4 What do you do?

1.1 › Daily tasks	1.2 › A work plan	1.3 › A survey	1.4 › Work skills: Talking about people and roles	1.5 › Business workshop: We want to meet you …
Vocabulary: Jobs and tasks **Pronunciation:** → The -s ending (p.96) **Communicative grammar:** Facts and routines **Video:** ▶ Working day **Task:** Introducing yourself and talking about your job and routine	**Vocabulary:** Work tasks and activities **Reading and listening:** ◆ Scheduling meetings **Writing:** An email to schedule a meeting	**Reading:** An employee survey **Communicative grammar:** Questions **Pronunciation:** → Questions (p.96) **Writing:** A survey about facilities in the workplace	**Video:** ▶ What do you do? **Speaking:** Talking about people and roles	**Reading:** A webpage; an email **Speaking:** Arranging to meet; an interview about your job; talking about your company and travel

Review p.87

UNIT 2 › DOING BUSINESS p.17
Videos: 2.1 The Good Eating Company   2.4 Agreeing contract details

2.1 › Orders and deliveries	2.2 › Placing orders on the phone	2.3 › Email enquiries	2.4 › Work skills: Making agreements	2.5 › Business workshop: Planning a work party
Vocabulary: Orders and deliveries **Communicative grammar:** Things you can and can't count **Video:** ▶ The Good Eating Company **Task:** Asking and answering questions about quantities	**Listening:** ◆ An order by phone **Vocabulary:** An order by phone **Pronunciation:** → /iː/, /ɪ/ and /aɪ/ (p.96) **Grammar:** can/can't **Speaking:** Placing an order	**Reading:** Frequently Asked Questions (FAQs) **Pronunciation:** → /tʃ/ and /dʒ/ (p.97) **Communicative grammar:** Saying something exists **Writing:** A response to an email enquiry	**Video:** ▶ Agreeing contract details **Speaking:** Making agreements	**Reading:** Information from a catering company **Speaking:** Comparing information about an order **Writing:** reply to an order enquiry

Review p.88

UNIT 3 › CHANGES p.27
Videos: 3.1 How we started   3.4 How did the project go?

3.1 › A company's story	3.2 › New office	3.3 › Company performance	3.4 › Work skills: How did it go?	3.5 › Business workshop: Our first year
Vocabulary: A company's story **Communicative grammar:** Talking about the past (1) **Pronunciation:** → The -ed ending (p.97) **Video:** ▶ How we started **Task:** Completing a timeline	**Vocabulary:** Email phrases **Grammar:** Giving instructions **Reading:** An email about meeting room rules **Listening:** ◆ A conversation about an office move **Writing:** An email giving instructions	**Reading:** Past successes and challenges **Pronunciation:** → /ɜː/ and /ɔː/ (p.98) **Communicative grammar:** Talking about the past (2) **Writing:** An email describing successes and challenges	**Video:** ▶ How did the project go? **Speaking:** Talking about projects	**Reading:** A timeline about a new company **Writing:** Preparing for a move **Speaking:** Asking questions about a new company; discussing a project

Review p.89

UNIT 4 › TRAVELLING FOR WORK p.37
Videos: 4.1 Away on business   4.4 Technical problems

4.1 › I'm flying to Tokyo tomorrow	4.2 › The 12.05 is delayed	4.3 › An update email	4.4 › Work skills: Setting up a video call	4.5 › Business workshop: A business trip
Vocabulary: Travel arrangements **Communicative grammar:** Talking about arrangements **Pronunciation:** → /ŋ/, /ŋk/ and /n/. The -ing ending (p.98) **Video:** ▶ Away on business **Task:** Arranging a time to meet	**Vocabulary:** Airports and train stations **Reading and listening:** ◆ Dealing with delays **Grammar:** will/won't **Writing:** Writing a text message about an announcement	**Reading:** Emails to a project manager **Communicative grammar:** Things happening now **Writing:** An update email	**Video:** ▶ Technical problems **Grammar:** Making suggestions **Speaking:** Problems with teleconferencing **Pronunciation:** → /ɪə/ and /eə/ (p.98)	**Reading:** Travel arrangements **Listening:** ◆ A change in plans **Speaking:** Arranging a meeting **Writing:** Text messages giving updates

Review p.90

UNIT 5 > ORGANISING p.47

Videos: 5.1 Graduate Fashion Week   5.4 What do you think of the trade fair?

5.1 > Trade shows and exhibitions	5.2 > Phoning about a conference	5.3 > Invitations	5.4 > Work skills: Socialising with clients	5.5 > Business workshop: The conference
Vocabulary: Organising an exhibition **Communicative grammar:** Talking about intentions **Pronunciation:** /æ/, /e/ and /eɪ/ (p.99) **Video:** Graduate Fashion Week **Task:** Talking abut plans for a trade fair	**Vocabulary:** Leaving a message **Listening:** Organising a conference **Speaking:** Taking and leaving phone messages	**Reading:** Messages about an invitation **Communicative grammar:** Invitations with *would* and *want* **Pronunciation:** /θ/ and /ð/ vs. /s/, /z/, /f/, /v/, /t/, /d/ (p.99) **Writing:** Informal messages of invitation	**Video:** What do you think of the trade fair? **Speaking:** Socialising with clients	**Speaking:** Phoning to compare conference details **Writing:** An email about a conference **Speaking:** Making conversation at a conference dinner

Review p.91

UNIT 6 > PRODUCTS p.57

Videos: 6.1 Industry futures   6.4 How many do you want to order?

6.1 > Future products	6.2 > A problem with an order	6.3 > The production process	6.4 > Work skills: Placing an order	6.5 > Business workshop: Buy natural
Vocabulary: Technology and the environment **Communicative grammar:** Speculating about the future **Video:** Industry futures **Task:** Talking about the future	**Listening:** A problem with an order **Vocabulary:** Helping with a problem **Pronunciation:** /ɑː/ and /ʌ/ (p.99) **Speaking:** Phoning and answering as customer services	**Reading:** Environment and ethics **Communicative grammar:** Describing production **Pronunciation:** /uː/ and /ʊ/ (p.100) **Writing:** A description for a company website	**Video:** How many do you want to order? **Speaking:** Placing an order	**Reading:** A company website about ethical products **Speaking:** Placing an order; making a complaint about an order

Review p.92

UNIT 7 > COMPETITION p.67

Videos: 7.1 Comparing sports cars   7.4 Our products and services

7.1 > Should I upgrade?	7.2 > Services	7.3 > The best providers	7.4 > Work skills: Presentations	7.5 > Business workshop: The big contract
Vocabulary: Product qualities **Listening:** Talking about using a product **Communicative grammar:** Comparing (1): comparatives **Video:** Comparing sports cars **Task:** Comparing two models	**Vocabulary:** Fees **Pronunciation:** /əʊ/ and /aʊ/ (p.100) **Listening:** Comparing recruitment agencies **Writing:** An advertisement for services	**Reading:** An email comparing services **Communicative grammar:** Comparing (2): superlatives **Writing:** An email summarising survey results **Pronunciation:** /p/, /b/, /f/ and /v/ (p.100)	**Video:** Our products and services **Speaking:** Presenting	**Reading:** An email about a trade show **Speaking:** Giving presentations **Writing:** A summary email giving a recommendation

Review p.93

UNIT 8 > JOBS p.77

Videos: 8.1 Skills and experience   8.4 The job interview

8.1 > Work experience	8.2 > The best person for the job	8.3 > Professional profiles	8.4 > Work skills: A job interview	8.5 > Business workshop: The interviewer and the candidate
Vocabulary: Skills and personal qualities **Communicative grammar:** Talking about experience **Video:** Skills and experience **Task:** Asking and answering interview questions	**Vocabulary:** Job requirements **Listening:** Choosing job candidates **Pronunciation:** The vowel /ɒ/. The letter 'o' as /ɒ/, /əʊ/ and /ʌ/ (p.101) **Speaking:** Describing and comparing candidates	**Reading:** A professional profile **Communicative grammar:** Talking about experiences and completed past events **Pronunciation:** Silent letters (p.101) **Writing:** An employee profile	**Video:** The job interview **Speaking:** Job interviews	**Speaking:** Interview questions; choosing the best candidate for the job

Review p.94

Pronunciation p.95   Grammar reference p.102   Irregular verbs list p.114   Additional material p.115   Videoscripts p.129   Audioscripts p.133

Contents

	Introduction	**5**
Unit 1	**Working day**	**19**
	Unit overview	19
	Unit vocabulary list	20
	Teaching notes	21–30
Unit 2	**Doing business**	**31**
	Unit overview	31
	Unit vocabulary list	32
	Teaching notes	33–41
Unit 3	**Changes**	**42**
	Unit overview	42
	Unit vocabulary list	43
	Teaching notes	44–53
Unit 4	**Travelling for work**	**54**
	Unit overview	54
	Unit vocabulary list	55
	Teaching notes	56–64
Unit 5	**Organising**	**65**
	Unit overview	65
	Unit vocabulary list	66
	Teaching notes	67–75
Unit 6	**Products**	**76**
	Unit overview	76
	Unit vocabulary list	77
	Teaching notes	78–86
Unit 7	**Competition**	**87**
	Unit overview	87
	Unit vocabulary list	88
	Teaching notes	89–98
Unit 8	**Jobs**	**99**
	Unit overview	99
	Unit vocabulary list	100
	Teaching notes	101–109
	Resource bank	110
	Videoscripts	145
	Audioscripts	149

Introduction

Overview

Business Partner is students' 'Employability Trainer' because it focusses on both language and skills for work. The beginner and elementary levels are designed for learners who have had little exposure to English, or who may have studied English before, at school or privately, but what they learnt has not been very useful for them in their job, or they just don't remember much.

- Now they need to study business English in order to better communicate in a workplace that is increasingly international.
- To achieve this, they need to improve their knowledge of the English language but also develop key work skills.
- They need a course that is relevant to their professional needs.

Business Partner has been designed to enable teachers to meet these needs without spending many hours researching their own materials. The content and structure of the course is based on these key concepts: **employability**, **learner engagement and relevance**.

Course aims and key concepts

Employability

Balance between language and work skills training

In order to be more comfortable in an international workplace, learners of all ages and professional contexts need to improve their knowledge of the English language as it is used in the workplace. They must also develop key communication skills.

In addition to building their vocabulary and grammar, the key principle of *Business Partner* is to build learning around situations in which our A2 students may find themselves and help them to acquire language to function in these situations. Students learn through engaging content which is divided into short, manageable chunks and is relevant to their experience.

Learner engagement and relevance

One key element of learner engagement is to make sure that students relate to the material they use; that it is relevant to their needs. All the content in *Business Partner* is rooted in real needs of real people in real life, and pair work or group work requires learners to be themselves, and to practise the language that they will need to use in their real job.

Using business English teaching materials with learners who have little or no work experience can be particularly challenging, even more so at elementary level. *Business Partner* has been carefully designed for such students, as well as for in-work professionals. In the case of collaborative speaking tasks and roleplays, the situation used will either be:

- one that we can all relate to as customers and consumers.
- a mix of professional and everyday situations.

Both will allow learners to practise the skill and language presented in the lesson, but in a context that is most relevant to them, and with as much or as little language as they may have acquired at any given point.

In order to engage learners, two lessons in each unit (Lesson 1 and Lesson 4) are based around video materials. In Lesson 1 videos, learners will watch professionals talking about their work experience, and the businesses and industries they work in. Videos in Lesson 4 will show workplace situations in which professionals interact. For more on videos in the course, see page 6.

Approach to teaching

Vocabulary

The acquisition of vocabulary and functional language is the number one priority for many students in business English classes. The vocabulary and functional phrases in each unit focus on industries and work environments that are relevant to students to help them function in a variety of professional situations.

This vocabulary has been selected to answer learner's needs at work and may seem high level or technical compared to a general English course; it is, however, based on the frequency with which the given topics come up in a work situation and reflects the basic professional vocabulary that learners need in order to function in their jobs.

Introduction

Vocabulary sets are introduced in Lessons 1 and 2. Extra activities, available in MyEnglishLab and at the Pearson English Portal, are signposted in lessons and offer additional vocabulary practice. Students can revise unit vocabulary on their own through Extra vocabulary practice worksheets. These worksheets are available for students in MyEnglishLab and to teachers in MyEnglishLab and at the Pearson English Portal. See page 18 for a detailed list of additional materials.

Grammar

The grammar syllabus comes from the communicative needs of learners at elementary level and is taught through a communicative approach. This means that the Communicative grammar boxes aim to teach grammar through its function: whole sentences are presented in these boxes so that students can use the phrases appropriately without having to worry about rules and explanations. Full explanations and additional grammar practice activities are available in the Grammar reference at the back of the book.

As with vocabulary, some of the grammar points may seem higher than A2 level compared to a general English course, but this is done to ensure that students have the grammar they need to function in specific work situations.

Grammar is introduced in Lessons 1 and 3, with additional grammar points appearing throughout the unit, where relevant.

Listening

The course has a listening syllabus based on both videos and audio recordings. The listening activities are based on work scenarios and are mostly business calls or business meetings.

Listening activities appear in Lessons 1, 2, 4 and some Business workshops. They serve three purposes: to demonstrate a model professional interaction, to reinforce key language, and to help develop comprehension skills by hearing language in context.

Lesson 1 video: the video material provides beginner and elementary-level learners with accessible authentic content. The videos are mostly interviews with professionals who talk about their work life or company. The video appears at the end of Lesson 1 and recycles the vocabulary and structures from the lesson. It is followed by a comprehension task and a speaking task. The videos can also be used as a model for students in the final speaking task.

Lesson 4 video: A short Work skills video in Lesson 4 of each unit shows people in a range of typical work situations. The videos present functional language used in work situations and offer students a model for the speaking task.

All of the video and audio material is available in MyEnglishLab and at the Pearson English Portal and includes a range of British, U.S. and non-native-speaker English, so that learners are exposed to a variety of accents, to reflect the reality of their working lives.

See page 18 for a detailed list of additional materials.

Speaking

Speaking is a central feature of the course. It is essential to give students the ability to speak from the very early stages of learning. There are plenty of opportunities for speaking practice in relevant and engaging activities in each lesson. The objective is to make apprehensive students feel comfortable developing this skill, which is essential for the workplace.

The main focus of Lesson 4 is speaking based on the authentic interactions that have been presented in the lesson's video. In addition, every Lesson 1 and four Lesson 2s end with a speaking task based on the content practised during the lesson. All Business workshops have speaking activities that elicit the language taught in the unit. Throughout the book there are also many 'embedded' speaking opportunities, for example the communicative practice of vocabulary and grammar points.

Extra speaking lessons are available to the teacher in MyEnglishLab and at the Pearson English Portal. These lessons offer additional speaking practice for the language introduced in Lesson 4 of each unit.

The Photocopiable materials section of the Teacher's Books offers additional speaking activities. See page 18 for a detailed list of additional materials.

Writing

Learners at this level need to respond to emails and other functional pieces of writing. The writing activities provide a model for students to follow, showing the grammar structures they need to use when writing, and functional language stems to help them. The writing tasks allow freer practice of the target vocabulary and grammar and offer elements of personalisation where possible.

The main focus of Lesson 3 is writing, with a focus on practising longer forms of writing such as emails. Four Lesson 2s practise shorter guided forms of writing, whereas the writing tasks in the Business workshops require students to use language from the whole unit, and therefore act as a form of revision.

Pronunciation

Two pronunciation points are presented and practised in every unit and are linked to the content of the unit. The Pronunciation bank is at the back of the Coursebook with signposts from the relevant lessons. This section also includes a phonetic chart for British English and American English.

Business workshop lessons at the end of each unit give learners the opportunity to consolidate and activate the language and skills from the unit. They provide interesting and engaging scenarios where students simulate real-life professional situations. Students will have been exposed to and will have practised in the previous lessons enough language to successfully communicate in these situations, thereby adding to their sense of progression and achievement. The Business workshops can also be used by the teacher to informally assess how well students managed to acquire the language from the unit and if any language needs revisiting.

Flexibility

Business Partner offers the teacher the possibility to be flexible with the material. The following signposts in the Coursebook indicate where additional materials offering further practice of the language covered are available:

> **T** Teacher's resources: extra activities

These are PDFs that can be found in the Teacher's Resources folder in MyEnglishLab or Resources section of the Pearson English Portal. Teachers can download and print them or display them on screen.

> Grammar reference: page 000

This section at the back of the book has complete grammar explanations and additional grammar practice activities.

> → page 000 See Pronunciation bank

This section at the back of the book introduces two pronunciation points per unit, which are directly linked to the language used in the lesson.

There are additional worksheets available for the teacher at the Pearson English Portal and in MyEnglishLab. For a list of all the extra materials available at the Pearson English Portal and in MyEnglishLab see page 18.

Approach to testing and assessment

Business Partner provides a balance of formative and summative assessment. Both types of assessment are important for teachers and learners and have different objectives. Regular reviews and ongoing assessment allow students to evaluate their own progress and encourage them to persevere in their studies. Formal testing offers a more precise measurement of the progress made in their knowledge and proficiency.

Formative assessment: Each Coursebook lesson is framed by a clear lesson outcome which summarises the learning deliverable. The lesson ends with a short self-assessment objective which encourages students to reflect on their progress in relation to the lesson outcome.

The course also contains one review page per unit at the back of the book to recycle and revise the key vocabulary, grammar and functional language presented in the unit. The Business workshop can also be used as part of formative assessment as the tasks are designed to elicit language students learnt in the unit.

Introduction

Summative assessment: Unit tests and an end-of-year test can be found in MyEnglishLab in the Teacher's Resources folder and at the Pearson English Portal. They are available in PDF and Word formats so that you can adapt them to suit your purposes. They are also available as interactive tests that you can allocate to your students if you wish to do so. These tests can also be used as additional revision material.

The Global Scale of English

The Global Scale of English (GSE) is a standardised, granular scale from 10 to 90 which measures English language proficiency. The GSE Learning Objectives for Professional English are aligned with the Common European Framework of Reference (CEFR). Unlike the CEFR, which describes proficiency in terms of broad levels, the Global Scale of English identifies what a learner can do at each point on a more granular scale – and within a CEFR level. The scale is designed to motivate learners by demonstrating incremental progress in their language ability. The Global Scale of English forms the backbone for Pearson English course material and assessment.

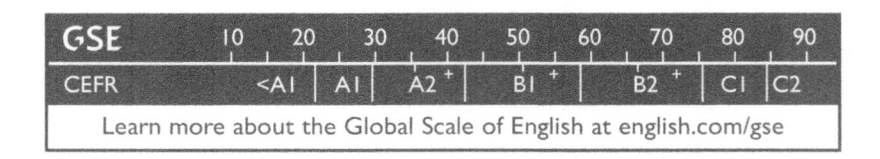

GSE	10	20	30	40	50	60	70	80	90
CEFR	<A1	A1	A2+		B1+		B2+	C1	C2

Learn more about the Global Scale of English at english.com/gse

Business Partner has been written based on these Learning Objectives, which ensure appropriate scaffolding and measurable progress. Each lesson outcome in each lesson in the Coursebook encapsulates a number of special Learning Objectives which are listed in this Teacher's Resource Book in the Teaching notes. The GSE Learning Objectives for the whole coursebook are listed in the GSE Mapping Booklets, which are available for download from https://www.pearson.com/english/catalogue/business-english/business-partner/levels.html.

Course structure

Business Partner is an eight-level course based on the Global Scale of English (GSE) and representing the CEFR levels: A1, A2, A2+, B1, B1+, B2, B2+, C1.

	For the teacher	For the student
print		Coursebook (with Digital Resources) Workbook
blended	Teacher's Resource Book with MyEnglishLab	Coursebook with MyEnglishLab (= interactive workbook practice)
digital	Presentation tool (Pearson English Portal)	Coursebook ebook

Introduction

Business Partner is a fully hybrid course with two digital dimensions that students and teachers can choose from. MyEnglishLab is the digital component that is integrated with the book content.

Access to MyEnglishLab is given through a code printed on the inside front cover of this book. As a teacher, you have access to both versions of MyEnglishLab, and to additional content in the Teacher's Resource folder.

Depending on the version that students are using, they will have access to one of the following:

Digital Resources includes downloadable coursebook resources, all video clips, all audio files, Extra Coursebook activities (PDFs), Extra vocabulary practice worksheets and additional interactive activities.

MyEnglishLab includes all of the **Digital Resources** plus the full functionality and content of the self-study interactive workbook with automatic gradebook. Teachers can also create a group or class in their own MyEnglishLab and assign workbook activities as homework.

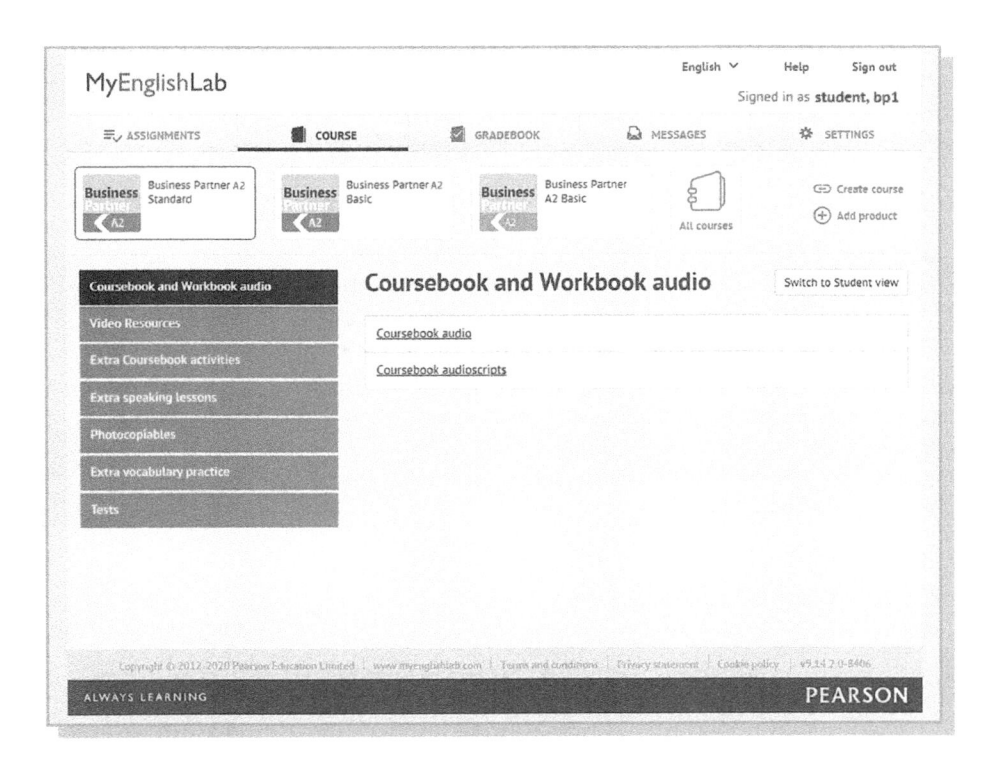

Components for the learner

Coursebook
(with access code for MyEnglishLab)

- Eight units, each containing five lessons (see pages 12–17 for unit overview)
- Eight Business workshop lessons relating to each of the eight units
- A one-page Review per unit to revise key language and grammar
- A Pronunciation section which practises two points from each unit
- A Grammar reference with detailed explanations, examples and additional grammar practice
- Videoscripts and audioscripts
- A list of key vocabulary by lesson

Coursebook video and audio material is available on MyEnglishLab.

MyEnglishLab digital component

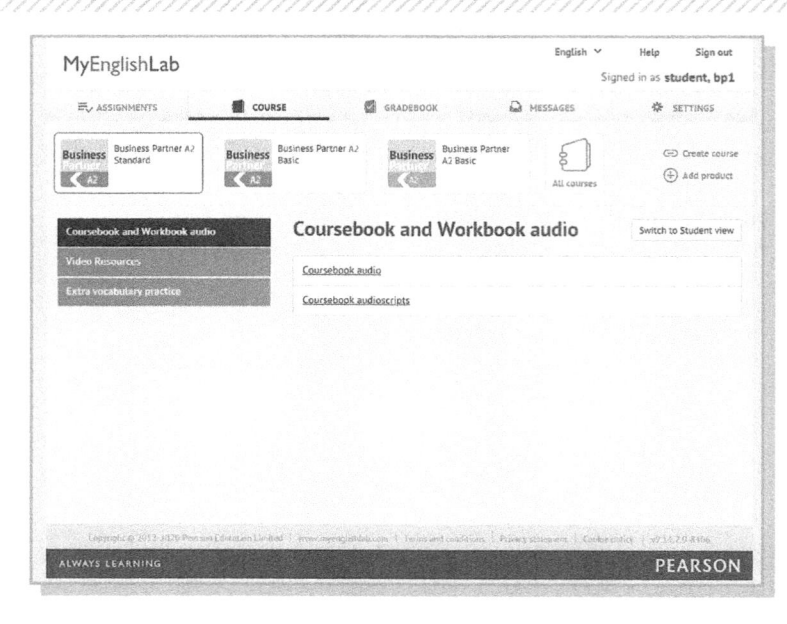

Accessed using the code printed on the inside cover of the Coursebook. Depending on the version of the course that you are using, learners will have access to one of the following options:

Digital resources powered by MyEnglishLab
- Video clips
- Audio files and scripts
- Extra vocabulary practice worksheets
- Additional interactive activities
- Workbook audio files and scripts

Full content of MyEnglishLab
- All of the above
- Interactive self-study Workbook with automatic feedback and gradebook

Workbook

- Additional self-study practice activities. Activities cover vocabulary, grammar, functional language, reading, listening and writing.
- Additional self-study practice activities for points presented in the Coursebook Pronunciation bank
- Answer key
- Audioscripts

Workbook audio is available on MyEnglishLab.

Components for the teacher

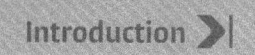

Teacher's Resource Book (with access code for MyEnglishLab)

- Teaching notes for every lesson including warm-ups, background /culture notes and answer keys
- Active/Passive vocabulary list
- Photocopiable activities – two per unit with teaching notes and answer keys
- Extra vocabulary practice worksheets
- Videoscripts and audioscripts

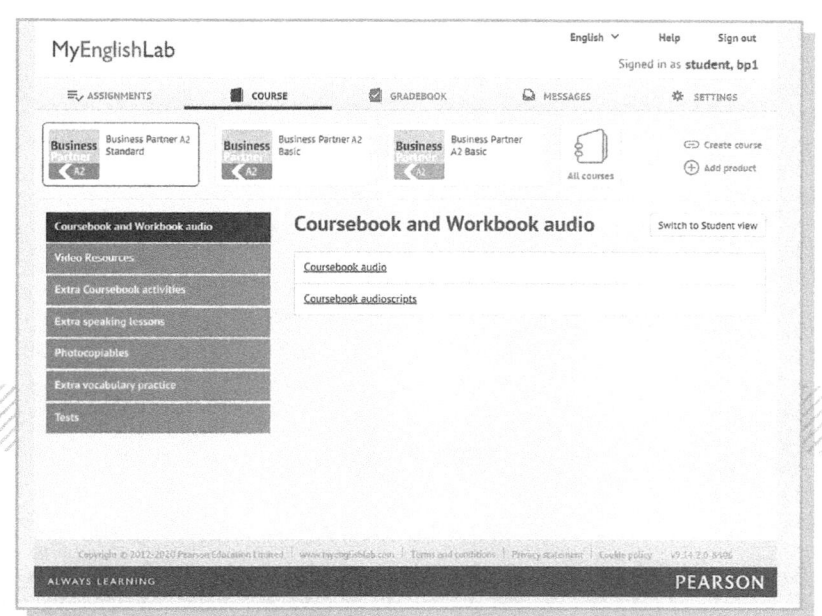

MyEnglishLab digital component

Accessed using the code printed on the inside cover of the Teacher's Resource Book.

Coursebook resources
- Video clips and scripts
- Audio files and scripts
- Extra Coursebook activities (PDFs)

Workbook resources
- Self-study interactive version of the Workbook with automatic feedback and gradebook
- Teachers can assign Workbook activities as homework
- Workbook audio files and audioscripts

Teacher's Book resources
- Extra speaking lessons
- Photocopiable activities + teaching notes and answer keys
- Extra vocabulary practice worksheets

Tests
- Unit tests (PDFs and Word), including exam task types
- Interactive Unit tests, with automatic gradebook
- Tests audio files
- Tests answer keys

Pearson English Portal

- Digital version of the Teacher's Resource Book
- Digital version of the Coursebook with classroom tools for use on an interactive whiteboard
- Video clips and scripts
- Audio files and scripts
- Extra Coursebook activities (PDFs)
- Extra speaking lessons
- Extra vocabulary practice worksheets

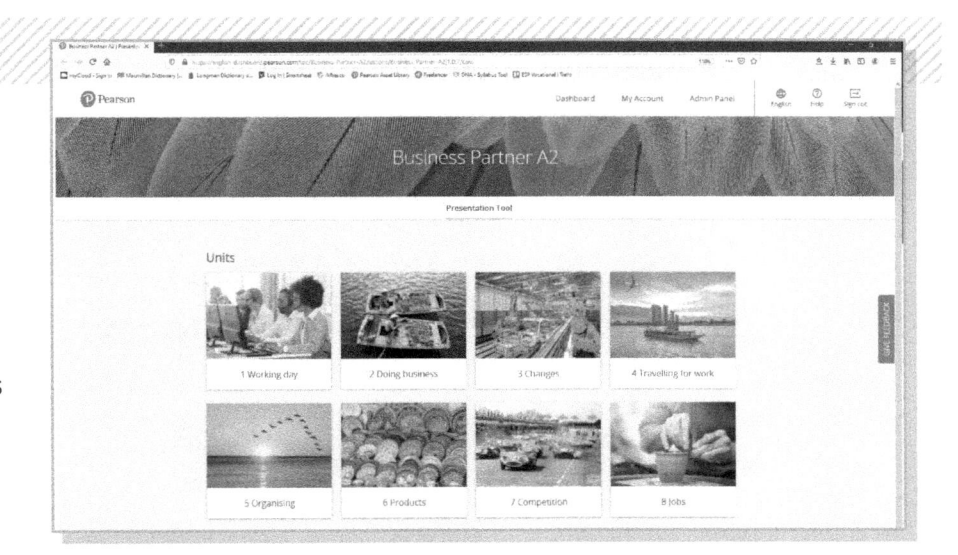

A unit of the Coursebook

Unit overview page

①▶ The unit overview summarises the contents of each lesson as well as the lesson outcomes.
②▶ There are also references to content at the back of the book, which supplements the main unit.

Travelling for work 4▶

> Are you travelling for work next week?

①▶ Unit overview

4.1▶ I'm flying to Tokyo tomorrow
Lesson outcome: Learners can talk about travel arrangements.

Vocabulary: Travel arrangements
Communicative grammar: Talking about arrangements
Video: Away on business
Task: Arranging a time to meet

4.2▶ The 12.05 is delayed
Lesson outcome: Learners can write a text message to apologise and explain why they are late.

Vocabulary: Airports and train stations
Reading and listening: Dealing with delays
Writing: Writing a text message about an announcement

4.3▶ An update email
Lesson outcome: Learners can write an update email about work they are doing now.

Reading: Emails to a Project Manager
Communicative grammar: Things happening now
Writing: An update email

4.4▶ Work skills: Setting up a video call
Lesson outcome: Learners can set up a video call and fix problems.

Video: Technical problems
Speaking: Problems with teleconferencing

4.5▶ Business workshop: A business trip
Lesson outcome: Learners can deal with arrangements for a business trip.

Reading: Travel arrangements
Listening and speaking: A change in plans
Writing: Text messages giving updates

②▶ **Review 4:** p.90 | **Pronunciation:** 4.1 /ŋ/, /ŋk/ and /n/. The -ing ending 4.4 /ɪə/ and /eə/ p.98 | **Grammar reference:** 4.1 Talking about arrangements 4.2 will / won't 4.3 Things happening now 4.4 Making suggestions p.106

Lesson 1 ▸ Vocabulary and Grammar

The aims of this lesson are:
- to present and practise topic vocabulary in business contexts.
- to present and practise grammar using a communicative approach.
- to engage students with the unit topic by exploring a video about real people and real companies, which reinforces the vocabulary and grammar presented in the lesson.
- to encourage students to activate the language they have learnt by collaborating in pairs in the final task.

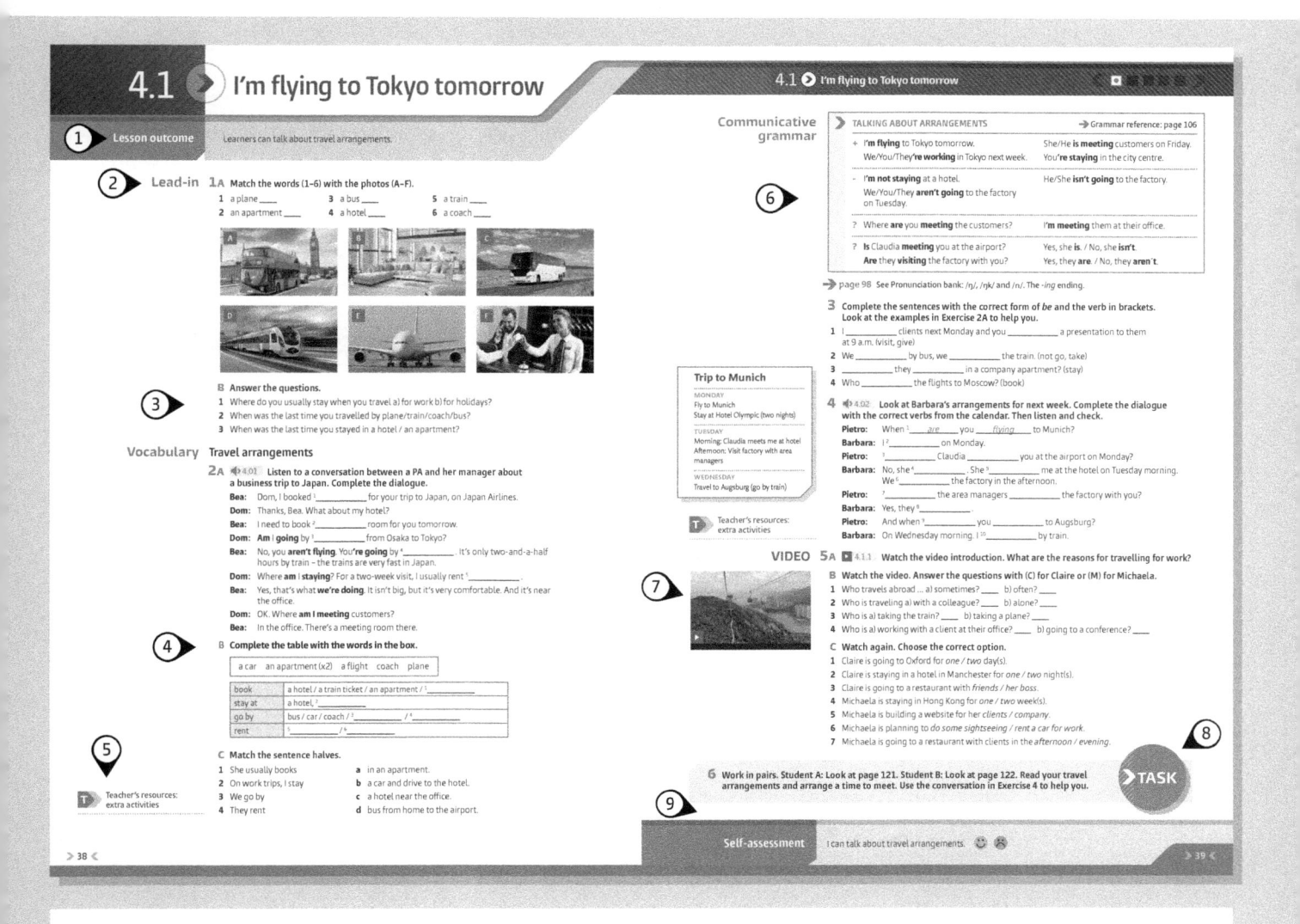

① The lesson outcome defines a clear learning outcome for every lesson. Each lesson outcome encapsulates a number of specific Learning Objectives for Professional English which are listed in this Teacher's Resource Book in the Teaching notes.

② Every lesson begins with a short Lead-in activity to engage learners with the lesson topic.

③ The tasks and questions in the lesson provide an opportunity for personalisation.

④ The lesson vocabulary set is presented, practised and then recycled in the video before being activated in the task.

⑤ **Teacher's resources: extra activities** Extra activities are clearly signposted. These are PDFs in MyEnglishLab and Pearson English Portal to display on-screen or print. They can be used to extend a lesson or to focus in more depth on a particular section.

⑥ Every Lesson 1 has a Communicative grammar box, presenting the first of two main grammar points in a unit, followed by practice activities.

⑦ Every Lesson 1 has an authentic video with comprehension activities, which can be used as a model for students in the final speaking task.

⑧ The Task at the end of Lesson 1 is a collaborative pairwork activity with a strong emphasis on communication.

⑨ Every lesson ends with a short Self-assessment section which encourages learners to think about the progress they have made in relation to the lesson outcome.

Introduction

Lesson 2 » Reading or Listening

The aims of this lesson are:
- to provide examples of real-life workplace written or spoken communication through reading or listening activities.
- to present and practise topic vocabulary in business contexts.
- to encourage students to activate the vocabulary point they have practised through communicative speaking or writing activities.

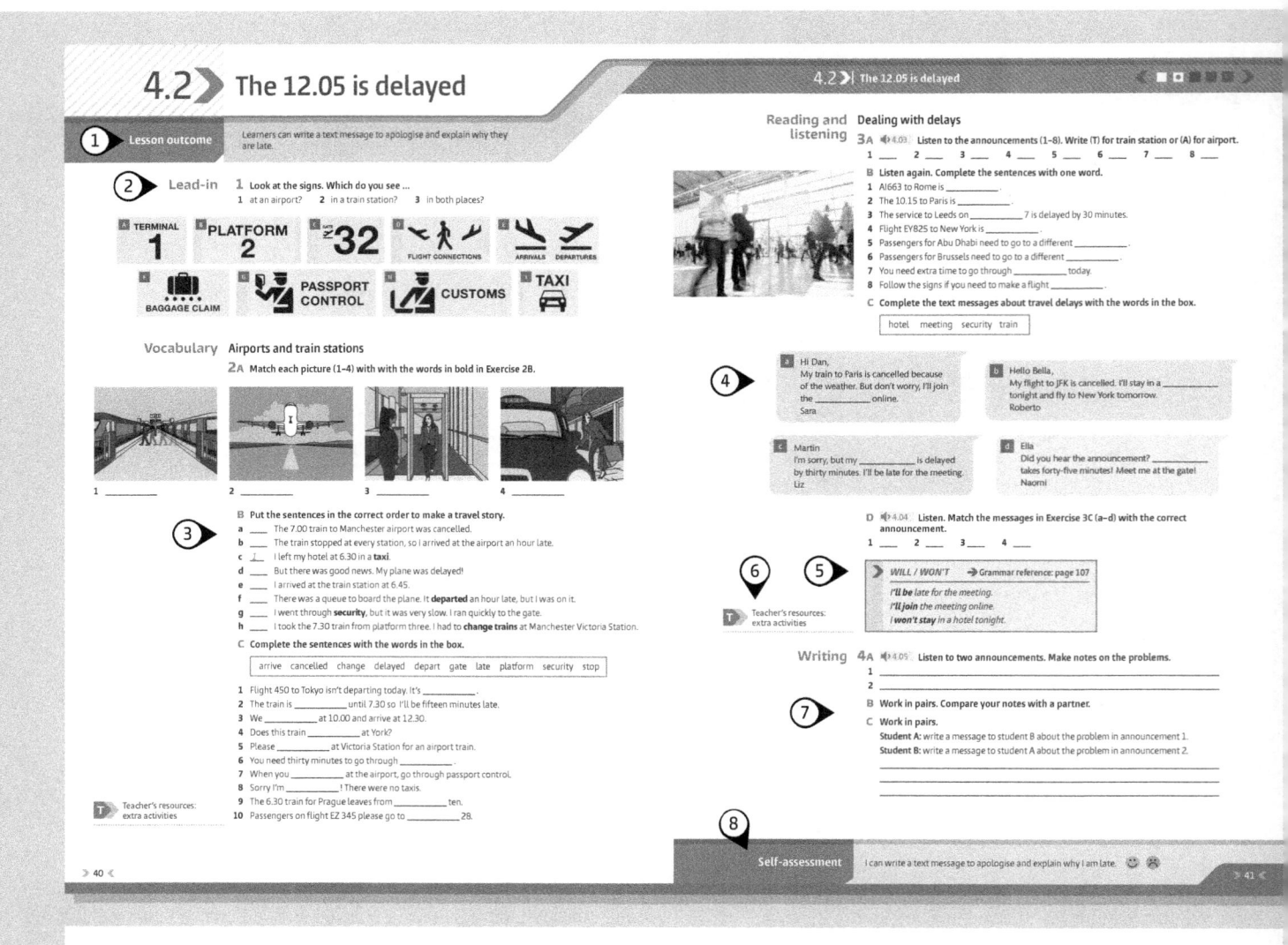

① The lesson outcome defines a clear learning outcome for every lesson. Each lesson outcome encapsulates a number of specific Learning Objectives for Professional English which are listed in this Teacher's Resource Book in the Teaching notes.

② Every lesson begins with a short Lead-in activity to engage learners with the lesson topic.

③ The lesson vocabulary set is presented, practised and then recycled in the listening or reading section before being activated in the final speaking or writing exercise.

④ The reading or listening section often features a business-related form of communication, such as a chat message, an email or phone call.

⑤ In some units, there are extra grammar boxes which highlight additional useful bite-size grammar points that appear in the reading or listening. More practice of these grammar points appears in the grammar reference.

⑥ **Teacher's resources: extra activities** Extra activities are clearly signposted. These are PDFs in MyEnglishLab and Pearson English Portal to display on-screen or print. They can be used to extend a lesson or to focus in more depth on a particular section.

⑦ The final exercise in this lesson is either Speaking or Writing, depending on the unit. It enables the learner to use English in the situational business contexts of the lesson.

⑧ Every lesson ends with a short Self-assessment section which encourages learners to think about the progress they have made in relation to the lesson outcome.

Introduction

Lesson 3 ▶ Grammar and Writing

The aims of this lesson are:
- to present and practise grammar, using a communicative approach.
- to present and practise the skills involved with written business communication.

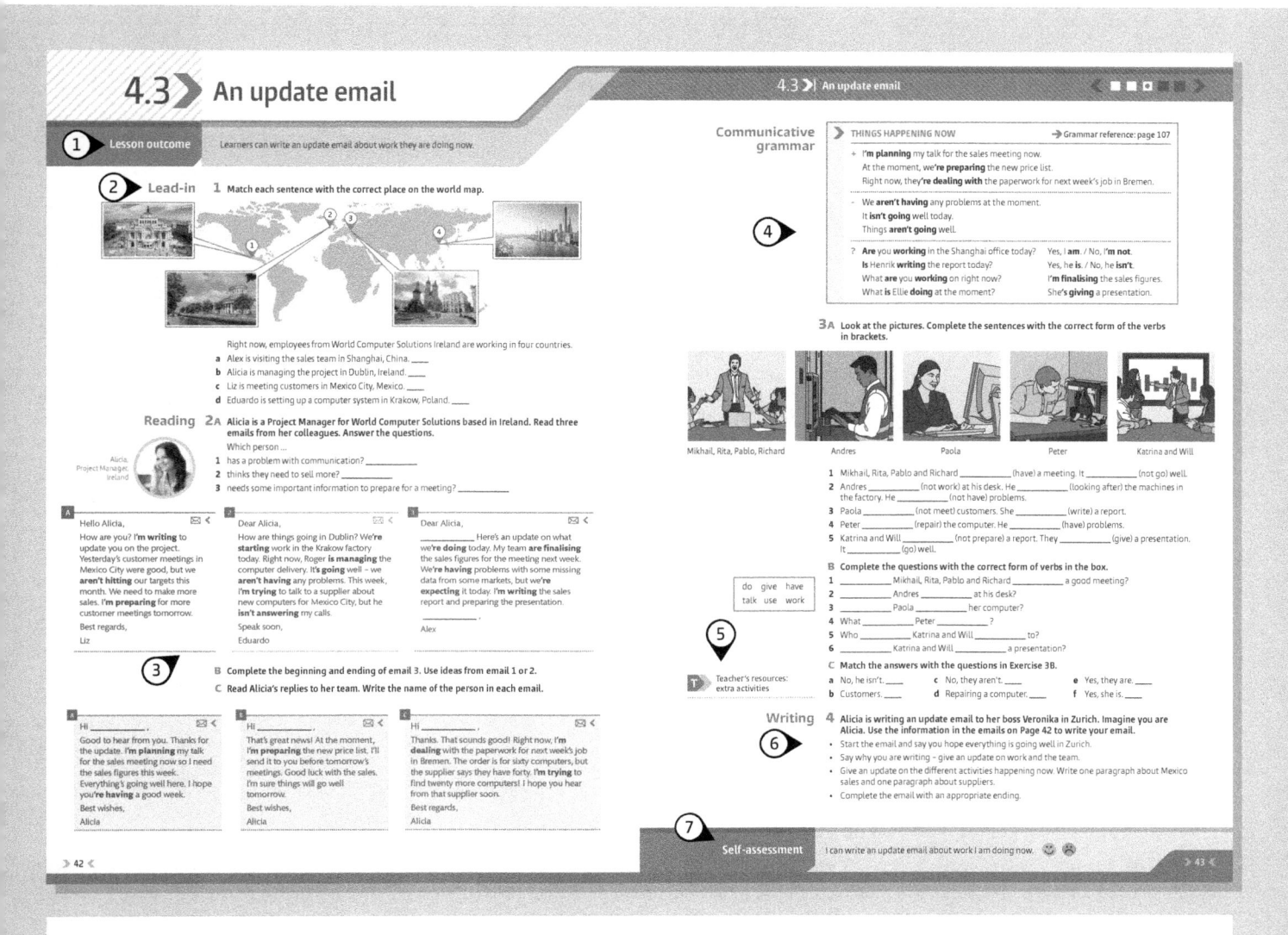

① The lesson outcome defines a clear learning outcome for every lesson. Each lesson outcome encapsulates a number of specific Learning Objectives for Professional English which are listed in this Teacher's Resource Book in the Teaching notes.

② Every lesson begins with a short Lead-in activity to engage learners with the lesson topic.

③ Every writing lesson has a model text, which includes the target grammar in context, in a specific form of business communication.

④ Every Lesson 3 has a Communicative grammar box, presenting the second of two main grammar points in a unit, followed by practice activities.

⑤ **Teacher's resources: extra activities** Extra activities are clearly signposted. These are PDFs in MyEnglishLab to display on-screen or print. They can be used to extend a lesson or to focus in more depth on a particular section.

⑥ The final Writing section allows students to actively reproduce the model reading text, using the grammar taught in the lesson.

⑦ Every lesson ends with a short Self-assessment section which encourages learners to think about the progress they have made in relation to the lesson outcome.

15

Introduction

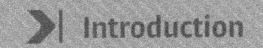

Lesson 4 ▶ Work skills

The aims of this lesson are:
- to present a model of best-practice communication for customer-facing interactions or internal communications within the team, such as meetings or presentations.
- to enable students to successfully communicate in different workplace situations through roleplay.

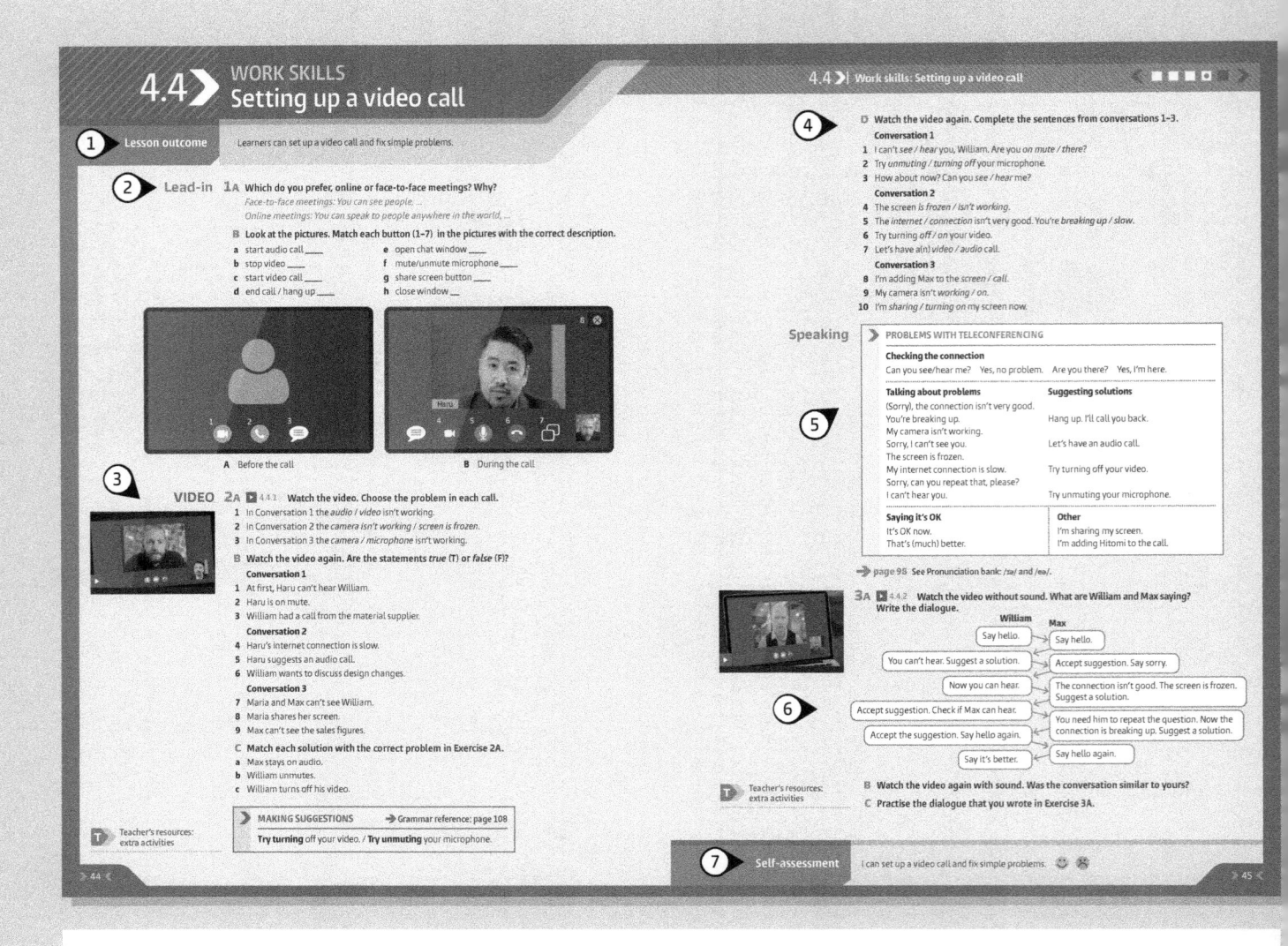

① The lesson outcome defines a clear learning outcome for every lesson. Each lesson outcome encapsulates a number of specific Learning Objectives for Professional English which are listed in this Teacher's Resource Book in the Teaching notes.

② Every lesson begins with a short Lead-in activity to engage learners with the lesson topic. The tasks and questions in the lesson provide an opportunity for personalisation.

③ The video demonstrates best practice in workplace situations and also presents the functional language necessary to perform the final task in the lesson.

④ The video is followed by practice of functional language from the video.

⑤ The Speaking box focusses on key functional language necessary to successfully perform in the final speaking task. The language is grouped clearly by functional purpose.

⑥ The final Speaking task enables students to perform in English in a workplace situation, using the functional language from the Speaking box.

⑦ Every lesson ends with a short Self-assessment section which encourages learners to think about the progress they have made in relation to the lesson outcome.

Business workshops

The aims of the Business workshops are:
- to encourage students to actively use the vocabulary, grammar and functional language from previous lessons in the unit in a series of related productive tasks in a specific workplace scenario.
- to provide further opportunity for students to demonstrate in freer practice the language they have learnt, by replicating the productive tasks from previous lessons in the unit.
- to enable teachers to review students' progress over the course of the unit and identify gaps in their learning.

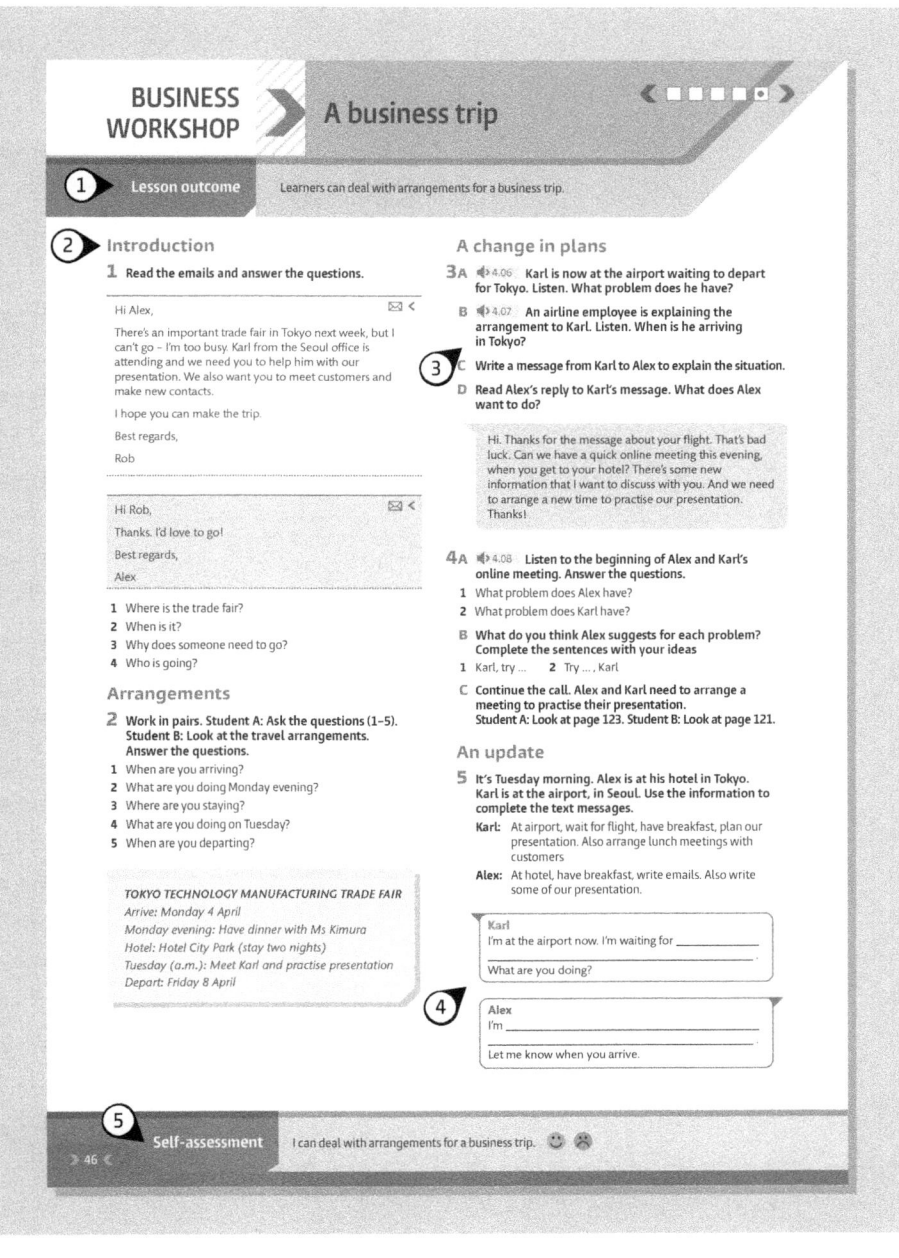

(1) The lesson outcome encompasses learning outcomes from previous lessons, making it clear which language and skills from the unit the lesson revises.

(2) The first exercise introduces a problem or a scenario that students will need to deal with and participate in.

(3) Every Business workshop includes productive tasks that echo real work-life situations, in which students need to actively use the language from the unit. In the Unit 4 Business workshop, Exercise 3 links back to Lesson 4.2, Exercise 4 to Lesson 4.4 and Exercise 5 to Lesson 4.3.

(4) During certain exercises, students are given additional scaffolding and/or revision of the target language needed for the productive tasks.

(5) Every Business workshop ends with a short Self-assessment section which encourages learners to think about the progress they have made in relation to the lesson outcome.

Introduction

Extra material

Content	For the teacher Available on MyEnglishLab and at the Pearson English Portal	For the learner Available on MyEnglishLab	Notes
Extra coursebook activities with answer key	✓	✗	Available for every **lesson 1-4**, offering additional language practice
Extra speaking lessons with teaching notes and answer keys	✓	✗	Additional speaking lessons reinforcing language from **Lesson 4**
Photocopiables with teaching notes and answer keys	✓	✗	Grammar (either from Lesson 1 or 3) and **Work skills** revision designed for use in class
Extra vocabulary practice worksheets with answer key	✓	✓	Revision of unit vocabulary for self-study or use in class
Irregular verbs list with audio	✓	✓	Available as a printable PDF page with audio recordings of irregular verbs
Coursebook audio	✓	✓	Available as downloadable MP3s
Workbook audio	✓	✓	Available as downloadable MP3s
Tests – in PDF format	✓	✗	Eight Unit tests consisting of a Language section (testing grammar, vocabulary and functional language) and a Skills section (testing reading, listening, and writing) One End-of-level test.
– in Word	✓	✗	
– interactive tasks	✓	✗	Tests tasks are only visible to students if assigned by the teacher
Tests answer key, audio and audioscript	✓	✗	
Additional interactive activities	available on MEL	✓	Self-study interactive activities, which can also be assigned by the Teacher through MyEnglishLab

Working day 1

Unit overview

	CLASSWORK	FURTHER WORK
1.1 Daily tasks	**Lead-in** Students talk about different jobs in their place of work. **Vocabulary** Students look at vocabulary related to jobs and tasks. **Communicative grammar** Students study and practise the affirmative and negative forms of the Present Simple. **Video** Students watch a video of people talking about their jobs. **Task** Students practise introducing themselves and talking about their job.	**MyEnglishLab:** Teacher's resources: extra activities; Additional interactive activities **Grammar reference:** p.102 Facts and routines **Pronunciation bank:** p.96 The -s ending **Teacher's book:** Resource bank Extra vocabulary practice p.136 Exercises 1 and 2 **Workbook:** p.4 Exercises 1 and 2; p.5 Exercises 1 and 2; p.44 Exercises 1–3
1.2 A work plan	**Lead-in** Students talk about their work tasks and activities. **Vocabulary** Students look at vocabulary related to work tasks and activities. **Reading and listening** Students read emails and listen to people scheduling meetings. **Writing** Students write emails to schedule a meeting.	**MyEnglishLab:** Teacher's resources: extra activities; Additional interactive activities **Teacher's book:** Resource bank Extra vocabulary practice p.136 Exercises 3 and 4 **Workbook:** p.4 Exercises 3 and 4; p.6 Exercises 1–4
1.3 A survey	**Lead-in** Students discuss the facilities they have at their place of work or study. **Reading** Students read an employee survey. **Communicative grammar** Students study and practise the question form of the Present Simple. **Writing** Students write and carry out a survey about improving facilities at their place of work or study.	**MyEnglishLab:** Teacher's resources: extra activities; Additional interactive activities **Grammar reference:** p.102 Questions **Pronunciation bank:** p.96 Questions **Teacher's book:** Resource bank Photocopiable 1.3 p.112 **Workbook:** p.5 Exercises 3 and 4; p.7 Exercises 1–3; p.44 Exercises 1 and 2
1.4 Work skills: Talking about people and roles	**Lead-in** Students look at conversations where the speakers introduce people and their roles. **Video** Students watch a video of people introducing themselves and others. **Speaking** Students look at useful language for making introductions and talking about people and roles.	**MyEnglishLab:** Teacher's resources: extra activities; Extra speaking lessons; Additional interactive activities **Grammar reference:** p.103 Subject and object questions **Teacher's book:** Resource bank Extra vocabulary practice p.136 Exercise 5; Photocopiable 1.4 p.113 **Workbook:** p.8 Exercises 1–4
Business workshop: We want to meet you ...	**Reading** Students read a page from a travel sales website. **Writing** Students write emails to arrange a meeting. **Speaking** Students roleplay a phone call to reschedule a meeting; roleplay an interview with a business professional.	

Teacher's notes

Unit vocabulary list

Active vocabulary

1.1

- analyse (sales) data
- answer the phone
- call customers
- do research
- finish work
- go to meetings
- make calls
- process orders
- start work
- travel for work
- write emails
- write reports

- always
- never
- often
- rarely
- sometimes
- usually

1.2

- budget meeting
- client meeting
- management meeting
- planning meeting
- project meeting

- book a meeting room
- calculate (production) costs
- create a brief
- get an update
- prepare a presentation
- send out the agenda

Passive vocabulary

1.2

- Admin Assistant
- Digital Designer
- Finance Officer
- IT Specialist

- Production Engineer
- Project Manager
- Sales Assistant
- Sales Manager

1.3

- area for relaxing
- canteen
- car park

- kitchen area
- meeting room
- workspace

1.4

- department
- manage (a team)
- office facilities

- planning
- production team
- update

1.1 Daily tasks

GSE learning objectives

- Can understand information related to people's daily routines.
- Can answer simple questions about habits and routines.
- Can describe their daily routines in a simple way.
- Can use a range of common adverbs of frequency.
- Can correctly place adverbs of frequency in longer sentences.

Lead-in

Students talk about different jobs in their place of work.

1A You could start the lesson by putting students in small groups and giving them a few minutes to brainstorm as many jobs as they can in English. When they have finished, elicit their answers and write them on the board. Go through all eight jobs from the exercise with the class and check understanding with focussed questions, e.g. *Which person creates things on a computer?* (Digital Designer), especially for the two jobs that are not shown in the photos (Digital Designer, Admin Assistant). Get students to complete the exercise individually, then check answers with the class.

A 2,3 **B** 8 **C** 1 **D** 6,7

1B Read the question with the class and if necessary, give students 1–2 minutes to think about their answers. Pre-service students can discuss their place of study or a company they know well instead. When they are ready, put students in pairs to discuss their answers, then nominate a few students to share their answers with the class.

Vocabulary: Jobs and tasks

Students look at vocabulary related to jobs and tasks.

2A Explain to students that they are going to read short descriptions of two jobs. Explain the activity and tell them not to worry about new vocabulary at this stage, just to focus on guessing each job. Give them 2–3 minutes to read the descriptions and write the jobs, then check answers with the class.

A Sales Manager **B** Admin Assistant

2B Look at the example with the class, and ask students to show you where the phrase in bold is in the descriptions in Exercise 2A. Students complete the rest of the expressions individually, then compare answers in pairs. Check answers with the class, and be prepared to offer explanations or examples where necessary. Students may complete some answers with the third person *-s* for answers with verbs because they have seen them in the text in this form. Explain that this is not incorrect and depends on the subject *I, you, they* or *he/she*.

1 go to **2** call **3** orders **4** research **5** make **6** travel
7 analyse **8** reports **9** the phone **10** start, finish

3 Ask students to close their books. Copy the 0%–100% line on the board and write *sometimes* in the middle, below it. List the other adverbs of frequency on the board (*never, rarely, often, usually, always*), and elicit where they should go on the line. Write (or invite students to write) them on the line. Put students in pairs to discuss the questions and encourage them to give more information where possible. Monitor and help where necessary. When they have finished, ask a few students to share any interesting information they found out about their partner with the class.

Extra activities 1.1

A This activity provides extra practice of the vocabulary in Exercise 2. Ask students to do it individually, and tell them that they can refer to Exercises 2A and 2B in their Coursebook if they need help. Check answers with the class.

1 goes **2** process **3** write **4** start **5** analyse
6 writes **7** do **8** travel for **9** finish **10** make

Pronunciation bank
p.96: The -s ending

1 🔊 P1.01 This exercise focusses on the sounds /s/ and /z/ and the notion of voicing. Demonstrate the sounds /s/ and /z/. Tell students that they are both articulated in the same way and the difference between them is that /s/ is unvoiced and /z/ is voiced. This means that when we pronounce /z/, the vocal cords vibrate, whereas the production of /s/ does not involve any movement of the vocal cords. You can feel the vocal cords vibrating by touching your throat while pronouncing /z/. Ask students to put their hands on their throats and say the prolonged sounds: /s/ and then /z/. Play the recording and ask students to repeat the sounds and words. Draw their attention to the spelling and point out that the sound /s/ is usually represented by the letter *s*, while /z/ can be written as *z* or *s*.

2 🔊 P1.02 The aim of this exercise is to make students aware of the difference in the pronunciation of the *-s* ending. While you do not need to explain the phonological rules to students, note that the *-s* ending can be pronounced /s/ or /z/, depending on the final sound in a word. If the word ends with an unvoiced consonant (/t/, /k/, /p/, /f/, /θ/), the *-s* ending is pronounced /s/. If the word ends with a voiced consonant (/b/, /g/, /d/, /ð/, /v/, /l/, /r/, /m/, /n/, /ŋ/) or any vowel sound, the *-s* ending is pronounced /z/. Play the recording and ask students to repeat. You could then put them in pairs to practise saying the words.

3 🔊 P1.03 Explain to students they are going to practise saying short sentences with the words from Exercise 2. Play the recording and ask them to repeat. Again, students could then practise saying the sentences in pairs.

Teacher's notes

4A 🔊 P1.04 Explain the activity and play the recording. Elicit the answer or explain that when we add the -s ending to a word that ends with a so-called hissing consonant, such as /s/, /z/, /ʃ/, /tʃ/, /ʒ/ or /dʒ/, we add the full syllable /ɪz/.

> Because they add another syllable to the base word.

4B If you think your students need more help with the target sounds, start by playing the recording again and getting them to repeat as a group. Then put them in pairs to practise saying the sentences.

5A Explain the activity and look at the example with the class, then put students in pairs and give them 2–3 minutes to complete the exercise. Do not confirm answers yet – students will check them in the next activity.

> /s/ assistants tasks makes starts
> /z/ emails phones answers travels
> /ɪz/ addresses spaces misses watches

5B 🔊 P1.05 Play the recording for students to check their answers to Exercise 5A. Play it again and ask them to repeat the words as a group or individually, then get them to practise saying the words in pairs or small groups. Monitor and correct pronunciation as necessary.

Communicative grammar: Facts and routines

Students study and practise the affirmative and negative forms of the Present Simple.

Facts and routines

Go through the Grammar box with students and highlight the form of the negatives and contractions. Point out the absence of the third person -s after *doesn't*. Using -s after *doesn't* can be a common error, so you may wish to highlight this on the board: *He doesn't ~~calls~~ call customers*. Go over the use of adverbs of frequency, and explain that they usually go before the main verb but after the verb *be*. Refer students back to the job descriptions in Exercise 2A so they can look again at the target language in context – draw their attention to the verbs and phrases in bold in the texts. At this point, you may wish to refer students to the Grammar reference on page 102, go through the explanations and examples with them and answer any questions they may have. Pay particular attention to the spelling rules for verbs ending in -s, -sh, -ch and consonant + -y. Students could then do the extra grammar activities there, in class or as homework.

Grammar reference answer key: page 30

4 Explain the activity and elicit the first answer as an example. Students then complete the rest of text individually, referring to the Grammar reference to help them if necessary. Check answers with the class.

> 1 work 2 isn't 3 's/is 4 are 5 start 6 don't finish
> 7 analyse 8 'm/am not 9 'm/am

5 Elicit the first sentence as an example and write it on the board. Students then complete the exercise individually and if there is time, compare answers in pairs before class feedback. As an extension, you could ask students to write four similar sentences about what they do at work. Monitor and help with vocabulary, writing any new words/phrases on the board. When they have finished, put students in pairs to compare their sentences, then invite a few students to share their sentences with the class.

> 1 I often start work at eight o'clock.
> 2 We always call customers on Fridays.
> 3 They sometimes have a team meeting. / Sometimes they have a team meeting.
> 4 You never write emails after lunch.
> 5 They don't analyse data.
> 6 She doesn't usually call customers.

Extra activities 1.1

B This activity provides extra practice of the affirmative and negative forms of the Present Simple. Students should complete it individually and then, if there is time, compare answers in pairs before class feedback.

> 1 'm 2 doesn't 3 are 4 arrives 5 go 6 are
> 7 finish 8 have

C This activity looks at adverbs of frequency. Draw students' attention to the table and explain that it shows how often the people do the activities. Explain the task and do the first item as an example with the class, then ask students to complete the rest of the exercise individually. Check answers with the class.

> 1 Liz often goes to meetings.
> 2 Johan rarely starts work at 8 o'clock.
> 3 David and Beth sometimes answer the phone.
> 4 Liz always starts work at 8 o'clock.
> 5 Johan never answers the phone.
> 6 David and Beth always go to meetings.
> 7 Liz usually answers the phone.
> 8 Johan sometimes goes to meetings.
> 9 David and Beth usually start work at 8 o'clock.

Teacher's notes

Video

Students watch a video of people talking about their jobs.

6A ▶ 1.1.1 Explain to students that they are going to watch a video of people talking about their jobs. Go through the job titles in the box with them and check understanding of each one. Elicit students' ideas as to what tasks each job might involve. Before students watch, you may wish to pre-teach the following vocabulary from the video: *travel abroad*, *take a break*, *pharmaceutical research*, *cycle* and *company account*. Play the video for students to watch and match the people to the job titles, then check answers with the class.

> 1 Student Services Manager 2 Senior Research Manager
> 3 Chief Executive Officer (CEO)

6B ▶ 1.1.1 Go through the tasks in the left-hand column of the table with students, so they know what to listen for. Play the video again, twice if necessary, then check answers with the class.

Who …	Liz	Ellen	Muj
starts work at 7.30?			✓
finishes work at 5.30?		✓	
travels to other countries for work?			✓
has lunch at 1 o'clock?	✓	✓	
analyses data?		✓	
writes reports?			✓

6C Put students in pairs, explain the activity and look at the example with the class. If necessary, let students watch the video again and make notes, or let them refer to videoscript 1.1.1 on page 129 during the activity. When they have finished, ask a few students to share their sentences with the class.

Task

Students practise introducing themselves and talking about their job.

7A Explain the activity, look at the example with the class and before students practise in pairs, give them a few minutes to think about what they are going to say and make notes if they want to. Monitor and help with ideas and vocabulary as necessary. When students are ready, put them in pairs to introduce themselves and talk about their job and routine. Encourage them to use vocabulary from Exercise 2 and adverbs of frequency from Exercise 3. Also explain that they are going to talk about their partner's job in the next activity, so they may want to make notes while listening to their partner. During the activity, monitor and note down any common errors or examples of good language use to highlight with the class during feedback after Exercise 7B.

> **Model answer**
> My name's Nick. I'm a factory worker. I help make cars. I always start work at seven-thirty. I never finish before five-thirty but I often finish at six o'clock. I sometimes travel for work. I visit other factories. My boss always processes orders on Mondays, so we have a meeting. We plan the work for the week.

7B Join pairs together into groups of four, explain the activity and look at the example with the class. Again, encourage students to use language from the lesson and remind them to refer to their notes from Exercise 7A if they have them. When they have finished, nominate a student from each group to share anything interesting they found out about the people in their group with the rest of the class. Finally, go over any points you noted while monitoring.

> **Model answer**
> This is Nick. He's a factory worker. He helps make cars. He always starts work at seven-thirty. He never finishes before five-thirty he but often finishes at six o'clock. He sometimes travels for work. He visits other factories. His boss always processes orders on Mondays, so they have a meeting. They plan the work for the week.

MyEnglishLab: Teacher's resources: extra activities; Additional interactive activities
Grammar reference: p.102 Facts and routines
Pronunciation bank: p.96 The -s ending
Teacher's book: Resource bank Extra vocabulary practice p.136 Exercises 1 and 2
Workbook: p.4 Exercises 1 and 2; p.5 Exercises 1 and 2; p.44 Exercises 1–3

1.2 ▶ A work plan

> **GSE learning objectives**
> - Can understand information related to people's daily routines.
> - Can identify key information (e.g. places, times) from short audio recordings, if spoken slowly and clearly.
> - Can use language related to the working day.
> - Can understand a simple work schedule.
> - Can understand short, simple emails on work-related topics.
> - Can write simple sentences about what they and other people do.
> - Can write simple plans and arrangements on a calendar or in a diary.

Lead-in

Students talk about their work tasks and activities.

1 Go through the tasks in the box with the class and quickly check they remember them from Lesson 1.1. Put students in pairs or small groups to discuss which of the tasks they do, and encourage them to give more information (e.g. the type of research they do, how often they go to meetings). Pre-service students can talk about a job they would like to do or know well.

2 Go through the words in the box and check students understand them by asking for examples of activities during each type of meeting or the purpose of each one. Students can discuss the question in pairs or small groups. When they have finished, ask a few students to share their answers with the class.

Teacher's notes

Vocabulary: Work tasks and activities

Students look at vocabulary related to work tasks and activities.

3 Draw students' attention to the calendar and the to-do list, and ask if students use these items in their work/study. Explain the activity, pointing out the phrases in bold, then give students time to read the information and complete the exercise individually. Check answers with the class, and be prepared to offer any further explanations/examples where necessary. In weaker classes, you could do this as a whole-class activity: give students time to read the information first, then elicit the correct definition for each phrase in turn, clarifying meanings as you go.

> **1** d **2** c **3** a **4** f **5** e **6** g **7** b

4 Ask students to complete the exercise individually, referring to the definitions in Exercise 3 if they need help. If there is time, get them to compare answers in pairs before checking with the class.

> **1** book **2** budget **3** agenda **4** brief **5** presentation **6** update **7** calculate

Extra activities 1.2

A/B These activities provide extra practice of vocabulary related to work tasks and activities. Ask students to complete both exercises individually and remind them that they can refer to Exercise 3 if they need help. Get them to compare answers in pairs before class feedback. For Exercise B, write (or invite students to write) the answers on the board, so students can check their spelling.

> **A** **1** b **2** e **3** a **4** h **5** c **6** g **7** f **8** d
> **B** **1** book **2** send **3** update **4** prepares **5** creates **6** production **7** budget

Reading and listening: Scheduling meetings

Students read emails and listen to people scheduling meetings.

5A Explain that the five emails are between two colleagues who are trying to schedule a meeting. Point out that email C is the first one. Students number the emails in order individually, then compare answers in pairs. Check answers with the class.

> **A** 2 **B** 3 **C** 1 **D** 5 **E** 4

5B Before students do this activity, go through the ways of telling the time in the box. You could then put students in pairs to test each other: the student being tested covers the words with a notebook or their hand, and the other student points to one of the numbers/abbreviations for their partner to say it. Students then swap roles and repeat. Individually, they then look back at the emails in Exercise 5A and mark the time and date of the meeting on David's calendar. Check the answer with the class.

> 2.00 p.m. on Thu 28 (in Susan's office)

6A 🔊 1.01 Explain to students that David is now calling Susan to reschedule the project planning meeting that they read about in the emails in Exercise 5A. Go through the work tasks with them, so they know what to listen for, then play the recording. Give students a chance to compare answers in pairs, then play the recording again if necessary. Check answers with the class.

> - Presentation: Fri 29 until 11.00 a.m.
> - Phone call: Fri 29 12.00–1.00 p.m.
> - New project planning meeting (new time): Fri 1.00–2.00 p.m.

6B 🔊 1.02 Tell students that they are going to look at useful phrases for scheduling meetings and point out that the sentences are from David and Susan's phone call. Give them a minute to look at the words in the box and ask you about any they do not understand, then ask them to complete the sentences individually. Play the recording for students to check their answers, then check answers with the class, checking understanding of each phrase.

> **1** date **2** available **3** about **4** busy **5** Shall **6** then **7** fine **8** See

Extra activities 1.2

C This activity provides extra practice of the useful phrases for scheduling meetings from the listening. Ask students to complete it individually, then check answers with the class.

> **1** Shall **2** change, about, See **3** then, fine **4** available, busy

Writing

Students write emails to schedule a meeting.

7 Put students in pairs. If you have an odd number of students, have one group of three with two Student Bs. Explain that students are going to practise scheduling a meeting, then direct them to their relevant pages. Give them time to read the information in Part 1 while you go round and help as necessary. When they are ready, ask students to write their emails. Remind them of the useful phrases in Exercise 6B, and that they can refer to the model emails in Exercise 5A if they need help. Draw attention to how David and Susan open and close their emails in Exercise 5A, and tell students to open and close their emails in an appropriate way. Encourage them to use their mobile devices if possible in order to replicate authentic conditions. If this is not possible, they can write their emails on paper and exchange them. Monitor and check students' writing, offering help and corrections. When they have finished, move on to Parts 2 and 3. Ask students to swap emails and write a reply. Students continue exchanging emails until they have agreed a time and a place for the two meetings. In feedback, ask each pair where and when they are meeting.

Teacher's notes

Model exchange beginning with Student A

Hi Student B,
As you know, we need to have a planning meeting by Friday 29 March. I'm available on Tuesday 26th. Are you available then?
Best regards,
Student A

Hi Student A,
Thanks for your message. I'm usually at the factory on Tuesdays. And on Wednesday 27 March I have client meetings all day. How about Thursday 28 March at 10.00 a.m.? We can meet in my office.
Best regards,
Student B

Hi Student B,
Sorry, I have a management meeting on Thursday. Is Friday 29 March at 10.00 a.m. OK?
Best regards,
Student A

Hi Student A,
I'm working at home on Friday morning. How about Friday afternoon at 2.00 p.m.?
Best regards,
Student B

Hi Student B,
Perfect. See you at 2.00 p.m. on Friday.
Best regards,
Student A

Model exchange beginning with Student B

Hi Student A,
As you know, we need to have a budget meeting by Friday 29 March. I'm available on Monday 25th. Are you available then?
Best regards,
Student B

Hi Student B,
Thanks for your message. I'm usually at the factory on Mondays. And on Wednesday 27 March I have a sales meeting all day. How about Tuesday 26 March at 10.00 a.m.? We can meet in my office.
Best regards,
Student A

Hi Student A,
Sorry, I'm at the factory on Tuesdays. Is Thursday 28 March at 10.00 a.m. OK?
Best regards,
Student B

Hi Student B,
Sorry, I have a management meeting all day on Thursday. How about Friday afternoon at 4.00 p.m., after our planning meeting?
Best regards,
Student A

Hi Student A,
Perfect. See you at 4.00 p.m. on Friday.
Best regards,
Student B

MyEnglishLab: Teacher's resources: extra activities; Additional interactive activities
Teacher's book: Resource bank Extra vocabulary practice p.136 Exercises 3 and 4
Workbook: p.4 Exercises 3 and 4; p.6 Exercises 1–4

1.3 > Writing
A survey

GSE learning objectives
- Can answer simple questions in a face-to-face survey.
- Can ask simple questions in a face-to-face survey.
- Can understand simple phrases related to familiar, everyday activities.
- Can understand short, simple texts about everyday activities.
- Can form questions with 'what' and 'which' as adjectives.
- Can form questions with 'How often' in the present tense.
- Can write simple sentences about what they and other people do.

Lead-in

Students discuss the facilities they have at their place of work or study.

1A Draw students' attention to the photos and captions, and clarify meanings as necessary. With stronger classes, you could ask students to cover the captions and just look at the photos and try to name the facilities, then look at the captions to check their answers. Put students in pairs or small groups to discuss the question, then invite students from different pairs/groups to share their answers with the class.

1B Students discuss the question in the same pairs/groups as Exercise 1A, saying what they use each facility for. When they have finished, elicit answers from a few students and find out if others have the same answers.

Reading

Students read an employee survey.

2A To introduce the topic of surveys, you could briefly discuss the following questions with the class: *Do you ever answer surveys at work? What about in your personal life? What kind of questions do you answer?* Draw students' attention to the form and explain that a company is carrying out a survey of their employees in order to improve staff facilities at work – look at the introductory text in the survey with the class. Explain the activity and before students begin, go through the headings in the box with them and check understanding. Give students 3–5 minutes to complete the exercise individually, then check answers with the class. Answer any questions students have about the vocabulary in the survey.

Teacher's notes

> A The work day B The workplace
> C Meetings and meeting rooms D Other facilities

2B Explain the activity, making sure that students understand the answers only match six of the questions in the survey, and if necessary, elicit the first answer as an example. Ask students to complete the exercise individually, then check answers with the class.

> **a** 4 **b** 2 **c** 10 **d** 11 **e** 3 **f** 12

2C Put students in pairs to ask and answer the questions in the survey. Pre-service students could invent their answers, talking about a company they know well and/or would like to work for. If there is time, give students 1–2 minutes to think about their answers first, before they practise in their pairs. When they have finished, ask a few students to share any interesting answers with the class.

Communicative grammar: Questions
Students study and practise the question form of the Present Simple.

> **Questions**
>
> Go through the Grammar box with the class, clarifying any points as necessary. Remind students of the use of *don't/doesn't* in negative sentences, and explain that questions are also formed using the auxiliary *do/does*. Again, point out that we do not use the third person *-s* after *does*: When does your working day ~~starts~~ start? For some quick practice, you could put students in pairs and ask them to take turns to ask and answer the questions in the Grammar box. Then refer them to the Grammar reference on page 102, go through it with them and clarify any points as necessary. Students could then do the extra grammar activities there, in class or as homework.
>
> **Grammar reference answer key:** page 30

3 Ask students to complete the exercise individually and if necessary, do the first item as an example with the class. Remind students that they can refer to the Grammar box and/or the Grammar reference if they need help. If there is time, get them to compare answers in pairs before checking with the class.

> 1 What are your working hours?
> 2 Does your office have enough workspaces?
> 3 Does your office have an area for relaxing?
> 4 Do you use the gym?
> 5 Where is the kitchen area?
> 6 What time do you start work?
> 7 When does your day finish?
> 8 Does your company have a car park?

> **Pronunciation bank**
> **p.96: Questions**
>
> **1A** 🔊 P1.06 Play the recording and ask students to just listen. Tell them that for each verb, they heard the weak forms first, followed by the strong forms. Explain that *are*, *do* and *does* in questions sound weak and are pronounced /ə/, /də/ and /dəz/, respectively. Point out that by 'weak', we mean that the words are not stressed and are therefore 'weakened' in speech. The same verbs in short answers sound strong and are pronounced /ɑː/, /duː/ and /dʌz/. Play the recording again and ask students to repeat.
>
> **1B** 🔊 P1.07 Play the recording and ask students to repeat in chorus. Remind them to pay attention to the correct pronunciation of weak and strong forms.
>
> **2A** 🔊 P1.08 Explain to students that intonation is about how we say things to create expression and variation in speech; it is how our voice goes up or down to convey our attitude and emotions. Tell them that they are going to hear the questions from this exercise and think about intonation – they should decide whether the speaker's voice goes up or down at the end. Start the recording, pause after the example and ask students if they could hear the difference. Then play the rest of the recording for them to complete the exercise. Check answers with the class, then ask students if they can work out a rule. Elicit an answer or explain that in *yes/no* questions we use rising intonation, while *wh-* questions are pronounced with falling intonation. You may want to play the recording again and ask students to repeat in chorus.
>
> > In each item, the first question has rising intonation (goes up at the end) and the second falling intonation (goes down at the end).
>
> **2B** Put students in pairs to practise saying the questions in Exercise 2A. Monitor and correct intonation as necessary.

4A Explain the activity and point out that students need to write one word in each gap. Ask them to complete the questions individually and if there is time, get them to compare answers before class feedback.

> **1** is **2** Does **3** do **4** are **5** is **6** Do **7** Does
> **8** How

4B Students could do this individually or, if time is short, you could do it as a quick, whole-class activity, checking answers as you go. As an extension, you could put students in pairs to practise asking and answering the questions.

> **1** c **2** e **3** a **4** d **5** f **6** b **7** h **8** g

Teacher's notes

Extra activities 1.3

A This activity provides further practice of Present Simple questions. Ask students to complete it individually, then check answers with the class.

1 are 2 do 3 do 4 Does 5 Do 6 is 7 do 8 do

B Explain the activity and point out to students that they should look carefully at the verbs in the answers in order to complete the questions. If necessary, do the first item as an example with the class. After checking answers, you could put students in pairs to practise the conversations.

1 Do you have 2 Do you eat 3 Where is
4 Does, have 5 How do you get 6 Where is
7 What are / When are 8 When is

Writing

Students write and carry out a survey about improving facilities at their place of work or study.

5A Read the instructions with the class and go through the topics with them. Explain that students should use the topics to help them, but they can also invent some of their own to make the survey relevant to their place of work or study. Encourage them to use language from the lesson when writing their questions, and remind them that they can use the survey in Exercise 2A as a model if they need help. During the activity, monitor, checking students are forming their questions correctly and helping them with any vocabulary they may need.

Possible questions

What is your workspace like?
Are there enough meeting rooms?
Do you have lots of meetings?
Are there enough computers/Is there enough IT equipment?
Is it easy to access your workspace? (Is there a lift? Are there stairs?)
Is there a quiet area?
What other facilities are there?
What time do you start work?
When does your work day end?
How do you get to work?
Who do you work with?
What time is lunch break?
Where is the canteen?
Is there a gym?
Are there areas to relax?
What do you have for lunch?
What is the best way to spend break time?
Do you go out with colleagues after work?
Does your company have a fitness centre?

5B Put students in pairs and explain that they are going to swap surveys and write their answers to their partner's questions. When they have finished, ask a few students to share any interesting information they found out with the class. As feedback, go over any common errors or difficulties you noted during this and the previous activity.

MyEnglishLab: Teacher's resources: extra activities; Additional interactive activities
Grammar reference: p.102 Questions
Pronunciation bank: p.96 Questions
Teacher's book: Resource bank Photocopiable 1.3 p.112
Workbook: p.5 Exercises 3 and 4; p.7 Exercises 1–3; p.44 Exercises 1 and 2

1.4 > Work skills
Talking about people and roles

GSE learning objectives

- Can understand basic information about someone when introduced to them using simple language.
- Can identify simple information in a short video, provided that the visual supports this information and the delivery is slow and clear.
- Can ask and answer questions about what they do at work and in their free time.
- Can respond politely when introduced to someone, using a few basic fixed expressions.

Lead-in

Students look at conversations where the speakers introduce people and their roles.

1 As a brief warm-up, students could discuss the following questions in pairs, small groups or as a class: *How often do you meet new people at work? What type of people are they? Do you like working with lots of people or just a few? Why?* Draw students' attention to the photos and ask them what they think the situation is in each one. Elicit a few ideas, then explain that the conversations below match each photo, but they are in the wrong order. Students complete the exercise individually, then compare answers in pairs. In feedback, clarify meanings as necessary then, if there is time, put students in pairs to practise the conversations.

A 1 b 2 c 3 a
B 1 d 2 a 3 c 4 b
C 1 b 2 c 3 a

Video

Students watch a video of people introducing themselves and others.

2A ▶ 1.4.1 As this is the first work skills video for your class, you may wish to give students some background information about Sleek, the company in the videos. Refer them to page 6 of the Coursebook and go through the Introduction with them. Also refer them to the summary for the Unit 1 video. Then explain the activity and go through the questions with the class so they know what to watch for. Play the video for students to watch and answer the questions, then check answers with the class.

27

Teacher's notes

1 In the London office.
2 No, they don't.
3 Yes, she does.
4 No, she doesn't.

2B ▶ 1.4.1 Ask students to complete the exercise individually – point out that they should only use one word in each gap. Play the video for them to check their answers, then go over them with the class.

1 this, from 2 Which, work 3 know, visits 4 visit, sales
5 presentation, update

2C ▶ 1.4.1 Explain to students that these are some useful phrases from the video and ask them to do the matching task individually. Play the video again for them to check their answers, then go over them with the class, clarifying meanings as necessary. As an extension, you could put students in pairs to practise the exchanges.

1 d 2 a 3 e 4 f 5 c 6 b

Extra activities 1.4

A This activity provides further practice of the functional language from the video. You could do it after Exercise 2C or after going through the Speaking box with the class. Ask students to complete the exercise individually and then to compare answers in pairs before class feedback.

1 c 2 a 3 d 4 b 5 g 6 e 7 f

B Again, this activity can be done after Exercise 2C or after students look at the Speaking box which follows. Students could it individually and then compare answers in pairs before class feedback. Alternatively, if time is short, you could do it as a whole-class activity, checking answers as you go along. As an extension, students could practise the exchanges in pairs.

a 3 b 1 c 6 d 4 e 2 f 7 g 5

Speaking: Talking about people and roles

Students look at useful language for making introductions and talking about people and roles.

Talking about people and roles

Tell students they are going to look at useful phrases for making introductions and talking about people and roles. Explain that the phrases in the first section are for introducing someone else, and the other two sections are for asking and answering about roles and activities. Give students 1–2 minutes to look at the phrases in the Speaking box, then go through them with the whole class, clarifying meanings as necessary. You may also need to help students with the pronunciation of some of the phrases. For some quick practice, you could put students in groups of three and get them to have quick exchanges using phrases from the box.

Unit 1 Extra speaking lesson

This lesson gives further practice of speaking related to talking about people and roles. To access the lesson go to MyEnglishLab > Extra speaking lessons.

Subject and object questions

Write on the board: _Martha_ manages _the Madrid team_. Point to _Martha_, elicit the question needed to find out this information (_Who manages the Madrid team?_) and write it on the board, with an arrow pointing to _Martha_ in the sentence. Elicit or explain that _Martha_ is the subject of the sentence. Then point to _the Madrid team_, elicit the question needed to find out this information (_What does Martha manage?_), write it on the board and draw an arrow pointing to _the Madrid team_ in the sentence. Elicit or explain that _the Madrid team_ is the object of the sentence. Explain that questions about the subject simply replace the subject with a question word, while questions about the object use the auxiliary _do/does_. Go through the examples in the Grammar box with students, then refer them to the Grammar reference on page 103, go through it with them and clarify any points as necessary. Students could then do the extra grammar activity there, in class or as homework.

Grammar reference answer key: page 30

Extra activities 1.4

C This activity provides further practice of subject and object questions. Ask students to complete it individually, referring to the Grammar reference on page 103 if they need help, then check answers with the class.

1 Who manages that team?
2 Which team do you manage?
3 Where do you work?
4 Where is your office?
5 How much does the phone cost?
6 Which employees work hard?

3A Look at the example profile with the class, then ask students to complete their own profile individually. Pre-service students could invent some information about themselves. Go round and help with any vocabulary students may need.

3B Put students in groups of three and go through the instructions with them. With weaker classes, look at videoscript 1.4.1 on page 129 with students before they begin and point out the different stages of the conversations. You could then demonstrate a conversation with two stronger students (or ask three stronger students to demonstrate to the class). Finally, remind students to use phrases from the Speaking box in their conversations. Monitor while students are writing, offering help as necessary and noting down any common errors or difficulties to highlight during feedback after the next exercise.

3C Students now practise their conversations in their groups. When they have finished, ask them to swap roles and practise again. If there is time, you could then ask a few groups to perform their dialogues for the class. Finally, have a brief feedback session, highlighting any points you noted while monitoring.

Teacher's notes

MyEnglishLab: Teacher's resources: extra activities;
Extra speaking lessons; Additional interactive activities
Grammar reference: p.103 Subject and object questions
Teacher's book: Resource bank Extra vocabulary practice p.136 Exercise 5; Photocopiable 1.4 p.113
Workbook: p.8 Exercises 1-4

Business workshop
We want to meet you …

> **GSE learning objectives**
> - Can make an appointment on the phone.
> - Can ask simple questions to find out about a subject.
> - Can ask and answer questions about what they do at work and in their free time.
> - Can understand short, simple emails on work-related topics.
> - Can give basic information to introduce themselves in work-related situations (name, job, etc.).

Introduction
Students read a page from a travel sales website.

1 Go through the questions with the class and check that they understand *professional* (n) and *contact* (v). Give students 3-4 minutes to read the text and answer the questions individually, then get them to compare answers in pairs before checking with the class.

> 1 *U-Trav-L* is a travel sales website for business travellers.
> 2 For their blog. The blog shows work life and business travel.
> 3 They would like to interview you about your job and business travel.

Arranging a meeting
Students write emails to arrange a meeting.

2A Explain that Ms Lawrie has written to the *U-Trav-L* website and that the email is a reply from the company to her. Students read the email, then answer the question in pairs. Check the answer with the class.

> Maria wants to interview Ms Lawrie at her office. She wants to interview her in March.

2B If you think your students will find this activity difficult, review the Reading and Listening section of Lesson 1.2. Put students in pairs and explain that they are going to arrange a meeting between Ms Lawrie and Maria Alvarez, the Editor of *U-Trav-L*. Direct them to their relevant pages and give them time to read the information. Explain that Student B should write the first email. Students could use their actual email addresses if they are comfortable sharing them, and write to their partner immediately to get instant replies. Otherwise, each pair could write their emails on paper and pass them around. Students who are waiting for an email response can look at their previous response and attempt self-correction. Go round and offer help where necessary.

> They can meet on Friday 4 April at 2.00 p.m.
>
> **Model answers**
>
> **Student B** (Angela Lawrie responds to the initial email)
>
> Hi Maria,
> Thanks for your message. I usually work on the financial results in March. I'm available for one day in the last week of March. How about Friday 28 March?
> Best regards,
> Angela
>
> Hi Angela,
> Thanks for your message. I'm not available in the last week in March. Is Wednesday 2 April OK? I'm available all day.
> Best regards,
> Maria
>
> Hi Maria,
> Sorry, I usually work from home on Wednesdays. I'm available at 2.00 p.m. on Friday 4 April. Are you available then?
> Best regards,
> Angela
>
> Hi Angela,
> Perfect. I'm available on Friday 4 April at 2.00 p.m.
> See you then,
> Maria

A phone call
Students roleplay a phone call to reschedule a meeting.

3 If you think your students will find this activity difficult, review the Reading and listening section of Lesson 1.2. Students can stay in the same pairs as in Exercise 2 for this activity. Go through the instructions with them, then direct them to their relevant pages and give them time to read the information. You could introduce or elicit the first line of the conversation (see model conversation below) to help them. With weaker classes, students can write out the conversation first and then practise it. Otherwise, students continue after the first line. Monitor students' conversations, making notes on any common errors/examples of good language use for later feedback. When they have finished, ask what time and day they are meeting. Go through any common errors on the board as a class.

> The only time they're both available is 12:00 on Friday.
>
> **Model conversation**
> **A:** Hi, Angela. It's Maria Alvarez from *U-Trav-L*.
> **B:** Oh hi, Maria. How are you?
> **A:** I'm good, thanks. How are you?
> **B:** I'm OK, but I'm not available on Friday 4 April. I'm sorry, but we need to change the date of the interview. Are you available on Thursday 10th, in the morning?
> **A:** Sorry, no, I'm not. I have a budget meeting at that time. How about Friday?
> **B:** I'm available all afternoon - from 12.00 p.m. Shall we meet at your office?
> **A:** Yes, that's fine. How about 12.00 p.m., then?
> **B:** 12.00 p.m. is good. I'll see you then!
> **A:** See you then!

Teacher's notes

The interview

Students roleplay an interview with a business professional.

4A If you think your students will find this activity difficult, review the Communicative grammar section of Lesson 1.3. Read the example with the class, then ask students to write the rest of the questions individually. When they have finished, ask students to compare answers in pairs, then check answers with the class.

> 1 Which department do you work in?
> 2 What do you do?
> 3 Where do you work?
> 4 How do you get to work?
> 5 How long is your journey to work?
> 6 How often do you travel abroad?
> 7 Where do you travel to?
> 8 Why do you travel for work?
> 9 Do you work when you're on the train or plane?
> 10 What's your favourite travel destination?

4B Put students in pairs and explain that Maria Alvarez wants to interview Angela Wright, and students are going to roleplay the interview. Ask them to turn to page 116 and give them time to read the information and ask you any questions they may have. Explain that they are going to take turns to be Maria and Angela, and give them time to think about any language they want to use in their answers as interviewees. When they are ready, ask them to conduct their interviews. Monitor and make notes on students' language use for later feedback. When they have finished, students swap roles and repeat the interview. If they are comfortable doing so, you could ask students to film themselves doing the interviews using the cameras on their mobile devices. They could then watch them and self-correct where necessary.

Talking about your company and travel

Students roleplay an interview with a business professional.

5A Put students in new pairs, assign roles and explain that they are going to roleplay an interview between Maria Alvarez and a business professional. Direct them to their relevant pages, and give them time to read it and prepare for their interviews. Explain that they are going to take turns to be Maria and the business professional, so they should both prepare for both roles. They should look at their questions as interviewers and invent their information as interviewees. During the preparation stage, monitor and help where necessary. When students are ready, they carry out their interviews. Monitor and note down any points to highlight during feedback after Exercise 5B.

5B If you think your students will find this activity difficult, review the Speaking section of Lesson 1.4 before you start. Put students in new pairs and explain the activity. Before they begin, elicit useful phrases they could use and/or introduce the model language below, and write it on the board for students to refer to during the activity. Students then share their information and choose the best candidate for the webpage. When they have finished, ask a few students who they chose and why. Finally, go over any points you noted while monitoring.

Model language
He/She works in the ... department.
He/She's a Manager.
He/She works in London.
It takes him/her one hour to get to work.
He/She travels abroad 3–5 times a year.
He/She travels to ... a lot.
He/She often works on the train or plane.
His/Her favourite travel destination is ...

Grammar reference ◄ 1

1.1

> **1** 1 Mike and Lisa often go to meetings.
> 2 Joe rarely works from home.
> 3 Mike and Joe usually start work at 8.00.
> 4 Lisa often works from home.
> 5 Lisa and Joe often go to the factory.
> 6 Lisa always starts work at 8.00.
> 7 Mike never goes to the factory.
> 8 Joe never goes to meetings.

1.2

> **1** 1 Are you an Engineer?
> 2 Do Paolo and Imran go to meetings?
> 3 When do you start work?
> 4 Where is the kitchen?
> 5 Is Helena an IT Specialist?
> 6 Does your boss work from home?
> 7 How does Ewan get to work?
> 8 What are their names?

1.4

> **1** 1 answers 2 does 3 are 4 does David need
> 5 works 6 do you get 7 is 8 do

Review ◄ 1

> **1** 1 have 2 go to 3 call 4 do 5 analyse 6 write
> 7 answer 8 make 9 travel 10 go to 11 start
> 12 finish
> **2** 1 have 2 available 3 How about 4 meet 5 fine
> 6 calculate 7 send out 8 book
> **3** 1 He always starts work at eight o'clock.
> 2 I often travel to other countries for work.
> 3 We usually have meetings on Fridays.
> 4 They sometimes work with me on projects.
> 5 Her English is excellent, but she never studies!
> 6 We often go to meetings with customers.
> **4** 1 is 2 'm / am not 3 don't finish 4 work 5 start
> 6 travel 7 isn't / is not 8 're / are
> **5A** 1 are 2 is 3 do 4 Is 5 Do 6 Does
> **5B** 1 Where is their office?
> 2 Why does Helena need a computer?
> 3 Who books (the) meeting rooms?
> 4 When are your meetings?
> 5 Who manages the sales team?
> 6 How does he get to work?
> **6** 1 f 2 d 3 e 4 b 5 c 6 a

Doing business 2

Unit overview

	CLASSWORK		FURTHER WORK
2.1 Orders and deliveries	Lead-in	Students talk about food delivery apps they use.	**MyEnglishLab:** Teacher's resources: extra activitie; Additional interactive activities
	Vocabulary	Students look at vocabulary related to orders and deliveries.	**Grammar reference:** p.103 Things you can and can't count
	Communicative grammar	Students study and practise countable/uncountable nouns and quantifiers.	**Teacher's book:** Resource bank Extra vocabulary practice p.137 Exercise 1; Photocopiable 2.1 p.114
	Video	Students watch a video about a contract caterer in London.	**Workbook:** p.9 Exercises 1–3; p.10 Exercises 1 and 2
	Task	Students practise countable/uncountable nouns and quantifiers by asking and answering questions about themselves.	
2.2 Placing orders on the phone	Lead-in	Students practise asking and answering questions to complete an order form.	**MyEnglishLab:** Teacher's resources: extra activities; Additional interactive activities
	Listening	Students listen to a customer placing an order by phone.	**Grammar reference:** p.104 *can/can't*
	Vocabulary	Students look at vocabulary related to taking and placing orders by phone.	**Pronunciation bank:** p.96 /iː/, /ɪ/ and /aɪ/
	Speaking	Students practise placing and taking an order by phone.	**Teacher's book:** Resource bank Extra vocabulary practice p.137 Exercises 2 and 3
			Workbook: p.9 Exercises 4 and 5; p.11 Exercises 1–4; p.45 Exercises 1–3
2.3 Email enquiries	Lead-in	Students talk about returning and exchanging things they buy.	**MyEnglishLab:** Teacher's resources: extra activities; Additional interactive activities
	Reading	Students read a company's FAQs and replies to customers' email enquiries.	**Grammar reference:** p.104 Saying something exists
	Communicative grammar	Students study and practise *there is / there are*.	**Pronunciation bank:** p.97 /tʃ/ and /dʒ/
	Writing	Students write a response to an email enquiry.	**Workbook:** p.10 Exercises 3 and 4; p.12 Exercises 1–4; p.45 Exercises 1–3
2.4 Work skills: Making agreements	Lead-in	Students talk about the cleaning service at their home and place of work/study.	**MyEnglishLab:** Teacher's resources: extra activities; Extra speaking lessons; Additional interactive activities
	Video	Students watch a video of a meeting about a cleaning contract.	**Teacher's book:** Resource bank Extra vocabulary practice p.137 Exercises 4 and 5; Photocopiable 2.4 p.115
	Speaking	Students look at useful language for making business agreements.	**Workbook:** p.13 Exercises 1–3
Business workshop: Planning a work party	Reading	Students read an email about arranging an employee's anniversary party.	
	Writing	Students complete an enquiry email and write a reply.	
	Speaking	Students practise taking and placing an order by phone, and making a business agreement.	

Teacher's notes

Unit vocabulary list

Active vocabulary

2.1

deliver
order (*verb*)
supply

delivery
order (*noun*)
supplier

2.2

(X) speaking. How can I help you?
I'd like to order (some) ...
Do you have the (product reference numbers)?
How much is/are (the) ... ?
How much does delivery cost?
How many (boxes) do you need?
Can you deliver by (tomorrow)?
I'm very sorry, we can't. / Yes, we can.
I'd like to order (the) ... (please).
Certainly, I'll put your order on the system.
How much is that in total?

Passive vocabulary

2.1

distribution centre
regional centre
truck
warehouse

import (*noun*)
export (*noun*)
online platform
operate
region

2.2

What's the order number?
What's the company address?
What's the product code number?

2.3

exchange
purchases
refund
return
in stock
Click here
Customer Services

Please find attached
Please contact us
Thank you for your enquiry
In response to your enquiry

2.4

clean the desks
clean the floor
empty the bins
vacuum the carpet
wash dishes/cups

catering
charge (*noun*)
cupboard
floor
hot/cold
materials
plates/glasses
products
specialist company
stairs

Teacher's notes

2.1 ▶ Orders and deliveries

GSE learning objectives
- Can use language related to amounts.
- Can ask about quantities using 'how much/many' with count and uncountable nouns.
- Can use 'some' as a quantifier with count and mass nouns.
- Can identify simple information in a short video, provided that the visual supports this information and the delivery is slow and clear.

Lead-in
Students talk about food delivery apps they use.

1 Draw students' attention to the photo and elicit what students can see (someone delivering food). Put students in pairs or small groups to discuss the question. When they have finished, invite a few students to share their answers with the class.

Vocabulary: Orders and deliveries
Students look at vocabulary related to orders and deliveries.

2A Explain to students that they are going to read a short description of how a food delivery app called Jangle works. Give them one minute to read the description, then ask: *Is this similar to any apps you use?* Elicit a few answers, then draw students' attention to the first word in bold in the text (*delivers*) and ask if it is a verb or a noun (verb). Students do the same for the other words in bold, then compare answers in pairs. Check answers with the class. As an extension, you could elicit the verb and noun forms of each word and write them on the board. For the nouns, write both the singular and the plural forms:
- *deliver* (v) – *delivery, deliveries* (n)
- *order* (v) – *order, orders* (n)
- *supply* (v), *supplier, suppliers* (n); *supplies* (n pl)

1 verb **2** verb **3** noun **4** noun **5** verb **6** noun

2B Explain the activity and encourage students to think about what type of word is needed for each sentence – a verb or a noun – before they complete it. Students complete the sentences individually, then compare answers in pairs, referring to the forms on the board from Exercise 2A (if you went through them). Check answers with the class.

1 order **2** delivers **3** deliveries **4** supplier **5** order

Extra activities 2.1

A This activity provides extra practice of the vocabulary from Exercises 2A and 2B. Students should complete it individually, then compare answers in pairs before class feedback. Encourage students to read each sentence carefully first, and think about what type of word is needed before they choose the correct alternative for it.

1 delivers **2** deliveries **3** deliver **4** delivery
5 order **6** orders **7** order **8** order **9** supplies
10 supplier **11** suppliers **12** supply

3 Go through the instructions with the class and check understanding of *distribution centre* and *chain*. Read through the questions with the class, then ask them to complete the exercise individually. If students ask about the words/phrases in bold in the text, explain what they mean but avoid going into detail about their use, as they will look at them in detail in the Communicative grammar section that follows.

1 b **2** d **3** a **4** c

Communicative grammar: Things you can and can't count
Students study and practise countable/uncountable nouns and quantifiers.

Things you can and can't count
Go through the Grammar box with students and highlight the words and phrases in bold, explaining that some (e.g. *a lot of*) can be used with both types of nouns, while others (e.g. *how many / how much*) can only be used with one type of noun. Refer students back to the webpage in Exercise 3 so they can look again at the target language in context – draw their attention to the quantifiers in bold in the text. You could then refer them to the Grammar reference on page 103, go through it with them and clarify any points as necessary. Students could then do the extra grammar activity there, in class or as homework.
Grammar reference answer key: page 41

4A Explain the activity and if necessary, do the first item as an example with the class. Students complete the rest of the exercise individually, then compare answers in pairs. Check answers with the class.

1 T-shirts (C) **2** winter jackets (C) **3** coffee (U)
4 money (U) **5** pasta (C) **6** jumpers (C)

4B Ask students to complete the sentences individually, and remind them that they can refer to the Grammar box and/or the Grammar reference on page 103 if they need help. Check answers with the class, clarifying any errors/difficulties as necessary.

1 a lot of / many **2** any **3** a lot of **4** any
5 much / a lot of **6** many / a lot of

5 Before starting the exercise, remind students of when we use *a*, *an* and *some* (*a/an* for singular nouns we can count; *some* for plural nouns we can count and nouns we can't count). Ask them to complete the sentences individually, then check answers with the class.

1 an, some **2** a, some **3** an, some **4** an, a

6 This activity is best done in two stages. Start by drawing students' attention to the questions and explaining that they need to complete them with *many* or *much* – elicit or remind them when we use each word (*many* for things we can count and *much* for things we can't count). Check answers with the class, then ask students to match the questions with the answers.

Teacher's notes

Point out that they need to look carefully at the quantifier in each answer – this will help them choose the right question. Check answers with the class. As an extension, you could put students in pairs to practise the questions and answers.

1 many, c 2 much, b 3 many, a 4 much, e 5 much, f
6 many, d

Extra activities 2.1

B This activity provides further practice of countable and uncountable nouns, and quantifiers. Ask students to complete it individually and if there is time, get them to compare answers in pairs before checking with the class.

1 many 2 much 3 an 4 How 5 lot 6 a
7 many 8 much 9 lot 10 many

Video
Students watch a video about a contract caterer in London.

7A ▶ 2.1.1 Tell students that they are going to watch a video about a company called The Good Eating Company, and look at the question with them. You may want to pre-teach the following words from the video: *chef, freshly prepared, flat white* and *fresh produce*. Play the introduction (0:00–0:17), then elicit the answer.

The Good Eating Company runs/manages cafés and restaurants.

7B ▶ 2.1.1 Explain to students that they are now going to watch the full video and complete a text about the Good Eating Company. Give them time to read the text before they watch – to help them, you could tell them that they need to write a number in each gap. Play the video, twice if necessary, then check answers with the class.

1 28/twenty-eight 2 6/six 3 5/five
4 500/five hundred 5 25/twenty-five 6 20/twenty
7 over 300 / over three hundred

7C ▶ 2.1.1 Explain the activity and give students time to read the sentences before they watch the video again. Go through the definitions in the box with them, and also check understanding of *CEO, international, local, flat whites* and *dessert*. In stronger classes, you could ask students to try and answer as many of the questions as they can before watching, then play the video again for them to check/complete their answers.

1 Operations Manager 2 Ireland 3 Chef 4 sells a lot of
5 local 6 suppliers 7 morning 8 hot dishes

Task
Students practise countable/uncountable nouns and quantifiers by asking and answering questions about themselves.

8A Remind students of the questions in Exercise 6. Put them in pairs to discuss the questions, and encourage them to give more information where possible. When they have finished, ask a few students to report back anything interesting they found out about their partner to the class.

8B Refer students to page 126, explain the activity and look at the example with them. Give them plenty of time to complete the sentences while you monitor and help them with any vocabulary they may need. When they are ready, put them in pairs and explain that they should take turns to read their sentences to their partner, for him/her to guess the company. When they have finished, ask a few students to read out their sentences for the class to guess the company.

MyEnglishLab: Teacher's resources: extra activities; Additional interactive activities
Grammar reference: p.103 Things you can and can't count
Teacher's book: Resource bank Extra vocabulary practice p.137 Exercise 1; Photocopiable 2.1 p.114
Workbook: p.9 Exercises 1–3; p.10 Exercises 1 and 2

2.2 ▶ Placing orders on the phone

GSE learning objectives

- Can understand simple work-related questions asked on phone calls.
- Can conduct very simple business transactions using basic language.
- Can make simple purchases by stating what is wanted and asking for the price.
- Can answer simple questions on the phone using fixed expressions.

Lead-in
Students practise asking and answering questions to complete an order form.

1 You could introduce the topic by discussing the following questions with the class: *What orders do you place on the phone for work / in your daily life? What kind of information do people usually ask for when you place a phone order?* Put students in pairs and explain that they are going to complete an order form. Direct Student Bs to page 118, look at the order forms with the class and check understanding of *reference number, product code number* and *quantity*. Before students begin, point out the questions in the speech bubbles and explain that they will need to ask these questions in order to complete their forms. During the activity, monitor and help where necessary. When students have finished, they can look at each other's forms to check their answers.

Teacher's notes

> 1 S342091BE 2 Donaldson Group
> 3 187 High Street, Burham 4 CR88510765V
> 5 GB100463Y 6 250

Listening: An order by phone

Students listen to a customer placing an order by phone.

2A 🔊 2.01 Use the picture and table to pre-teach *catalogue* and *takeaway boxes*. Draw students' attention to the table and explain that it is the online catalogue of Eco Boxes, a company which sells takeaway boxes. Check that they understand the information in each column. Explain that they are going to listen to a customer calling for information, and that they need to make notes on the information the customer needs. Play the recording, then elicit the answer.

> prices for takeaway boxes (400 small white boxes and 500 medium natural boxes)

2B 🔊 2.01 Give students a minute to read through the information so they know what to listen for, then play the recording again for them to choose the correct alternatives. Alternatively, students could attempt the activity from memory, then listen again to check/complete their answers. Check answers with the class.

> 1 2.50 2 3.00 3 2.00 4 natural, white 5 400 6 500
> 7 26th 8 115

Vocabulary: An order by phone

Students look at vocabulary related to taking and placing orders by phone.

3 🔊 2.02 Explain to students that they are going to look at some useful phrases from the recording for taking and placing orders by phone. Give them time to read the phrases before they begin, and go through the definition of *in stock* with them. Students complete the phrases individually. Monitor and offer help where necessary, but do not confirm the answers yet. Play the recording for students to check their answers, then go over the answers with the class, checking understanding of each phrase.

> 1 speaking 2 order 3 have 4 much 5 delivery
> 6 many 7 deliver 8 sorry 9 put 10 much

Extra activities 2.2

A/B These activities practise the functional language from Exercise 3. Ask students to do both exercises individually and if there is time, get them to compare answers in pairs before class feedback. If you are short of time, you could do Exercise B as a whole-class activity, checking answers as you go. As an extension, you could put students in pairs to practise the exchanges.

> A 1 help 2 like 3 have 4 need 5 much 6 cost
> 7 deliver
> B a 5 b 1 c 2 d 4 e 7 f 6 g 3

4 Elicit the first answer as an example, then ask students to categorise the rest of the phrases individually. Check answers with the class.

> 1 S 2 C 3 S 4 C 5 C 6 S 7 C 8 S 9 S 10 C

> ### Pronunciation bank
> p.96: /iː/, /ɪ/ and /aɪ/
>
> **1** 🔊 P2.01 🔊 P2.02 🔊 P2.03 Write the words *eat* and *cheese* on the board, and tell students that they contain the sound /iː/. This is a long vowel in which the lips are spread really wide, as if you were smiling broadly, and the centre of the tongue is raised quite high. You may also mention the phrase 'say cheese', which we often use to make people smile when we are taking their photograph. This might work as a helpful hint on how the vowel is articulated. Play recording P2.01 and get students to repeat the words with the vowel /iː/ in chorus and then individually. Point out that the sound /iː/ is often spelt with the letters *ee* and *ea*, but there are other spellings too, e.g. k*ey* and mach*i*ne.
>
> Now write the words *it* and *chip* on the board, and explain that they contain the sound /ɪ/. This is a short vowel in which the lips are quite wide and the centre of the tongue is raised in the mouth, but not as high as for the vowel /iː/. Play recording P2.02 and get students to repeat the words with /ɪ/ as a group and then individually. Tell them that the vowel /ɪ/ is usually spelt with the letter *i*, but there are common exceptions such as g*y*m and w*o*men.
>
> Finally, write the pronoun *I* and the verb wr*i*te on the board. Explain to students that the words contain the sound /aɪ/. Play recording P2.03 and get students to repeat the words with /aɪ/ as a group and then individually. Point out that /aɪ/ is usually spelt with the letters *i*, *y* or *igh*, but there are common exceptions such as *eye* or b*uy*.
>
> **2** 🔊 P2.04 This exercise focusses on words that only differ in the target vowel sounds. Play the recording and get students to repeat the threes of words individually. Remember that it may be hard for students to hear this difference, especially between /iː/ and /ɪ/, if their first language has fewer or considerably different vowel sounds.
>
> **3A** 🔊 P2.05 Explain the activity and point out that only one word in each sentence contains the /iː/ sound. Play the recording, twice if necessary, then put students in pairs to compare their answers. Do not confirm answers yet – students will check them in Exercise 3D.
>
> > 1 m*ea*ls 2 m*ea*t 3 l*i*tre 4 pl*ea*se 5 gr*ee*n
> > (Note: In *litre* /iː/ is represented by the letter *i*, which typically represents the vowel /ɪ/.)

Teacher's notes

3B 🔊 P2.05 Explain to students that they are going to listen to the recording again but this time they should identify and circle the words containing the vowel /ɪ/. Play the recording, then get students to compare answers in the same pairs as Exercise 3A.

1 de**li**ver   2 f**i**sh   3 dr**i**nks, **i**n   4 m**i**lk   5 **i**s, b**i**g

3C 🔊 P2.05 Play the recording once again and ask students to underline one word in each sentence with the sound /aɪ/. Get them to compare answers in their pairs.

1 motorb**i**kes   2 r**i**ce   3 suppl**y**   4 b**uy**   5 s**i**ze

3D 🔊 P2.05 Tell students that they are going to listen again to check their answers in Exercises 3A–3C. Play the recording, then check answers with the class. Finally, ask students to practise saying the sentences in their pairs, while you monitor and correct pronunciation of /iː/, /ɪ/ and /aɪ/ as necessary.

can/can't

Go through the Grammar box with students, and explain that we use *can* when something is possible, and *can't* when something is not possible. At this point, you may wish to briefly go over the grammar of modal verbs, explaining that they are verbs we use before other verbs, and that the form is the same in all persons. Point out the inversion in questions, and tell students that in negative sentences, the full form is *cannot* – point out that it is (typically) written as one word. You could then refer students to the Grammar reference on page 104 and go through it with them, clarifying any points as necessary. Students could then do the extra grammar activity there, in class or as homework.

Grammar reference answer key: page 41

Extra activities 2.2

C This activity offers extra practice of using *can* and *can't* in sentences expressing possibility. Ask students to do the exercise individually and if there is time, get them to compare answers in pairs before class feedback. As an extension, you could put students in pairs to roleplay appropriate questions and answers using the sentences in this exercise.

1 We can deliver the computers tomorrow, it's not a problem.
2 Can you send the order to us later today?
3 I'm sorry, but we can't give you that information.
4 Our company can help you find new clients.
5 John is very busy today. He can't help me. He doesn't have time.
6 When can you deliver the order?

Speaking

Students practise placing and taking an order by phone.

5 Put students in pairs and direct Student Bs to page 116. Explain that they are going to practise taking and placing orders by phone. Give them time to read their information for roleplay 1. Encourage them to think about which phrases from Exercise 3 they are going to use, and refer to audioscript 2.01 on page 133 if they need help. When they are ready, students roleplay their conversation in pairs. Monitor carefully and make notes on students' language use for later feedback. When they have finished, ask them to swap roles and repeat the above steps for roleplay 2. At the end of the activity, praise any good use of language and go over any common errors/difficulties with the class. As an extension, students could change partners, swap roles and do the roleplays again after feedback and correction work. You could also invite a few pairs to act out their conversations for the rest of the class.

MyEnglishLab: Teacher's resources: extra activities; Additional interactive activities
Grammar reference: p.104 *can/can't*
Pronunciation bank: p.96 /iː/, /ɪ/ and /aɪ/
Teacher's book: Resource bank Extra vocabulary practice p.137 Exercises 2 and 3
Workbook: p.9 Exercises 4 and 5; p.11 Exercises 1–4; p.45 Exercises 1–3

2.3 ❯ Writing
Email enquiries

GSE learning objectives

- Can understand short, simple emails on work-related topics.
- Can read a simple text and extract factual details.
- Can use 'some' as a quantifier with count and mass nouns.
- Can use 'some' and 'any' as quantifiers in negative statements and questions with mass and count nouns.
- Can write short, simple notes, emails and messages relating to everyday matters.
- Can write a simple email/letter in response to a request for information.

Lead-in

Students talk about returning and exchanging things they buy.

1A Depending on the level of the class, you could do this as a whole-class activity, checking answers and clarifying meanings as you go. Alternatively, ask students to complete the exercise individually and then get them to compare answers in pairs before checking with the class. Clarify meanings as necessary during feedback.

1 c   2 a   3 d   4 b

Teacher's notes

1B You could introduce the discussion by giving the class examples of things you sometimes return or exchange yourself. Students can then discuss the questions in pairs, small groups or as a class. If they work in pairs/groups, invite a few students to share their answers with the class.

Reading

Students read a company's FAQs and replies to customers' email enquiries.

2 Write the abbreviation *FAQs* on the board, ask if anyone knows what it means and elicit or give the answer (*Frequently Asked Questions*). Explain to students that they are going to read the FAQs from a company's website. You may also want to pre-teach the following words from the text and questions: *charge* (n), *free of charge*, *discount*, *Customer Services*, *change* (v), *cancel*, *purchase* (n). Students complete the exercise individually, then compare answers in pairs. Check answers with the class.

> **1** b **2** d **3** c **4** a

3A Explain to students that the two emails are replies to customers' enquiries about sections of the FAQs in Exercise 2. Ask them to ignore the gaps for now, and give them 1–2 minutes to read each email quickly and match it to the relevant section of the FAQs. Check answers with the class.

> The first email is replying to an enquiry about returns (question 1 in Exercise 2). The second email is a reply to an enquiry about delivery charges (question 2 in Exercise 2).

3B Go through the phrases in the box with the class, clarifying meanings as necessary. Ask students to complete the exercise individually, and if there is time, get them to compare answers in pairs. Check answers with the class.

> **1** In response to your enquiry, **2** Please find attached
> **3** Please contact us **4** Thank you for your enquiry.

> **Pronunciation bank**
> **p.97:** /tʃ/ and /dʒ/
>
> **1** ◆ P2.06 ◆ P2.07 While you do not need to explain the phonological rules to students, note that the consonants /tʃ/ and /dʒ/ are both pronounced with the tip of the tongue touching the alveolar ridge. The sound /tʃ/ is unvoiced, whereas /dʒ/ is a voiced consonant.
>
> Play recording P2.06 and ask students to repeat the words as a group. Draw their attention to the spelling: the sound /tʃ/ is usually represented by *ch*, *tch* or *t* when followed by *ure*. Then play recording P2.07 and ask students to repeat the words with the sound /dʒ/. Point out that its common spellings are *j* and *g* before *e* and *dge*.

2A ◆ P2.08 The aim of this exercise is to help students notice some exceptional pronunciations of the letters *ch*. Play the recording and ask students to underline the words in which *ch* represents the sound /tʃ/. Check answers with the class. Note that in the words *chemical*, *school* and *technical*, *ch* is pronounced as /k/, while in *machine* and *schedule* (s)*ch* represents /ʃ/, and that the American English pronunciation /ˈskedʒuːl/ can also sometimes be heard in British English.

> **ch**arge, ex**ch**ange, pur**ch**ase, resear**ch**

2B ◆ P2.08 Play the recording again and ask students to repeat as a group and then individually.

3 Give students a minute to look at Exercise 2A and find the words which contain both sounds, then check answers with the class.

> **ch**ar**g**e, ex**ch**an**g**e

4A ◆ P2.09 Explain the activity and play the recording, pausing after each sentence for students to write their answers. If necessary, play the recording a second time for students to check/complete their answers. Check answers with the class. You may also want to ask students whether the missing words contain the sounds /tʃ/ or /dʒ/.

> (/tʃ/ sounds are underlined; /dʒ/ sounds are in bold)
> **1** sandwi<u>ch</u>es, lun<u>ch</u> **2** a**g**enda **3** re**g**ional
> **4** Ea<u>ch</u> bu**dg**et **5** Di**g**ital pro**j**ects

4B ◆ P2.09 Play the recording again, pausing after each sentence for students to repeat as a group. Then put them in pairs to practise saying the sentences. Monitor and correct pronunciation of the /tʃ/ and /dʒ/ sounds as necessary.

Communicative grammar: Saying something exists

Students study and practise *there is* / *there are*.

> **Saying something exists**
>
> Go through the Grammar box with students, clarifying any points as necessary. Point out that we use *there is* with both singular countable nouns and uncountable nouns, and *there are* with plural countable nouns. Highlight the different quantifiers used with each form. You could then refer students to the Grammar reference on page 104, go through it with them, then get them to do the extra grammar activities there, in class or as homework.
>
> **Grammar reference answer key:** page 41

> Teacher's notes

4 Ask students to complete the exercise individually, and remind them that they can refer to the Grammar box and/or the Grammar reference if they need help. Encourage them to look at the quantifier before each noun to help them choose the correct verb form each time. If they need to choose the correct quantifier, they should look carefully at the verb form before it. Check answers with the class, clarifying any errors/ difficulties as necessary.

> 1 are 2 is 3 are 4 is 5 any 6 any 7 aren't 8 isn't

5A Students should complete the conversations individually, then compare answers in pairs if there is time. Do not confirm the answers yet – students will check them in the next exercise.

5B ♦ 2.03 Play the recording for students to check their answers, then go through the answers with the class. Students then practise the conversations in pairs. When they have finished, you could ask them to swap roles and practise again.

> 1 Is there 2 there's 3 Is there 4 there isn't 5 Are there 6 there's 7 Is there 8 there isn't

Extra activities 2.3

A This activity provides further practice of *there is / there are*. Ask students to match the question halves individually, then check answers with the class.

> 1 b 2 c 3 d 4 h 5 f 6 i 7 g 8 e 9 a

B Explain the activity and if necessary, do the first item as an example with the class. Students should complete the exercise individually and then, if there is time, compare answers in pairs before class feedback.

> 1 There is some paper in the boxes.
> 2 There aren't any deliveries today.
> 3A Is there a new model of this phone?
> 3B Yes, there is.
> 4 There are some problems with the new product.
> 5A Are there any new products in the warehouse?
> 5B No, there aren't.
> 6 There isn't any money to buy this at the moment.

Writing

Students write a response to an email enquiry.

6 Explain that the email is another customer's enquiry to the company from Exercise 2. Give students 1–2 minutes to read the email, then ask: *What does the customer want to know?* (prices, if there is a discount for large orders and any delivery charges). Explain the writing task, then refer students back to the model emails in Exercise 3 and point out that students need to open and close their emails in an appropriate way, using phrases to sound polite. Remind them that they can refer back to these emails if they need help. Point out that they should use phrases from Exercise 3 and *there is/are*, then ask them to write their replies, inventing any information they need. With weaker classes, students could plan their emails in pairs, then write them individually. When they have finished, put students in pairs to give each other feedback. Write these questions on the board: *Does the email answer the customer's questions? Does it use phrases from Exercise 3? Does it use 'there is/are' correctly? What does your partner do well? What can he/she improve?* Ask students to read their partner's email and think about the questions on the board, then give feedback to their partner. Alternatively, collect students' emails to mark yourself. Students could then write a second draft for homework.

Model answer

Dear Ms Kuliešienė,

Thank you for your enquiry. We are sorry you can't find the prices on the website. Yes, there is a discount for a large order. Please find attached information about prices and discounts. The delivery charge for orders €200 and under is €5. There are no delivery charges for orders over €200.

Please contact us if you have any questions.

Regards,

Helen Green

Customer Services

MyEnglishLab: Teacher's resources: extra activities; Additional interactive activities
Grammar reference: p.104 Saying something exists
Pronunciation bank: p.97 /tʃ/ and /dʒ/
Workbook: p.10 Exercises 3 and 4; p.12 Exercises 1–4; p.45 Exercises 1–3

2.4 > Work skills
Making agreements

GSE learning objectives

- Can understand what people say they can or can't do from simple sentences spoken slowly and clearly.
- Can recognise simple expressions of agreement and disagreement in short discussions, if conducted slowly and clearly.
- Can make simple arrangements to meet or do something.
- Can conduct very simple business transactions using basic language.
- Can ask for and provide everyday goods and services.

Lead-in

Students talk about the cleaning service at their home and place of work/study.

1 Draw students' attention to the photos and check that they understand what the phrases mean. Discuss the question as a class. You could also add other tasks depending on students' interest and level, e.g. *sweep the floor, mop the floor, water the plants, wash the dishes, wash the windows, dust the shelves*.

Teacher's notes

Video

Students watch a video of a meeting about a cleaning contract.

2 ▶ 2.4.1 Tell students that they are going to watch another video with employees at Sleek, and ask them what they remember about the company. Ask them if they remember who Izabel is (the Office Manager) and explain that in the video, she is meeting Robert, the owner of a cleaning company, to discuss a cleaning contract. Alternatively, refer them to page 6 of the Coursebook and look at the video summary with them. At this point, you may want to pre-teach the following vocabulary from the video: *contract*, *individual* (*office*), *cleaner*, *stairs*, *empty* (v), *provide*, *include*, *invoice* and *equipment*. Read the instructions and items 1–5 with the class, then play the video for students to number the items in the correct order. Check answers with the class.

1 d **2** c **3** b **4** e **5** a

3 ▶ 2.4.1 Give students time to read the notes and think about what type of information they need to complete each gap. When they are ready, play the video again for them to watch and complete the notes. Check answers with the class, writing (or inviting students to write) them on the board to make sure they have spelt them correctly.

1 meeting rooms **2** offices **3** clean (the) floors
4 Monday to Friday (5/five days) **5** 8.30 **6** 3/three hours
7 15/fifteen hours **8** 310 **9** kitchen

4 ▶ 2.4.1 Ask students to complete the exercise individually, then play the video again for them check their answers. Go over the answers with the class, clarifying meanings as necessary. Students could then practise asking and answering the questions in pairs.

1 f **2** d **3** e **4** a **5** b **6** g **7** h **8** c

Extra activities 2.4

A This activity provide further practice of the functional language from the video. You could do it after Exercise 4 or after going through the Speaking box in the next section with the class. Students should complete the exercise individually, then compare answers in pairs before class feedback.

1 there **2** about **3** fine **4** provide **5** much
6 many **7** include

B/C Follow the same procedure for both exercises. Go through the sentences in the box with the class and check understanding of each one. Get students to complete the conversations individually, then check answers with the class. If there is time, you could put students in pairs to practise the conversations.

B 1 A cold buffet at our office and some drinks.
  2 There are twenty-five staff here.
  3 How about next Friday at 1 o'clock?
  4 Yes, there is. How many chefs are there?
  5 Can the chefs clean the kitchen after the event?
C 1 Can you provide the plates and glasses?
  2 Does the price include the plates and cups?
  3 How much is that?
  4 And how much is the total for twenty-five staff?

Speaking: Making agreements

Students look at useful language for making business agreements.

Making agreements

Go through the phrases in the Speaking box with the class, clarifying meanings as necessary and pointing out the function of each group of phrases. You may need to help students with the pronunciation of some of the phrases, drilling them chorally and individually. For some quick practice, you could put students in pairs and ask them to take turns to choose a yes/no question from the first two sections of the Speaking box, for their partner to answer using phrases from the *Saying yes* and *Saying no* sections.

Unit 2 Extra speaking lesson

This lesson gives further practice of speaking related to making agreements. To access the lesson go to MyEnglishLab > Extra speaking lessons.

5 Put students in pairs and explain that they are going to practise making agreements. Direct them to their relevant pages and give them plenty of time to read their information and think about what to say. Remind them that they can refer to the Speaking box if they need help. Monitor and offer help where necessary, and when students are ready, ask them to practise their conversations. Monitor and check they are using the phrases correctly. Note down any common errors, then go over them with the class at the end of the activity.

6 Explain the activity and scenario, direct students to their relevant pages and give them time to read their information and think about what they are going to say. Since this roleplay is about a catering contact, you may want to pre-teach/elicit some useful vocabulary, such as *catering*, *buffet*, *glasses* and *plates*. Before they start, go through the conversation outline with the class and remind them to use phrases from the Speaking box. During the roleplays, monitor and note down any points to highlight during feedback. When students have finished, you could ask a few pairs to perform their conversations for the class. Finally, have a brief feedback session highlighting any points you noted while monitoring.

MyEnglishLab: Teacher's resources: extra activities; Extra speaking lessons; Additional interactive activities
Teacher's book: Resource bank Extra vocabulary practice p.137 Exercises 4 and 5; Photocopiable 2.4 p.115
Workbook: p.13 Exercises 1–3

Business workshop
Planning a work party

GSE learning objectives
- Can extract specific information (e.g. facts and numbers) from simple informational texts related to everyday life (e.g. posters, leaflets).
- Can understand short, simple emails on work-related topics.
- Can write a simple email/letter in a response to a request for information.
- Can make simple arrangements to meet or do something.
- Can conduct very simple business transactions using basic language.
- Can answer simple work-related questions on the phone using fixed expressions.

Introduction
Students read an email about arranging an employee's anniversary party.

1 Explain to students that they are going to practise planning a work party, and read the instructions with them. Draw their attention to the email, give them 2 minutes to read it, then ask: *What does the sender want you to organise?* (an anniversary party) *Who is the party for?* (Emilia, an employee). Check the answer with the class.

> contact a catering company and arrange a buffet lunch for 60 people on 14 March; organise an extra cleaning service after the party

Reading
Students complete an enquiry email and write a reply.

2 If you think your students will find this activity difficult, review the Communicative grammar sections in Lessons 2.1 and 2.3 before you start. Explain that students are going to hire a catering company for the party in Exercise 1 and that the email they are going to complete is an enquiry email to this company. Go through the information with the class and check understanding of *platter* and *canapés*. Then ask students to complete the questions in the email – point out that the first letter is given. Get them to compare answers in pairs, then check answers with the class. You could also point out the more formal style of this email, and highlight some useful phrases before students write their reply in the next activity. Explain that we use *Dear Sir/Madam* when we do not know the name of the person we are writing to, and *Regards* as a more formal way of finishing an email.

> **1** are there **2** How many **3** How many **4** how much **5** is there

3 Explain that students are now going to write a reply to the email in Exercise 2. Allow plenty of preparation time and encourage students to use appropriate phrases from Exercise 3A of Lesson 2.3 in their emails. Point out that they should answer all the questions in the email in Exercise 2. With weaker classes, you could let students plan their emails in pairs, then write them individually.

> **Model answer**
> Dear Ms Patterson,
> Thank you for your enquiry. Please find attached our sandwich menu with the vegetarian options. This information is also on the website. There are six canapés per person. You can select from twenty items on the menu. Each cake and dessert platter serves six to eight people. We deliver in the London area and do not charge for delivery. There is a 5% discount for orders of £500 and over.
> Please contact us again if you have any questions. You can also call 0938 665 0123 to speak to one of our team.
> Regards,
> Gonzalo

Speaking
Students practise taking and placing an order by phone, and making a business agreement.

4A If you think your students will find this activity difficult, review the phrases in Exercise 3 of Lesson 2.2 before you start. You could put some of the phrases on the board for students to refer to during their roleplays. Explain that students are now going to place an order for food for the party, put them in pairs and direct them to their relevant information. Give them time to read their information and think about what to say, while you monitor and offer help where necessary. When students are ready, they roleplay their phone calls. Point out that they should not show their notes / order form to their partner. During the roleplays, monitor and make notes on any common errors for later class feedback.

> **Student A:** £956.65 with 5% discount
> **Student B:** **2** 14 March **3** 60/sixty **4** 10/ten **5** 5/five **6** 3/three **7** 2/two **8** 10/ten **9** 8/eight **10** 11.30 a.m.

4B Students should do this in the same pairs as Exercise 4A. Explain that they should now compare the information they wrote down during the roleplays, and check that it is all correct. Check answers with the class, and highlight any points you noted while monitoring.

5 If you think your students will find this activity difficult, review the Speaking section of Lesson 2.4 before you start. It would be a good idea for students to change partners at this stage to ensure they practise with a variety of people. Put them in new pairs and explain that they are going to arrange a cleaning service for the party. Student A works for Best Cleaning Services, and Student B works for Benham Engineering. Direct students to their relevant pages, giving them plenty of time to read the information and prepare for their roleplay, while you monitor and offer help where necessary. Point out that Student As should complete the questions they are going to ask the customer, and then complete their notes during the roleplay; Student Bs should look carefully at what they want the cleaner to do, and then add the cost of the service to their notes. When they are ready, students roleplay their conversations. During the activity, monitor and make notes on any errors/difficulties to highlight during feedback, but do not interrupt the roleplays. When students have finished, ask them to compare their information and check that all the details of the agreement are correct. Finally, have a brief feedback session, highlighting any points you noted while monitoring.

Student A
Questions
1 What date do you want the extra cleaning service?
2 How many extra hours do you need?
3 What time do you want the cleaner to come?
4 Which rooms do you want the cleaner to clean?
5 What do you want the cleaner to do?
Notes
2 14 March
3 2/two
4 start after 5.30 p.m.
5 the conference room and staff kitchen
6 clean the tables, empty bins and vacuum the carpet in the conference room, wash the plates and glasses, clean the kitchen floor

Student B
Notes
£48 (£24/hour for two hours)

Review 2

1 1 deliveries 2 order 3 supplies 4 delivered
  5 suppliers 6 order
2A 1 How can I help you?
  2 I'd like to order some office desks.
  3 Do you have the product reference number?
  4 How many small boxes do you need?
  5 How much are the large boxes?
  6 How much does delivery cost?
  7 Can you deliver by Monday morning?
2B 1 d 2 g 3 c 4 b 5 a 6 f 7 e
3 1 many 2 much 3 much 4 much 5 many 6 many
  7 many 8 much
4 1 c 2 a 3 b 4 c 5 a 6 a
5 1 Is there 2 There are 3 There isn't / There is not
  4 Is there 5 There aren't / There are not 6 There's / There is 7 Are there 8 There isn't / There is not
6A 1 many, there 2 many, do 3 do 4 much 5 do
  6 much 7 Does 8 Is there 9 can
6B 1 S 2 S 3 S 4 C 5 S 6 C 7 C 8 S 9 C

Grammar reference 2

2.1

1 1 How much 2 How many 3 How much
  4 How much 5 a lot of 6 many 7 any 8 much

2.2

1 1 How can I help you?
  2 I can't see the prices.
  3 We can send you a new catalogue.
  4 Can we order 300 small boxes?
  5 We can deliver your order on Friday.
  6 We can't send any white boxes.

2.3

1A 1 There are 2 There is 3 There is 4 There are
  5 Is there 6 Are there 7 Is there 8 Are there
1B 1 There aren't any deliveries today.
  2 There isn't a meeting this morning.
  3 There isn't any new computer equipment.
  4 There aren't any visitors in reception.

3 Changes

Unit overview

		CLASSWORK		FURTHER WORK
3.1 A company's story	Lead-in	Students talk about a businessperson.		**MyEnglishLab:** Teacher's resources: extra activities; Additional interactive activities
	Vocabulary	Students look at vocabulary related to describing changes at work.		**Grammar reference:** p.104 Talking about the past (1)
	Communicative grammar	Students study and practise the Past Simple of regular verbs.		**Pronunciation bank:** p.97 The -ed ending
	Video	Students watch a video about the history of two companies.		**Teacher's book:** Resource bank Extra vocabulary practice p.138 Exercises 1
	Task	Students exchange information in order to complete a timeline.		**Workbook:** p.14 Exercises 1 and 2; p.15 Exercises 1 and 2; p.46 Exercises 1–3
3.2 New office	Lead-in	Students discuss work/study locations.		**MyEnglishLab:** Teacher's resources: extra activities; Additional interactive activities
	Vocabulary	Students look at useful language for emails giving instructions and practise imperatives.		**Grammar reference:** p.106 Giving instructions
	Reading and listening	Students complete an email giving instructions and listen to a conversation about an office move.		**Teacher's book:** Resource bank Extra vocabulary practice p.138 Exercises 2
	Writing	Students write an email giving instructions.		**Workbook:** p.14 Exercises 3 and 4; p.16 Exercises 1–3
3.3 Company performance	Lead-in	Students talk about communicating with their place of work or study.		**MyEnglishLab:** Teacher's resources: extra activities; Additional interactive activities
	Reading	Students read an email and look at useful vocabulary for describing a company's performance.		**Grammar reference:** p.106 Talking about the past (2)
	Communicative grammar	Students study and practise the Past Simple of irregular verbs.		**Pronunciation bank:** p.98 /ɜː/ and /ɔː/
	Writing	Students write an email about a company's performance.		**Teacher's book:** Resource bank Photocopiable 3.3 p.116
				Workbook: p.15 Exercises 3 and 4; p.17 Exercises 1–3; p.46 Exercises 1–3
3.4 Work skills: How did it go?	Lead-in	Students discuss production processes.		**MyEnglishLab:** Teacher's resources: extra activities; Extra speaking lessons; Additional interactive activities
	Video	Students watch a video of a feedback meeting.		**Teacher's book:** Resource bank Extra vocabulary practice p.138 Exercises 3–5; Photocopiable 3.4 p.117
	Speaking	Students look at useful language for talking about projects.		**Workbook:** p.18 Exercises 1–3
Business workshop: Our first year	Reading	Students read a timeline about a new company.		
	Writing	Students write an email giving instructions.		
	Speaking	Students talk about a new company's performance.		

Unit vocabulary list

Active vocabulary

3.1
create a company
expand (a/the/your/its) market
hire more employees
launch (a product / an award)
move (from ... to ...)
open a shop/store
produce (coffee)
start a company

3.2
To all staff
Dear employees
Please do the following
Please follow these instructions
Thank you for your help
We appreciate your cooperation
Best wishes
Regards

3.3
bought advertising
built relationships (with customers)
grew our business
had problems
hit our (sales) targets
made progress
spent (£/$/€) on (something)
went to events
won new business

Passive vocabulary

3.3
blog post
emails
intranet

newsletter
website

3.4
generally
in particular

design (*noun*)
test (a design)

deadline
instructions
manufacturing
material
shipping company
supplier
teamwork

Teacher's notes

3.1 A company's story

GSE learning objectives
- Can get the gist of short, simple stories if told slowly and clearly.
- Can talk about their life (e.g. family, home, job), using simple language.
- Can ask yes/no questions using the past tense of verbs.
- Can make affirmative statements using common regular Past Simple forms.
- Can answer simple questions about work experience or education using simple language.
- Can identify simple information in a short video, provided that the visual supports this information and the delivery is slow and clear.

Lead-in
Students talk about a businessperson.

1 Explain the activity and tell students that they can talk about someone they know or someone famous. Give them a few minutes to think about their answers and make notes if they want to, then put them in pairs to discuss the questions. When they have finished, invite a few students to share their answers with the class.

Vocabulary: A company's story
Students look at vocabulary related to describing changes at work.

2A Draw students' attention to the timeline and ask if they know the company and what they know about it. Give them time to read the timeline quickly and answer the question – tell them not to worry about any unknown words for now. Elicit the answer.

31

2B Explain the activity, check understanding of the verbs in bold in the timeline and answer any other questions students have about vocabulary. Read sentences a–h with the class, and check understanding of *coffee supply* and *employees*. Ask students to complete the exercise individually, then check answers with the class, but do not go into detail about the Past Simple yet – students will look at it in the Communicative grammar section that follows. If time is short, you could do this as a whole-class activity, checking answers as you go.

1 c **2** e **3** a **4** f **5** b **6** g **7** d **8** h

2C Explain the activity and if necessary, do the first item as an example with the class. Get students to do the exercise individually, then check answers with the class. Again, you could do this as a whole-class activity if time is short, checking answers as you go.

1 c **2** e **3** a **4** f **5** b **6** g **7** d **8** h

Extra activities 3.1

A This activity provides extra practice of the vocabulary in Exercise 2. Ask students to complete the exercise individually, and remind them that they can refer to Exercises 2B and 2C if they need help. Check answers with the class.

1 b **2** f **3** a **4** d **5** c **6** g **7** e **8** h

Communicative grammar: Talking about the past (1)
Students study and practise the Past Simple of regular verbs.

Talking about the past (1)
Go through the Grammar box with students and explain that there are two types of Past Simple forms: regular verbs and irregular verbs; we form the Past Simple of most regular verbs by adding *-ed* to the base form – refer students to the examples in the first section of the Grammar box. Then ask them to look at the other two sections, and try to elicit the rules for forming questions. Highlight the use of the base form of the verb (rather than the Past Simple form) after *did*, and also the difference between subject and object questions. Refer students back to the timeline in Exercise 2A so they can look again at the target language in context – draw their attention to the verbs in bold. You could then refer them to the Grammar reference on pages 104–105 and go through it with them (note that the negative form is covered on page 106, under *Talking about the past (2)*). Pay particular attention to the spelling rules as well as the section on subject and object questions. Students could then do the extra grammar activities there, in class or as homework.

Grammar reference answer key: page 53

Pronunciation bank
p.97: The *-ed* ending

1A ▶ P3.01 While you do not need to explain the phonological rules, it can be useful to be aware that the *-ed* ending can be pronounced /t/, /d/ or /ɪd/, depending on the final sound in the word. If the word ends with an unvoiced consonant (/s/, /k/, /p/, /f/, /θ/, /ʃ/, /tʃ/), the *-ed* ending is pronounced /t/. If the word ends with a voiced consonant (/b/, /g/, /z/, /ð/, /v/, /ʒ/, /dʒ/, /l/, /r/, /m/, /n/, /ŋ/) or any vowel sound, the *-ed* ending is pronounced /d/. In the past forms of verbs ending with /t/ or /d/, we add a full syllable, and *-ed* is pronounced /ɪd/. As a minimum, students should recognise that the *-ed* ending has different phonological realisations. Play the recording and ask students to repeat the verbs individually.

1B Ask the question to the whole class. You could play the recording again and repeat each verb ending exaggeratedly to help students hear the differences of sounds.

> The green past forms are different because they add an extra syllable at the end of the word, rather than just a phoneme. This is because the base form of the words (*start, found*) end in the sounds /t/ and /d/.

Teacher's notes

2A ◆ P3.02 Explain the activity, let students hear the first item and pause the recording to look at the example with them. Note that the sentences in each pair only differ by the verb forms: Present Simple or Past Simple. The object *it* linked to the preceding verb may make the understanding even more challenging. Play the recording, twice if necessary, then check answers with the class.

> 2 I liked it.
> 3 They supply it.
> 4 I used it.
> 5 We want it.
> 6 They needed it.

2B ◆ P3.03 Play the recording and get students to repeat the sentences as a group or individually.

3A ◆ P3.04 Play the recording and get students to repeat the verbs individually. Encourage them to exaggerate slightly with the careful pronunciation of the endings – this helps form a habit of paying attention to the word final sound. Pause after each pair of verbs and ask students how the *-ed* ending is pronounced.

> 1 /t/   2 /ɪd/   3 /d/   4 /d/   5 /t/   6 /ɪd/

3B ◆ P3.05 Play the recording and ask students to repeat the sentences in chorus. Then put them in pairs to practise saying the sentences. Monitor and focus individualised correction on the Past Simple forms themselves – do not draw attention to other errors students might make with the sentences.

3A Ask students what they know about Bill Gates and elicit answers around the class. Then draw their attention to the timeline, give them time to read it, and check understanding of *Chairman*, *Advisor* (American English) / *Adviser* (British English), *launch* (v) and *charity*. Explain the activity and if necessary, elicit the first answer as an example. Students then complete the rest of the exercise individually, referring to the Grammar reference if they need help. Check answers with the class, writing (or inviting students to write) the verbs on the board.

> 1 finished   2 studied   3 started   4 launched
> 5 changed   6 played

3B Get students to complete the exercise individually, then check answers with the class.

> 1 What did Bill Gates do in 1973?
> 2 Did he finish university?
> 3 When did he start Microsoft?
> 4 What did he launch in 1985?
> 5 Did his job at Microsoft change in 2000?
> 6 Who did he play tennis with in 2017?

3C Put students in pairs to ask and answer the questions in Exercise 3B. Point out that they will need to refer to the timeline in Exercise 3A for the answers. If necessary, do the first item as an example with the class. Give pairs 3–4 minutes to complete the exercise, then check answers with the class.

> 1 He finished school.
> 2 No, he didn't.
> 3 (He started Microsoft) in 1975.
> 4 He launched Windows.
> 5 Yes, he did.
> 6 (He played (tennis) with) Roger Federer.

Extra activities 3.1

B This activity provides extra practice of the Past Simple of regular verbs. Ask students to complete the exercise individually, and go through the verbs in the box with them before they begin. Encourage them to read the whole text quickly before they attempt the task – this will help them choose the correct verb for each gap. Check answers with the class.

> 1 moved   2 started   3 worked   4 produced
> 5 created   6 encouraged   7 loved   8 hired
> 9 opened   10 expanded

C Give students a minute or two to read the information and help them with vocabulary where necessary. Ask them to complete the questions individually, then check answers with the class.

> 1 Who   2 study   3 When   4 What   5 produce
> 6 launched   7 did   8 Did

D Explain the activity and do the first item as an example with the class if necessary. Students could write the answers individually or, in weaker classes, in pairs. Alternatively, if time is short, you could do this as an oral activity: put students in pairs and get them to take turns to ask a question from Exercise C for their partner to answer. Check answers with the class.

> 1 Richard Branson.   2 No, he didn't.   3 In 2014.
> 4 Start work. / They started work.   5 Yes, it did.
> 6 Richard Branson.   7 Business Administration.
> 8 No, they didn't.

4 You may want to give students a few minutes to think about their answers and make notes first. Draw students' attention to questions 2 and 3 and elicit that *was/were* are the past of *is/are*. Explain that this is an irregular form and these are looked at in more detail in Lesson 3.3. When they are ready, put them in pairs to ask and answer the questions. If students do not yet have any work experience, tell them that they can invent information. Monitor and check they are using the Past Simple correctly, noting down any common errors to highlight during feedback. When they have finished, ask a few students to share anything interesting they found out about their partner with the class. Finally, have a brief feedback session, highlighting any points you noted while monitoring.

Teacher's notes

Video

Students watch a video about the history of two companies.

5A ▶ 3.1.1 Explain to students that they are going to watch a video about the history of two companies. You may want to pre-teach the following vocabulary from the video – you could look at all the words now or teach the vocabulary from each part of the video before students watch it: *be based in*, *employ* (v), *hire*, *Sales Associate*, *Head of Operations*, *be valued* (at), *store design*, *feel* (n). Read the question with the class so they know what to listen for, then play the video introduction (0:00–0:22) and elicit the answer.

> Postmark sell cards and gifts. The Cambridge Satchel Company sell bags.

5B ▶ 3.1.1 Explain to students that Part 1 of the video is about Postmark. Give them time to read the questions and go through the definition of *annual turnover* with them. Encourage them to make notes in answer to the questions while watching, and play the first part of the video. In weaker classes, students may need to watch the video a second time in order to check/complete their answers. Check answers with the class.

> 1 Leona's husband, Mark.
> 2 In 2004.
> 3 a) In 2006 it was £120,000. b) Last year it was approximately £1.3 million.
> 4 Postmark has four stores and employs 24 people.
> 5 Morgan arrived in the UK in 2008. She worked as a Sales Assistant.
> 6 Morgan joined Postmark in 2013.

5C ▶ 3.1.1 Tell students that Part 2 of the video is about The Cambridge Satchel Company. Explain the activity and give them time to read the statements so they know what to listen for. Depending on the time available and the level of your class, you may want to do the activity in two stages: play the second part of the video for students to decide if the statements are true or false, and check answers with the class. Then play it a second time for them to correct the false statements. Get them to compare answers in pairs before class feedback.

> 1 T
> 2 F (They opened a factory in 2011.)
> 3 F (The company now has 155 employees.)
> 4 F (The company has five shops – one in Cambridge, London, Brighton, Oxford and Edinburgh.)
> 5 F (Max is Head of Special Projects.)
> 6 T

Task

Students exchange information in order to complete a timeline.

6 Explain to students that they are going to complete timelines about two successful businesspeople. Put them in pairs and direct them to their relevant pages. Explain the task and give them time to read the information, helping with vocabulary where necessary. Then ask them if they have heard of either of the people and what they know about them, feeding in information from the Notes below. Give students plenty of time to prepare their questions. Go round and offer help where necessary, and check that they are forming Past Simple questions correctly. When they are ready, students take turns to ask and answer their questions in order to complete their timelines. Monitor and make notes on any common errors for later feedback. When they have finished, ask students to look at each other's information and check it is correct. Check answers with the class, and go over any common errors you noted while monitoring.

> **Part 1**
> Student B's questions
> 1 Where did Liu Qing study? / At what university did Liu Qing study?
> 2 What (subject) did she study at Harvard?
> 3 When did she start work?
> 4 Who/Which company did she join / work for?
> 5 When did she change jobs?
> 6 What Forbes' list was she on in 2018?
> Student A's answers
> 1 (She studied at) Peking University.
> 2 (She studied) Computer Science.
> 3 (She started work) in 2002.
> 4 (She worked for) Goldman Sachs.
> 5 (She changed jobs) in 2014.
> 6 (She was in) Top 100 Businesswomen.
> Timeline
> 1 Peking 2 Computer Science 3 2002
> 4 Goldman Sachs 5 2014 6 Top 100 Businesswomen
> **Part 2**
> Student A's questions
> 1 When did Arash finish high school?
> 2 What did he launch in June 2007?
> 3 What did he do in September 2007?
> 4 What did he do from 2007 to 2016?
> 5 When did he change jobs/start a new job?
> Student B's answers
> 1 (He finished high school) in 2004.
> 2 (He launched) Dropbox (in 2007).
> 3 He finished university (at MIT) (with no degree).
> 4 He worked as Chief Technology Officer of Dropbox.
> 5 (He changed jobs / started a new job) in 2016.
> Timeline
> 1 2004 2 Dropbox 3 Finishes university (at MIT)
> 4 Chief Technology Officer 5 2016

> **Notes**
>
> **Liu Qing** (b. 1978) is a Chinese businesswoman and President of the mobile transportation platform Didi Chuxing (aka 'DiDi'). Daughter of the founder of the technology company, Lenovo, she studied Computer Science at Peking University and at Harvard University.
>
> **Arash Ferdowsi** (b. 1985) is an American entrepreneur and co-founder of Dropbox, a file-sharing and storage service. He studied Electrical Engineering and Computer Science at Massachusetts Institute of Technology (MIT), but dropped out in his final year to set up Dropbox.

MyEnglishLab: Teacher's resources: extra activities; Additional interactive activities
Grammar reference: p.104 Talking about the past (1)
Pronunciation bank: p.97 The *-ed* ending
Teacher's book: Resource bank Extra vocabulary practice p.138 Exercise 1
Workbook: p.14 Exercises 1 and 2; p.15 Exercises 1 and 2; p.46 Exercises 1–3

3.2 New office

GSE learning objectives

- Can use language related to giving instructions and orders.
- Can understand simple requests or instructions to carry out concrete work-related tasks.
- Can write very short, basic directions.
- Can use language related to in the office.

Lead-in

Students discuss work/study locations.

1 You could introduce the topic by asking students what changes are taking place in their place of work or study at the moment, and whether they think these changes are positive or negative. Invite a few students to share their answers with the class, then go through the questions in Exercise 1 with them, and check understanding of *location*. Look at the example with students, then put them in pairs or small groups to discuss the questions. Get brief feedback from the class.

Vocabulary: Email phrases

Students look at useful language for emails giving instructions and practise imperatives.

2A Draw students' attention to the subject line of the email and the questions, and elicit what students think the answers might be. Elicit a few ideas, then ask students to read the email to check them. Check answers with the class. During feedback, check understanding of the following vocabulary from the email: *arrangements, (the) following, remove, warehouse, attached*.

> 1 Beth Lowry, Office Manager
> 2 remove everything from their desk; put their things in a box; write their name of the box; not move the box; look at the plan and find their new workspace

2B Go through the phrases with the class, clarifying meanings as necessary, then ask students to complete the exercise individually. Check answers with the class. Elicit or explain that phrases a–d are more formal than the ones used in the email.

> **a** 4 **b** 1 **c** 3 **d** 2

Giving instructions

Go through the examples in the Grammar box with the class, and explain or elicit that we use the infinitive for positive instructions and *don't* + infinitive for negative instructions. Point out the last example in each column and highlight the use of *please* to sound more polite. You could then refer students to the Grammar reference on page 106, go through it with them, then get them to do the extra grammar activities there, in class or as homework. Note that 'please' can go at the beginning or end of sentences (e.g. 1, 2, 3 & 5), although a comma should precede 'please' when it is at the end of a sentence. This is more appropriate in spoken English, rather than in written instructions.

Grammar reference answer key: page 53

3 Ask students to complete the exercise individually, then check answers with the class. Alternatively, if time is short, you could do this as a whole-class activity, checking answers as you go.

> **1** b **2** f **3** c **4** e **5** a **6** d

Extra activities 3.2

A This activity provides extra practice of useful language for emails giving instructions and is best done after Exercise 2B. Ask students to complete it individually, then check answers with the class. During feedback, check understanding of each phrase.

> **1** f **2** d **3** a **4** e **5** c **6** g **7** b

B This activity provides further practice of imperatives and is best done after Exercise 3. Elicit the first answer as an example, then ask students to complete the rest of the exercise individually. Get them to compare answers in pairs before checking with the class. Note that 'please' could also go at the end of these sentences, although a comma should precede 'please' (a comma is not present in the exercise).

> 1 Please arrive at 9 o'clock. / Arrive at 9 o'clock, please.
> 2 Don't move your desk.
> 3 Make a reservation for a meeting room.
> 4 Please don't eat in your workspace. / Don't eat at your workspace, please.
> 5 Come to the meeting at noon.
> 6 Please pay with your credit card. / Pay with your credit card, please.

Reading and listening

Students complete an email giving instructions and listen to a conversation about an office move.

4 Ask students to complete the email individually. Encourage them to read it quickly first to get the gist before attempting the exercise. If there is time, get them to compare answers in pairs before class feedback.

> **1** Dear all **2** don't use **3** talk **4** make **5** don't have **6** Go **7** for your cooperation **8** Regards

5A ◆ 3.01 Explain to students that they are going to hear a conversation about an office move. Read the questions with them so they know what to listen for, and ask them to make notes in answer to the questions while listening. Play the recording, then check answers with the class.

> 1 The company hired ten new employees and needs to move to a bigger office.
> 2 A party. / There is a party to celebrate the move to the new offices.

Teacher's notes

5B 🔊 3.01 Explain the activity and give students time to read the notes before they listen. Encourage them to think about what kind of information is missing in each gap (e.g. 1 a number, 2 a place). Play the recording, twice if necessary, then check answers with the class.

> 1 10/ten 2 new, bigger 3 9.00 4 office 5 12.30
> 6 1.00 p.m. 7 change 8 6.00 p.m.

Writing

Students write an email giving instructions.

6A Explain the activity and point out that students will have to give both positive and negative instructions. Give them time to read the sentences before they begin and check that they understand *celebration* in sentence 7. Ask them to complete the instructions individually and if there is time, get them to compare answers in pairs before class feedback.

> 1 arrive 2 Put 3 Don't stay 4 Don't come
> 5 Find, don't change 6 find 7 join

6B Explain the writing task and ask students to write their emails individually. Remind them of the phrases in Exercise 2B and tell them that they can refer to the emails in Exercises 2A and 4, as well as the instructions they completed in Exercise 6A, if they need support. Monitor as they write and offer corrections as you go along. When they have finished, you could put students in pairs to compare their emails.

> **Model answer**
> Dear all,
> As you know, we need to move to new, bigger offices next week. Please follow these instructions on Thursday morning:
> - please arrive by 9.00 a.m.
> - put the things from your desk in boxes, but please don't move the boxes.
> - please leave before 12.30 p.m.
> On Friday:
> - don't come to work in the morning. Please arrive between 12.30 and 1.00 p.m.
> - find your desk. Please don't change desks with other employees.
> - you can find your office items on your new desk.
> - please join the party for our new office at 6 p.m.
> We appreciate your cooperation.
> Best wishes,
> Andrew

MyEnglishLab: Teacher's resources: extra activities
Grammar reference: p.106 Giving instructions
Teacher's book: Resource bank Extra vocabulary practice p.138 Exercise 2
Workbook: p.14 Exercises 3 and 4; p.16 Exercises 1–3

3.3 Writing
Company performance

> **GSE learning objectives**
> - Can understand short, simple emails on work-related topics.
> - Can read a simple text and extract factual details.
> - Can write short basic descriptions of past events and activities.
> - Can write short, simple notes, emails and messages relating to everyday matters.
> - Can make affirmative statements using common irregular Past Simple forms.

Lead-in

Students talk about communicating with their place of work or study.

1A As a brief warm-up, you could ask students what their most/least favourite ways of communicating with different people are and why. Next, introduce the exercise, go through the types of communication with students and check that they understand each one. Ask them to complete the exercise individually.

1B If there is time, let students discuss the questions in pairs or small groups first, then elicit answers around the class.

Reading: Past successes and challenges

Students read an email and look at useful vocabulary for describing a company's performance.

2A Go through the table with the class and explain the meanings of any new words. Also check they understand *succeed* in the instructions, and pre-teach *store* (another word for *shop*). Explain that the email is a company communication to all employees and ask students to complete the exercise individually – tell them not to worry about new vocabulary at this stage. Also encourage them to underline the parts of the email that give them the answers, and elicit these during feedback. If time allows, get students to compare answers in pairs before checking with the class.

> 1 No 2 Yes 3 Yes 4 No 5 Yes 6 No

2B Briefly explain that the verbs in bold in the email are all irregular Past Simple verbs, i.e. they are not formed by adding *-ed*, as regular Past Simple verbs are. Ask students to match them to their present forms, then check answers with the class, clarifying meanings as necessary. Alternatively, you could do this as a quick, whole-class activity, checking answers and clarifying meanings as you go.

> b made c won d had e built f grew g bought
> h spent i was j went k didn't hit l didn't win

2c Students use the email in Exercise 2A to answer the questions. If you are short of time, this could be done as an oral, whole-class activity, checking answers as you go. During feedback, answer any questions students have about vocabulary in the email.

> 1 ten   2 twelve   3 at bike events
> 4 in the Northside area   5 $10,000

Pronunciation bank
p.98: /ɜː/ and /ɔː/

1 🔊 P3.06 🔊 P3.07 The sounds /ɜː/ and /ɔː/ are long vowels. The sound /ɜː/ is a central unrounded vowel. The tongue is low and the lips are stretched out. By contrast, the vowel /ɔː/ is a back rounded vowel. The tongue is low and the lips are pushed together lightly. Demonstrate the two sounds and explain to students that they are going to hear groups of words containing each sound. Play recording P3.06 and get them to repeat the words individually or as a group. Draw their attention to the spelling and explain that the vowel /ɜː/ is commonly represented by *ir* (*sir*), *er* (*term*), *ear* (*earn*) and *ur* (*turn*). Then play recording P3.07 and get students to repeat the words with the sound /ɔː/. Explain that it has a wide range of spellings, such as *oor* (*door*), *ore* (*store*), *au* (*August*), *ough* (*thought*), *ar* (*war*) or *a* (*all*).

2A 🔊 P3.08 Explain to students that the spelling *or* can represent either /ɜː/ or /ɔː/. Play the recording and ask them to underline the words with /ɜː/. Check answers with the class.

> word, work, world, worse, worst

2B 🔊 P3.08 Play the recording again for students to circle the words with /ɔː/, then check answers with the class.

> forward, north, order, passport, New York

2c 🔊 P3.08 Play the recording again and get students to repeat the words, individually or as a group.

3A 🔊 P3.09 Explain to students that they are going to complete the sentences with one word and then decide whether each word contains an /ɜː/ or /ɔː/ sound. If necessary, complete the first sentence as an example with the class. Play the recording, pausing after each sentence; encourage students to say each word to themselves and decide which sound each word contains. Check answers with the class.

> 1 Thursday /ɜː/   2 survey /ɜː/   3 store /ɔː/
> 4 morning /ɔː/   5 prefer /ɜː/   6 exports /ɔː/

3B 🔊 P3.09 Play the recording, pausing after each sentence for students to repeat as a group. Then put students in pairs to practise saying the sentences. Monitor and correct pronunciation of the target sounds as necessary.

Communicative grammar: Talking about the past (2)

Students study and practise the Past Simple of irregular verbs.

Talking about the past (2)
Go through the examples in the Grammar box with students and remind them that irregular verbs do not form the Past Simple with the *-ed* ending – each verb has its own form. Also highlight the use of the verb *be*: point out that it does not use the auxiliary *did/didn't* in negatives and questions. Refer students back to the email in Exercise 2A so that they can look again at the target language in context – draw their attention to the verbs in bold. Point out that there is a list of irregular verbs on page 114 of the Coursebook. You could then refer them to the Grammar reference on page 106, go through it with them and clarify any points as necessary. Students could then do the extra grammar activities there, in class or as homework.

Grammar reference answer key: page 53

3 Ask students to complete the exercise individually and remind them that they can refer to the irregular verbs list on page 114 if they need help. Check answers with the class and write (or invite students to write) the verbs on the board, so students can check their spelling.

> 1 didn't meet   2 bought, didn't buy   3 hired
> 4 won, made   5 didn't grow   6 missed, made

Extra activities 3.3

A This activity practises Past Simple negatives. Ask students to complete it individually and if necessary, complete the first sentence as an example with the class. If time allows, get them to compare answers in pairs before checking with the class.

> 1 We didn't / did not spend (any) money on advertising.
> 2 We didn't / did not have (any) problems with our online booking system.
> 3 We didn't / did not buy (any) new equipment.
> 4 We didn't / did not win (any) new customers in the Gulf region.
> 5 Our sales profits didn't / did not grow in the China region.
> 6 We didn't / did not make (any) progress with our new product development.
> 7 We didn't / did not build (any) strong relationships with new customers.
> 8 We didn't / did not hit all our sales targets for the year.
> 9 We didn't / did not go to Japan to visit customers.
> 10 It wasn't / was not a very busy year for us.

B This activity practises the linkers *and*, *but*, *however* and *so*, and is best done after Exercise 4, as an introduction to the Writing section that follows. Start by writing *and*, *but*, *however* and *so* on the board, and ask students to look back at the email in Exercise 2 and find four sentences containing these words. (e.g. *We grew our retail business from ten stores to twelve **and** we built strong relationships with important corporate customers.*

> Teacher's notes

> *Unfortunately, we didn't hit our target of fourteen stores,* ***so*** *we need to investigate new areas for business. ...* ***However****, we didn't win any new business in the Overton area,* ***so*** *we want to make progress there next year.*)
> Explain that *and* adds information to a sentence, *but* contrasts information and *so* introduces a result. *However* also contrasts information but is normally used at the start of a sentence, whereas *but* is usually used in the middle. Ask students to complete the sentences individually, then check answers with the class.
>
> **1** so **2** and **3** so **4** and **5** but **6** However

4 Ask students to complete the summary individually, then check answers with the class. You could ask different students to come to the board and write the answers, so students can check their spelling.

> **2** made **3** hit **4** bought **5** won **6** didn't spend **7** didn't build **8** didn't grow

Writing

Students write an email about a company's performance.

5 Explain to students that they are going to write an email to the new Sales Manager of a company, about the company's performance in the last year. Refer them back to the model email in Exercise 2, and point out how the information is organised into paragraphs – tell students that they should do the same in their emails. Give them time to read the notes and answer any vocabulary questions they may have, then ask them to plan their emails – they could do this individually or, in weaker classes, in pairs. Encourage students to use the email in Exercise 2A as a model and, if you did Extra activity B, remind them to use *and*, *but*, *however* and *so*. When they have finished, you could put them in pairs for some peer-feedback: get them to read each other's emails and think about what their partner did well and what can be improved. Did their partner organise their email into paragraphs? Did they include all the necessary information from the notes? Did they use *and*, *but*, *however* and *so*? Students could then write a second draft for homework.

> **Model answer**
> Dear Anthony,
> Welcome to the team! Here is a summary of last year's sales report.
> At the start, we spent €16,000 on advertising and we won a lot of new business in North America. We also made some progress in areas where there is a lot of competition – Japan and South Korea.
> However, we also had some problems. We didn't hit our sales targets in Europe, so we didn't grow the export business. This is because customers didn't buy our new product immediately. However, we built some good relationships with new customers in Europe last year, so I'm confident we can increase sales in the first six months of this year. We want to hire more Sales Reps to sell new products in Europe.
> Overall, it was a good year.
> Regards,
> Dmitry

MyEnglishLab: Teacher's resources: extra activities; Additional interactive activities
Grammar reference: p.106 Talking about the past (2)
Pronunciation bank: p.98 /ɜː/ and /ɔː/
Teacher's book: Resource bank Photocopiable 3.3 p.116
Workbook: p.15 Exercises 3 and 4; p.17 Exercises 1–3; p.46 Exercises 1–3

3.4 > Work skills
How did it go?

> **GSE learning objectives**
> - Can identify key information (e.g. places, times) from short audio recordings, if spoken slowly and clearly.
> - Can identify basic factual information in short, simple dialogues or narratives on familiar everyday topics, if spoken slowly and clearly.
> - Can follow the sequence of events in a short, simple dialogue or narrative.
> - Can make simple references to the past using 'was/were'.
> - Can identify simple information in a short video, provided that the visual supports this information and the delivery is slow.
> - Can give a simple update on a work-related project.

Lead-in

Students discuss production processes.

1A Go through the three process steps with the class and check understanding, then ask students to complete the exercise individually or in pairs. Alternatively, do this as a quick, whole-class activity, checking answers as you go.

> **1** A, D, G **2** B, E, H **3** C, F, I

1B Again, students could do this individually or in pairs, or you could do it as a whole-class activity, checking answers as you go.

> **1** A, E, I **2** B, F, G **3** C, D, H

1C If there is time, let students share their answers in pairs or small groups first, then with the class.

Video

Students watch a video of a feedback meeting.

2A ▶ 3.4.1 Tell students that they are going to watch another video with employees at Sleek, and ask them what they remember about the company. Explain that in the video, William, the Product Manager, is having a meeting with the designers, Haru and Ellen. Alternatively, refer them to page 6 of the Coursebook and look at the video summary with them. Read the question with the class, then play the first part of the video (0:00–0:35) for students to answer it. Check the answer with the class.

> William arranged the meeting to talk about the production process of their products ('the winter collection').

50

2B ▶ 3.4.1 Go through the topics with students and check understanding of any vocabulary where necessary. Play the video, then check answers with the class. During feedback, you could play the video again and tell students to ask you to pause each time a topic is mentioned.

> the customers' comments about the new jacket; the design of the jacket; problems with manufacturing; communication problems; something that needs to change

2C ▶ 3.4.1 Give students time to read the sentences and check understanding of any vocabulary you think students will not know, e.g. *schedule*, *deadline*. Play the video, then check answers with the class.

> **a** 3 **b** 1 **c** 5 **d** 2 **e** 6 **f** 4

3A Students match the questions and answers individually, referring to videoscript 3.4.1 on page 130 if necessary. Check answers with the class, clarifying meanings as necessary. Alternatively, you could do this as a whole-class activity, checking answers and clarifying meanings as you go.

> **1** g **2** c **3** a **4** f **5** b **6** d **7** e

3B Put students in pairs to practise reading videoscript 3.4.1. When they have finished, you could ask them to swap roles and repeat.

Extra activities 3.4

A/B These activities provide further practice of the functional language from the lesson. You could do them after Exercise 3B or after going through the Speaking box on page 35 with the class. Ask students to complete both exercises individually, then check answers with the class. If there is time, you could then get students to practise the conversations in both exercises in pairs.

> **A 1** A go B had
> **2** A well B met
> **3** A didn't B problem
> **4** A do B changed
> **5** A happen B made
> **B 1** didn't go well **2** to a different material
> **3** communicate well **4** the problem **5** need to

Speaking: Talking about projects

Students look at useful language for talking about projects.

Talking about projects

Explain to students that they are going to look at useful phrases for talking about projects. Give them 1–2 minutes to look at the phrases, then go through them with the class, clarifying meanings as necessary. Students could practise the questions and answers in pairs, with one student asking questions in random order for their partner to reply. Students can then swap roles and repeat.

Unit 3 Extra speaking lesson

This lesson gives further practice of speaking related to talking about projects. To access the lesson go to MyEnglishLab > Extra speaking lessons.

4A Draw students' attention to the pictures and descriptions, give them a minute to read them and answer any vocabulary questions they have. Students can then answer the questions individually or in pairs. Check answers with the class.

> **1** shoes **2** a problem with the material; they missed a deadline; they had communication problems **3** yes

4B Put students in pairs and explain that they are going to write a dialogue about the project in Exercise 4A but before they do, they should answer some questions. Refer them to page 116 and give them time to discuss the questions – tell them that they should use the pictures from Exercise 4A to help them. When they are ready, go through the conversation outline and the example with them, then ask them to write their dialogue. Encourage them to use phrases from the Speaking box and remind them that they can also refer to videoscript 3.4.1 for ideas. Monitor while they are writing, noting down any points to highlight during feedback after Exercise 4C.

Model answer
(*Questions in brackets are optional*)
A: Congratulations! The shoes are in the shops today!
B: Thanks. Yeah, I'm very happy!
A: So how did the project go, generally?
B: It went well, thanks.
A: Tell me about it. What went well, in particular?
B: The teamwork. It was really good. The testing went very well. And now the shoes are in the shops and the customers really like them.
A: Yes, that's great. What didn't go well?
B: There were one or two problems. We had some problems with manufacturing. First, there was a problem with the material.
A: So what did you do?
B: We changed to a different material.
A: (OK, I see. And what happened then?)
B: We had problems with the schedule. We delivered a few days late. That was because we had problems with communication – with the shipping company.
A: (What was the problem?)
B: We didn't explain the change very well. At first, they didn't understand.
A: What do we need to change?
B: Instructions. Next time, I want to make the instructions in our communication very clear.
A: Yes, that's a good idea. But it's OK now, and everyone's really happy with the shoes.

4C Put students in pairs to practise their dialogues. If there is time, invite a few pairs to act it out for the class. Finally, have a brief feedback session, highlighting any points you noted while monitoring.

Teacher's notes

MyEnglishLab: Teacher's resources: extra activities; Extra speaking lessons; Additional interactive activities

Teacher's book: Resource bank Extra vocabulary practice p.138 Exercises 3–5; Photocopiable 3.4 p.117

Workbook: p.18 Exercises 1–3

Business workshop
Our first year

> **GSE learning objectives**
> - Can communicate in routine tasks requiring simple, direct exchanges of information.
> - Can talk about past events or experiences, using simple language.
> - Can write basic instructions with a simple list of points.
> - Can write a simple work-related email/letter expressing thanks.
> - Can answer simple questions and respond to simple statements in an interview.
> - Can read a simple text and extract factual details.
> - Can follow a basic sequence of events in a simple text on a familiar topic.

A company's first year

Students read a timeline about a new company and talk about its performance.

1A Remind students of the company timelines they read in Lesson 3.1 and explain that they are going to read a similar timeline about a new software company. Get them to complete the exercise individually or, in weaker classes, in pairs, then check answers with the class.

> 1 *Vai-Vai* 2 Software de Jogo 3 Brasilia 4 Campinas
> 5 hired a product manager and 2/two more engineers
> 6 5/five

1B If you think your students will find this activity difficult, review the Communicative grammar sections in Lessons 3.1 and 3.3 before you start. Put students in pairs and direct them to their relevant pages. Students prepare their questions individually. Monitor and help where necessary, and check the questions are correct before they continue. Students then ask and answer their questions, using the information in the timeline. Check answers with the class.

> **Student A**
> 1 Who started Software de Jogo? (João and Manuela Silva)
> 2 Who did João and Manuela hire in January? (two software engineers)
> 3 When did they create Software de Jogo? (in March)
> 4 Where did they rent an office? (in Brasilia)
> 5 When did they launch *Vai-Vai* in Portuguese? (in June)

> **Student B**
> 1 Where was *Vai-Vai* an instant success? (in Brazil and Portugal)
> 2 Who did they hire in August? (translators, for an English version)
> 3 When did they move to Brazil's Silicon Valley? (in October)
> 4 Why did they hire a product manager and two more engineers? (to produce more games)
> 5 How many games did they produce from December? (five)

Preparing for a move

Students write an email giving instructions.

2 If you think your students will find this activity difficult, review the Grammar box in Lesson 3.2 before you start. Go through the instructions with students and remind them of the scenario: refer them back to the 'October' section of the timeline in Exercise 1A. Explain that they are going to write an email from João and Manuela to their team about the office move. Give them time to read the notes, and point out that they should include all the points in them in their emails. Also remind them of the emails they wrote in Lesson 3.2 and tell them that they can use the models and phrases there to help them. Students write their emails individually, then compare them in pairs.

> **Model answer**
> Move to Campinas
> To all staff,
> As you know, we are moving to Campinas next week.
> Therefore, on Friday, please:
> • remove everything from your desk.
> • put all of your things in a box.
> • write your name on the box.
> • please don't move the box – leave it on your desk.
> Thank you for your cooperation. Have a great weekend!
> Best wishes,
> João Silva
> CEO

3 Explain the activity and scenario, and ask students to complete the exercise individually or, in weaker classes, in pairs. Encourage them to try to find links between each part of the email, and look carefully at reference words like *this*, *that*, etc. and think about what each one might refer to; this will help them put the sentences in the correct order. If students work individually, get them to compare answers in pairs before class feedback.

> 1 i 2 c 3 a 4 f 5 b 6 d 7 e 8 h 9 g

How the first year went

Students practise asking and answering questions about a new company's performance.

4 If you think your students will find this activity difficult, review the Speaking section of Lesson 3.4 before you start. Explain to students that they are going to ask and answer questions about Software de Jogo's performance in the last year. Divide the class into two groups, A and B, and direct them to the relevant pages. Explain that group A have the questions and group B have the answers, and ask them to complete Activity 1 individually. Check the answers to each group's items by only eliciting the actual answers (not the whole questions/sentences, as this would pre-empt the next stage of the activity). For Activity 2, put students in pairs and explain their roles: Student As are writers for a business blog and are going to interview Student Bs using their questions from Activity 1. During the interview, they should complete their notes. Student B's are João Silva and are going to answer the interviewer's questions using their sentences from Activity A and the notes in the box. Give pairs 1–2 minutes to prepare, then ask them to roleplay their interviews. During the activity, monitor and note down any errors or difficulties; highlight these in a brief feedback session at the end of the activity.

1
Student A
1 go 2 went 3 do 4 do 5 was 6 didn't go
Student B
a didn't hit b went c had d fixed e grew f want to

2
Model answer
A: How did it go, generally?
B: It went well.
A: What went well, in particular?
B: We grew our range of games from one to five.
A: What didn't go well?
B: We didn't hit our target of 100,000 sales.
A: What was the problem?
B: We had problems with the English translation.
A: What did you do?
B: We fixed the problems (e.g. … because we hired a new translator).
A: What do you want to do next?
B: We want to create more games.

Grammar reference ◀ 3

3.1

1 1 started 2 worked 3 finished 4 developed
  5 studied 6 showed 7 planned 8 hired
2 1 Who signed 2 did you stay 3 Who designed the car?
  4 What did John design?
3 1 Did the company expand its range?
  2 Did you start university in 2014?
  3 Did she change jobs in 2019?
  4 Who started the company?
  5 How did they improve their workplace?
  6 Where did you work last year?
  7 Which company launched the HJ laptop last year?
  8 Why did she close the shop?
  9 Who ordered a new computer?

3.2

1 1 Please help me.
  2 Come in and sit down, please.
  3 Don't use your mobile phone here, please.
  4 Choose a new chair.
  5 Don't take photos here, please.
  6 Write your name on your desk.

3.3

1 1 spend 2 bought 3 had 4 make 5 grew
  6 builds 7 win 8 had 9 went 10 was
2 1 didn't start 2 didn't work 3 didn't finish
  4 didn't grow 5 didn't go

Review ◀ 3

1 1 move 2 start 3 produce 4 open 5 creates
  6 hires 7 expands 8 launches
2 1 c 2 a 3 b 4 d
3 1 did 2 expand 3 did 4 move 5 started 6 did
  7 create/do 8 Did 9 hire 10 Did 11 launch
4A 1 worked 2 hired 3 stayed 4 studied 5 developed
  6 produced
4B 1 grew 2 built 3 was not / wasn't 4 had
  5 didn't win 6 didn't hit
5 1 b 2 a 3 c 4 a 5 c 6 b

4 Travelling for work

Unit overview

	CLASSWORK	FURTHER WORK
4.1 **I'm flying to Tokyo tomorrow**	**Lead-in** Students discuss their travel experiences. **Vocabulary** Students look at vocabulary related to travel arrangements. **Communicative grammar** Students study and practise the Present Continuous for future arrangements. **Video** Students watch a video about travelling for work. **Task** Students practise arranging a time to meet.	**MyEnglishLab:** Teacher's resources: extra activities; Additional interactive activities **Grammar reference:** p.106 Talking about arrangements **Pronunciation bank:** p.98 /ŋ/, /ŋk/ and /n/. The -ing ending. **Teacher's book:** Resource bank Extra vocabulary practice p.139 Exercise 1 **Workbook:** p.19 Exercises 1 and 2; p.20 Exercises 1-3; p.47 Exercises 1-4
4.2 **The 12.05 is delayed**	**Lead-in** Students look at typical travel signs. **Vocabulary** Students look at vocabulary related to airports and train stations. **Reading and listening** Students listen to announcements and read text messages about travel delays. **Writing** Students write a text message about an announcement.	**MyEnglishLab:** Teacher's resources: extra activities; Additional interactive activities **Grammar reference:** p.107 will / won't **Teacher's book:** Resource bank Extra vocabulary practice p.139 Exercises 2-4 **Workbook:** pp.19 Exercises 3 and 4; p.21 Exercises 1-3
4.3 **An update email**	**Lead-in** Students identify different cities around the world. **Reading** Students read update emails to a Project Manager. **Communicative grammar** Students study and practise the Present Continuous for things happening now. **Writing** Students write an update email.	**MyEnglishLab:** Teacher's resources: extra activities; Additional interactive activities **Grammar reference:** p.107 Things happening now **Teacher's book:** Resource bank Photocopiable 4.3 p.118 **Workbook:** p.20 Exercises 4 and 5; p.22 Exercises 1-3
4.4 **Work skills:** Setting up a video call	**Lead-in** Students talk about video calls and look at useful vocabulary. **Video** Students watch video calls with technical problems. **Speaking** Students look at useful language for talking about problems with teleconferencing and suggesting solutions.	**MyEnglishLab:** Teacher's resources: extra activities; Extra speaking lessons; Additional interactive activities **Grammar reference:** p.108 Making suggestions **Pronunciation bank:** p.98 /ɪə/ and /eə/ **Teacher's book:** Resource bank Extra vocabulary practice p.139 Exercises 5 and 6; Photocopiable 4.4 p.118 **Workbook:** p.23 Exercises 1-3; p.47 Exercises 1-3
Business workshop: A business trip	**Reading** Students read emails about a business trip. **Speaking** Students ask and answer questions about travel arrangements; roleplay an online meeting. **Listening** Students listen to conversations about travel problems; listen to an online meeting. **Writing** Students write text messages giving updates.	

Teacher's notes

Unit vocabulary list

Active vocabulary

4.1
book a hotel / a (train/plane) ticket / an apartment / a flight
go by bus/car/coach/plane/train
rent an apartment / a car
stay at an apartment / a hotel

4.2
terminal	arrive
flight connections	change at
arrivals	depart
departures	
baggage claim	cancelled
passport control	delayed
customs	late
taxi	
	gate
	platform
	security
	stop at

Passive vocabulary

4.1
apartment	bus
hotel	car
	coach
	flight
	plane
	train

4.4
close window	audio (call)
end call	camera
hang up	break up
mute (microphone)	(chat) window
open (chat window)	frozen (screen)
share screen (button)	internet connection
start (video call)	microphone
stop (video call)	screen
unmute (microphone)	video (call)

Teacher's notes

4.1 I'm flying to Tokyo tomorrow

GSE learning objectives
- Can use the Present Continuous with future reference.
- Can identify simple information in a short video, provided that the visual supports this information and the delivery is slow and clear.
- Can understand key information about arrangements in simple dialogues spoken slowly and clearly.
- Can make simple future arrangements and plans with reference to a diary or schedule.
- Can use language related to travel.

Lead-in
Students discuss their travel experiences.

1A To introduce the topic, you could write the following questions on the board, get students to discuss them in pairs or small groups, then get brief feedback from the class: *What's your favourite way to travel? Why? What's your least favourite way to travel? Why?* Move on to the exercise. Ask students to complete it individually, then check answers with the class, clarifying meanings as necessary. If you are short of time, you could also do this as a whole-class activity, checking answers and clarifying meanings as you go.

1 E   2 B   3 A   4 F   5 D   6 C

1B Give students a minute to read the questions and think about their answers, then put them in pairs or small groups to discuss the questions. When they have finished, nominate a few students to share their answers with the class.

Vocabulary: Travel arrangements
Students look at vocabulary related to travel arrangements.

2A ◆ 4.01   Go through the instructions with the class and check they understand *PA* (a Personal Assistant). Before they listen, ask them to read the conversation and think about what the missing words might be. Elicit their ideas, but do not confirm answers yet. Play the recording for students to complete the conversation, then check answers with the class. Note that the verb forms in bold are examples of the target language in the Communicative grammar section that follows, but they should only be looked at as lexical items here, to make sure students can follow the conversation. Do not go into detail about the Present Continuous yet – students will look at it in the exercises that follow.

1 a flight   2 a hotel   3 plane   4 train   5 an apartment

2B Go through the table with the class, checking understanding of the verbs and nouns, then go through the words in the box. Ask students to complete the exercise individually or, in weaker classes, in pairs – tell them that they can refer to the conversation in Exercise 2A if they need help. Check answers with the class, clarifying meanings as necessary.

1 a flight   2 an apartment   3 plane   4 coach   5 a car   6 an apartment

2C You could do this as a quick, whole-class activity, checking answers and clarifying meanings as you go.

1 c   2 a   3 d   4 b

Extra activities 4.1

A This activity provides extra practice of the vocabulary in Exercises 2A–2C. Students should complete it individually, referring to the table in Exercise 2B if they need help. Check answers with the class.

1 an apartment   2 plane   3 flight   4 booking
5 customers   6 rent   7 going by   8 stay at

Communicative grammar: Talking about arrangements
Students study and practise the Present Continuous for future arrangements.

Talking about arrangements
Explain to students that they are going to learn how to talk about future arrangements. Write on the board: *I'm flying to Tokyo tomorrow.* and ask: *Is this the past, present or future?* (future) *Have I got my ticket?* (Yes.) *Is it definite?* (Yes.) Underline *'m flying* in the sentence on the board and explain that this is the Present Continuous. Go through the examples in the Grammar box with the class and elicit or explain how to form Present Continuous sentences: subject + *am/is/are* + verb with *-ing*. You could write the pattern on the board for students to refer to when they do the practice exercises that follow. Refer students back to the examples in bold in the conversation in Exercise 2A so they can look again at the target language in context. You could then refer them to the Grammar reference on pages 106–107, go through it with them and clarify any points as necessary. Pay particular attention to the spelling rules for verb + *-ing*. Students could then do the extra grammar activity there, in class or as homework.

Grammar reference answer key: page 64

Pronunciation bank
p.98: /ŋ/, /ŋk/ and /n/. The *-ing* ending.

1 ◆ P4.01   ◆ P4.02   ◆ P4.03   This exercise focusses on the nasal consonants /ŋ/ and /n/. The sound /ŋ/ is produced in the same position as /k/ and /g/, with the back of the tongue raised and its front hanging. However, unlike /k/ and /g/, it is a sound with a continuous vibration, not a plosive. The consonant /n/ only differs from /ŋ/ in the place of articulation. When you say /n/, the tip of the tongue touches the alveolar ridge. When you produce /ŋ/ or /n/, you can feel your nose tingling. Notice whether your students have a tendency to say /n/ instead of /ŋ/.

Teacher's notes

Play recording P4.01 and ask students to repeat the words with the sound /ŋ/ in the final position. Ask them to point to where on their body they feel the pronunciation of /ŋ/ (they should point to their noses). This way they can establish that the sound is produced with the air going through the nose, not the mouth. Draw students' attention to the spelling. Explain that the letters *ng* at the end of a word represent the /ŋ/ sound and the letter *g* in this sequence is silent. Next, play recording P4.02 and ask students to repeat the words ending with /ŋk/. Explain that when the spelling is *nk*, /ŋ/ is always followed by the sound /nk/. Finally, play recording P4.03 and get students to repeat the words which end with the letter *n*, representing the sound /n/. You may want to play all three recordings again for students to repeat all the words in chorus.

2 ◆ P4.04 Ask students to look at the *-ing* forms and draw their attention to the fact that the common *-ing* ending is pronounced /ɪŋ/. Play the recording and get students to repeat as a group.

3 ◆ P4.05 Tell students that they are going to practise saying sentences with the *-ing* forms from Exercise 2. Pay special attention to how they pronounce the words ending in *-nking* and *-ning* (Sentences 1 and 2) as such clusters may be particularly challenging for some students.

4A ◆ P4.06 Explain to students that they are going to complete the sentences with one word. Play the recording, pausing after each sentence for students to write their answers, then check them with the class.

> 1 growing 2 advertising 3 cleaning
> 4 printing 5 booking 6 putting

4B Put students in pairs to practise saying the sentences. Monitor and correct pronunciation of the target sounds as necessary. You could play the recording first and ask students to repeat the sentences as a group before they practise in their pairs.

3 Students complete the sentences individually, then compare answers in pairs, using the Grammar box to help them if necessary. Check answers with the class.

> 1 am/'m visiting, are/'re giving 2 aren't / are not going, are/'re taking 3 Are, staying 4 is/'s booking

4 ◆ 4.02 Draw students' attention to the calendar to the side of the dialogue and explain the activity. Ask them to work individually and remind them that they can refer to the Grammar reference if they need help with forming the Present Continuous or spelling the *-ing* form of verbs. Play the recording for them to check their answers, then go through them with the class, writing the answers on the board so students can check their spelling. If there is time, get students to practise the conversation in pairs.

> 2 am/'m flying 3 Is, meeting 4 isn't 5 's/is meeting
> 6 're/are visiting 7 Are, visiting 8 are 9 are, travelling
> 10 am/'m going

Extra activities 4.1

B This activity provides extra practice of the Present Continuous for future arrangements. If necessary, do the first item as an example with the class, and write it on the board. Students then work individually to write the sentences, and compare answers in pairs before class feedback. In feedback, write (or invite students to write) the Present Continuous verbs on the board, so students can check their spelling.

> 1 I'm / am visiting the Paris office on Monday.
> 2 Who are you meeting on Friday?
> 3 They aren't / are not flying to Oslo on Wednesday.
> 4 Where's / is he staying on Thursday evening?
> 5 Are we going by coach?
> 6 We're / are booking a flight to Peru next month.
> 7 Is she meeting Paola on Monday?
> 8 He isn't / is not hiring a car in Krakow.
> 9 Is she staying in a hotel tomorrow night?
> 10 You're / are starting the meeting at ten o'clock.

Video

Students watch a video about travelling for work.

5A ▶ 4.1.1 Tell students that they are going to watch a video of people talking about travelling for work. Read the question with the class, ask them to make notes in answer to the question while watching, then play the video introduction (0:00–0:30) and check the answer with the class. In feedback, you may wish to pre-teach some key vocabulary from the video, e.g. *location*, *event* (*management*), *rent* (v), *travel somewhere and back*, (*travel*) *internationally*, *sightseeing*.

> to visit clients or customers, to see colleagues in a different location, to go to a conference

5B ▶ 4.1.1 Give students time to read the questions and options so they know what to listen for, and check that they understand *abroad*. Play the video, then check answers with the class.

> 1a M 1b C 2a C 2b M 3a C 3b M 4a M 4b C

5C ▶ 4.1.1 Give students a minute to read the sentences and ask you about any vocabulary they need to. When they are ready, play the video again for them to watch and choose the correct options, then check answers with the class.

> 1 one 2 one 3 friends 4 two 5 clients 6 do some sightseeing 7 evening

Task

Students practise arranging a time to meet.

6 Tell students that they are going to practise arranging a time to meet. Put them in pairs and direct them to the relevant pages, then give them time to read their information and ask any questions they have. Remind them of the conversation in Exercise 5 and tell them that they can use it as a model for their conversations. Before they begin, elicit different phrases

Teacher's notes

they can use to ask their partner about their plans/travel arrangements, e.g. *What are you doing on … ?, Are you free on … ?, Are you busy on … ?* You could put these on the board for students to refer to during their conversations. Students hold their conversations in pairs. During the activity, monitor and note down any errors/difficulties to highlight during feedback but do not interrupt students' conversations. When they have finished, ask a few pairs when they are meeting, and go over any points you noted while monitoring.

> **Model conversation**
> **B:** When are you going to Frankfurt?
> **A:** I'm going on Tuesday.
> **B:** What are you doing in the afternoon?
> **A:** I'm meeting suppliers, and then going to the company apartment. What are you doing on Tuesday evening?
> **B:** I'm having dinner with the Sales Team Manager. Are you busy on Wednesday morning?
> **A:** Yes, I am. Angela is meeting me at the apartment and then we're going to the office. What are you doing in the afternoon?
> **B:** I'm meeting clients all afternoon. I'm not busy in the evening. Are you busy then?
> **A:** Yes, I am. I'm having dinner with Mr Brandt. ...
>
> (The only time Students A and B can meet is on Thursday afternoon, after 2 p.m.)

MyEnglishLab: Teacher's resources: extra activities; Additional interactive activities
Grammar reference: p.106 Talking about arrangements
Pronunciation bank: p.98 /ŋ/, /ŋk/ and /n/. The *-ing* ending.
Teacher's book: Resource bank Extra vocabulary practice p.139 Exercise 1
Workbook: p.19 Exercises 1 and 2; p.20 Exercises 1–3; p.47 Exercises 1–4

4.2 ▶ The 12.05 is delayed

> **GSE learning objectives**
> - Can extract key factual information such as prices, times and dates from short clear, simple announcements.
> - Can identify key information (e.g. places, times) from short audio recordings, if spoken slowly and clearly.
> - Can use language related to trains, train travel and stations.
> - Can understand short simple messages about when and where to meet.
> - Can write short, simple notes, emails and postings to friends.
> - Can use language related to transport problems.
> - Can make and accept a simple apology.
> - Can leave simple phone messages using fixed expressions.
> - Can find specific, predictable information in everyday materials (e.g. menus, timetables).
> - Can extract specific information (e.g. facts and numbers) from simple informational texts related to everyday life (e.g. posters, leaflets).
> - Can understand the general meaning of short, simple informational material and descriptions if there is visual support.

Lead-in
Students look at typical travel signs.

1 You could do this as a whole-class activity, checking answers and clarifying meanings as you go. Alternatively, look at the signs with students before they complete the exercise, and check understanding of any new vocabulary. Get them to complete the exercise individually, then check answers with the class, clarifying meanings as necessary.

> **1** A, C, D, E, F **2** B **3** I
> (Students might suggest answers G and H for (3) because there is passport control and customs operating at some international train station, e.g. for the Eurostar service between the UK and France.)

Vocabulary: Airports and train stations
Students look at vocabulary related to airports and train stations.

2A Tell students that they are going to look at vocabulary related to airports and train stations, and ask them to look at the words in bold in Exercise 2B. With weaker classes, do this as a whole-class activity, checking answers and clarifying meanings as you go. With stronger classes, let students complete the exercise individually, then check answers with the class.

> **1** change trains **2** departed **3** security **4** taxi

2B Give students time to read the sentences and check understanding of *was cancelled, arrived, was delayed, queue, board, go through* (*security*) and *gate*. Explain that the sentences tell a travel story, but they are in the wrong order. Show that the first one is sentence c, then ask students to put the rest of them in order. If there is time, get students to compare answers in pairs before checking with the class.

> **a** 3 **b** 5 **c** 1 **d** 7/6 **e** 2 **f** 8 **g** 6/7 **h** 4

2C This activity practises vocabulary from Exercises 2A and 2B, so students should be able to complete it individually.

> **1** cancelled **2** delayed **3** depart **4** stop **5** change
> **6** security **7** arrive **8** late **9** platform **10** gate

> **Extra activities 4.2**
>
> **A/B** These activities provide extra practice of the vocabulary in Exercises 2A–C. Ask students to complete both exercises individually; to help them, explain that thinking about the meanings of the words in bold will help them choose the correct option each time. Check answers with the class. Activity A can also be done as a whole-class activity: read out each sentence in turn, pausing before the gap to elicit the answer from the class.
>
> **A** **1** b **2** c **3** a **4** c **5** a **6** b **7** c **8** b
> **B** **1** c **2** e **3** a **4** g **5** b **6** h **7** f **8** d

Teacher's notes

Reading and listening: Dealing with delays

Students listen to announcements and read text messages about travel delays.

3A 🔊 4.03 Teach or elicit the meaning of *announcement*. Explain that students will hear eight announcements and must decide if each one is at an airport or a train station. You may want to pre-teach some key vocabulary from the recording before students listen, e.g. *due to*, *technical (problem)*, *expect*, *we are sorry to announce*, *apologise*, *approximately*, *customer service desk*, *attention*, *allow* and *airline*. Play the recording, twice if necessary, then check answers with the class.

> 1 A 2 T 3 T 4 A 5 A 6 T 7 A 8 A

3B 🔊 4.03 Explain the activity and give students time to read the sentences and think about what the missing words might be – this will help them focus on what type of information they need to listen for. Play the recording again for students to complete the sentences, then check answers with the class.

> 1 delayed 2 cancelled 3 platform 4 cancelled
> 5 gate 6 platform 7 security 8 connection

3C Students should do this exercise individually. If time allows, get them to compare answers in pairs before class feedback.

> **a** meeting **b** hotel **c** train **d** Security

3D 🔊 4.04 Explain that students will hear four of the announcements from Exercise 3A again. They should match them to the text messages in Exercise 3C. Play the recording, then check answers with the class.

> 1 d 2 a 3 b 4 c

will / won't

Go through the examples in the Grammar box with the class and explain that we use *will* + infinitive to talk about future facts, make promises and offers, agree to do something and for decisions we make at the moment of speaking. Refer students to the Grammar reference on page 107 and go through it with them, clarifying any points as necessary. They could then do the extra grammar activity there, in class or as homework.

Grammar reference answer key: page 64

Extra activities 4.2

C This activity provides further practice of *will/won't*. Ask students to complete it individually, then check answers with the class. As an extension, you could put students in pairs to practise the exchanges.

> 1 I'll/will get her for you now.
> 2 We'll/will sell more of that model next month.
> 3 We won't / will not have time next week.
> 4 Great, I'll/will meet you there.
> 5 I won't / will not order any.
> 6 I won't / will not be there, either. I'll/will join it online.

Writing

Students write a text message about an announcement.

4A 🔊 4.05 Explain that students are going to hear two of the announcements from Exercise 3A again and that they should make notes on the problem in each one. Play the recording, but do not confirm answers yet – students will check them in the next activity.

4B Ask students to compare their notes from Exercise 4A in pairs, then play the recording again if necessary for them to check. In feedback, ask a different student to explain each problem using their notes.

> 1 Flight A1 1663 to Rome – delayed about one hour
> 2 Gate change – Flight CA 2424 to Abu Dhabi, now gate 10, not gate 7

4C Students should do this activity in the same pairs as Exercise 4B. Explain that they are going to write a text message to their partner about one of the announcements in Exercise 4B, using their notes. Point out that they need to keep their messages short and to the point – refer them to the model messages in Exercise 3C. Also encourage them to try to use *will* in their messages. If students are happy to do so, they could exchange numbers and send their messages via their phones. Otherwise, they could just write them on paper. As an extension, you could ask students to write two additional text messages for announcements 6 and 8 (see audioscript 4.03), in class or as homework.

> **Model answers**
> 1 Hi David. My flight to Rome is delayed about one hour, so I'm going to be late. Sorry! Peter
> 2 Nina, the gate is changing. It's not gate 10 now. It's gate 7. I'll see you there!

MyEnglishLab: Teacher's resources: extra activities; Additional interactive activities

Grammar reference: p.107 *will/won't*

Teacher's book: Resource bank Extra vocabulary practice p.139 Exercises 1–4

Workbook: p.19 Exercises 3 and 4; p.21 Exercises 1–3

Teacher's notes

4.3 > Writing
An update email

GSE learning objectives

- Can use the Present Continuous to refer to events at the time of speaking.
- Can use the Present Continuous to refer to temporary situations.
- Can understand short, simple emails on work-related topics.
- Can write short, simple notes, emails and messages relating to everyday matters.

Lead-in
Students identify different cities around the world.

1 Draw students' attention to the map and photos, and ask them if they can identify the cities, but do not confirm answers yet. Explain the task, give students time to read the sentences, and check that they understand *set up* in sentence d. Students complete the exercise individually, then compare answers in pairs before class feedback.

a 4 **b** 2 **c** 1 **d** 3

Reading
Students read update emails to a Project Manager.

2A Tell students that they are going to read emails from the people in Exercise 1 in which they update Alicia, the Project Manager based in Dublin, on a project. Use this as an opportunity to pre-teach *update*, which students will see later in the lesson. Read the questions with the class so they know what to read for, then ask them to read the three emails and answer the questions. Encourage them to underline the parts of the emails where they found the answers, and elicit these during class feedback. Check answers with the class.

1 Eduardo **2** Liz **3** Alex

2B You could do this as a whole-class activity, eliciting ideas from students and writing them on the board. Encourage students to think of other beginnings and endings they have seen in previous units, e.g. *I hope you're well* and *Best wishes*, and add them to the board.

(beginning) How are you? / How are things going in Dublin? (ending) Best regards, / Speak soon,

2C Explain that students are going to read Alicia's replies to the emails in Exercise 2A and decide who they are addressed to. Ask them to complete the matching task individually, then to compare answers in pairs. Check answers with the class. Again, encourage students to say which parts of each reply helped them decide.

a Alex **b** Liz **c** Eduardo

Communicative grammar: Things happening now

Students study and practise the Present Continuous for things happening now.

Things happening now
Remind students of the use of the Present Continuous to talk about arrangements from Lesson 4.1, and explain that we also use this form to talk about things happening now, at the time of speaking. Draw students' attention to the Grammar box and go through the examples with them. Refer them back to the emails in Exercise 2A so they can look again at the target language in context – draw their attention to the verb forms in bold in the emails. You could then refer them to the Grammar reference on page 108, go through it with them, and get them to do the extra grammar activities there, in class or as homework.

Grammar reference answer key: page 64

3A Draw students' attention to the pictures and explain that they are going to complete sentences about the people and situations in them. Give students time to read the sentences and check understanding of *go well*, *look after* and *repair*. Students complete the sentences individually, using the Grammar box and/or the Grammar reference on page 108 to help them if necessary. Check answers with the class.

1 are having, isn't going
2 isn't working, 's looking after, isn't having (any)
3 isn't meeting, 's writing
4 is repairing, 's having
5 aren't preparing, 're giving, 's going

3B Explain to students that they are going to complete questions about the people in Exercise 3A, using the Present Continuous of the verbs in the box. Elicit the first answer as an example, then ask students to complete the rest of the questions individually. Check answers with the class.

1 Are, having 2 Is, working 3 Is, using 4 is, doing
5 are, talking 6 Are, giving

3C Get students to complete the exercise individually, then check answers with the class. As an extension, you could ask them to practise asking and answering the questions in pairs. If time is short, the exercise could also be done as a quick, whole-class activity: read out the questions from Exercise 3B in turn, eliciting the correct answer for each one as you go.

1 c 2 a 3 f 4 d 5 b 6 e

Teacher's notes

Extra activities 4.3

A This activity looks at time phrases used with the Present Continuous. Ask students to do it individually, then check answers with the class.

1 today 2 this month 3 morning 4 right now

B This activity provides further practice of the Present Continuous. Again, students should complete it individually, as a consolidation exercise. Check answers with the class.

1 'm writing 2 moment 3 're testing 4 now
5 're having 6 's coming

Writing

Students write an update email.

4 Explain the writing task and go through the list of points to include with the class. Allow plenty of time for them to plan their answers – they could do this individually or in pairs. In weaker classes, you could also do this with the whole class: ask students to look back at the emails on page 42 and think about what they are going to write for each point. Elicit ideas around the class, and write them on the board so students have a plan to refer to during the writing task. Before they begin, remind them to: a) start and end the email in an appropriate way, b) include all the necessary information, c) organise the information about Mexico sales and suppliers in two clear paragraphs and d) use the Present Continuous to update Alicia on activities happening now. While they are writing, monitor and offer help as necessary. When they have finished, you could put them in pairs for some peer feedback. Ask them to read each other's emails and think about points a)–d) above. What has their partner done well? Can they make any suggestions for improvements? As an extension, you could ask students to write an update email about their own work, for their manager; they could do this in class or as homework.

Model answer:

Hi Veronika,

I hope everything is going well in Zurich. I'm writing to give you an update.

Alex's team are finalising sales figures at the moment, but they're waiting for some data. He's writing the sales report and preparing the presentation. I'm planning the sales meeting now and preparing the new price list for Liz.

Eduardo is at the factory today. He's trying to talk to a supplier about new computers for Mexico City. I'm dealing with the paperwork for the job in Bremen at the moment.

Best regards,
Alicia

MyEnglishLab: Teacher's resources: extra activities
Grammar reference: p.107 Things happening now
Teacher's book: Resource bank Photocopiable 4.3 p.119
Workbook: p.20 Exercises 4 and 5; p.22 Exercises 1–3

4.4 Work skills
Setting up a video call

GSE learning objectives

- Can understand enough to respond to direct requests expressed slowly and clearly.
- Can answer simple questions on the phone using fixed expressions.
- Can ask for repetition or clarification on the phone in a simple way.
- Can ask for repetition and clarification on the phone in a simple way.
- Can make and respond to suggestions.
- Can use simple expressions to explain a technical problem.
- Can identify simple information in a short video, provided that the visual supports this information and the delivery is slow and clear.

Lead-in

Students talk about video calls and look at useful vocabulary.

1A Depending on the time available, you could do this as a whole-class activity or let students discuss the question in pairs or small groups first, and then elicit answers around the class.

1B Draw students' attention to the pictures and check they understand *during* in the caption for picture B. Go through phrases a–h with the class, checking understanding of each one, then get students to complete the exercise individually and check answers with the class. Alternatively, if you are short of time, you could do this as a whole-class activity, checking answers and clarifying meanings as you go.

a 2 b 4 c 1 d 6 e 3 f 5 g 7 h 8

Video

Students watch video calls with technical problems.

2A ▶ 4.4.1 Tell students that they are going to watch a video of members of the team at Sleek having video calls. Explain that the people are having problems with their calls and students need to identify these problems while watching. At this point, you could pre-teach the following vocabulary from the video: *breaking up*, *add* (*someone to a call*), (*sales*) *figures*, *data* and *frozen* (*screen*). Play the video, then check answers with the class.

1 audio 2 screen is frozen 3 camera

2B ▶ 4.4.1 Give students time to read the statements and ask you any questions they have about the vocabulary. Check that they understand *be on mute*, (*slow*) *internet connection*, *audio call* and *share* (*your screen*). Play the video, then check answers with the class.

1 T 2 F 3 F 4 F 5 T 6 T 7 F 8 T 9 F

Teacher's notes

2C Remind students of the problems in Exercise 2A, then ask them to complete the exercise individually. Alternatively, do this as a whole-class activity, eliciting the problem for each solution in turn.

a 3   **b** 1   **c** 2

Making suggestions
Look at the examples in the Grammar box with students and elicit the meanings of the phrases in bold. Explain that we often use *try + -ing* to make suggestions. Refer students to the Grammar reference on page 108 and go through it with them, then get them to do the extra grammar activity there, in class or as homework.
Grammar reference answer key: page 64

Extra activities 4.4

A This activity looks at useful language from the video for talking about and suggesting solutions for technical problems. You could do it after Exercise 2C or after going through the Speaking box on page 45 with the class. Depending on which option you choose, you could let students complete the conversations individually and clarify meanings as necessary during feedback or let them refer to the Speaking box for help if they need to. Get students to compare answers in pairs before class feedback. If there is time, they can then practise the conversations in pairs.

1 problem **2** here **3** breaking **4** call **5** audio
6 mute **7** video **8** sharing **9** frozen **10** unmuting

2D ▶ 4.4.1 Stronger classes could do the exercise from memory, then watch the video again to check their answers. Otherwise, give students a minute to read the sentences, then play the video again for them to choose the correct alternatives. Check answers with the class, clarifying meanings as necessary.

1 hear, on mute **2** unmuting **3** hear **4** is frozen
5 connection, breaking up **6** off **7** audio **8** call
9 working **10** sharing

Speaking: Problems with teleconferencing
Students look at useful language for talking about problems with teleconferencing and suggesting solutions.

Problems with teleconferencing
Go through the Speaking box with the class, pointing out the different function of each group of phrases and clarifying meanings as necessary. For some quick practice, put students in pairs and get them to take turns to choose a phrase from the *Talking about problems* section for their partner to reply using an appropriate phrase from the *Suggesting solutions* section.

Unit 4 Extra speaking lesson
This lesson gives further practice of speaking related to problems with teleconferencing. To access the lesson go to MyEnglishLab > Extra speaking lessons.

Pronunciation bank
p.98: /ɪə/ and /eə/

1 ▶ P4.07 ▶ P4.08 The sounds /ɪə/ and /eə/ are diphthongs. In /ɪə/ the vowel quality changes from /ɪ/ to /ə/, whereas in /eə/ it changes from /e/ towards /ə/. Write the word *ear* on the board, say it out loud and explain that it is pronounced with the sound /ɪə/. Play recording P4.07 and get students to repeat as a group and then individually. Draw their attention to the spelling, and explain that /ɪə/ is commonly represented by *ear* (*fear*), *eer* (*deer*) and *ere* (*here*).

Follow the same procedure for /eə/. Write the word *air* on the board, say it out loud and explain that it contains the sound /eə/. Play recording P4.08 and get students to repeat as a group and then individually. You could tell students that common spellings for this sound are *air* (*fair*), *are* (*dare*) and *ere* (*where*). Notice that some spellings can represent either of the target sounds, for example: *ear* (*hear*, *pear*) or *ere* (*here*, *there*), which may be confusing to students.

2 ▶ P4.09 This exercise contrasts the diphthongs /ɪə/ and /eə/ in some minimal pairs. Play the recording and get students to repeat the words as a group and then individually.

3A ▶ P4.10 Explain the activity and point out that only one word in each sentence contains the /ɪə/ sound. Play the recording, then get students to compare answers in pairs before checking with the class.

3B ▶ P4.10 Tell students that they are going to listen to the sentences again but this time they should underline the /eə/ sound in **one** word in each sentence. Play the recording, get students to compare answers in pairs, then check them with the class.

1 st<u>ai</u>rs **2** rep<u>air</u> **3** squ<u>are</u> **4** ch<u>ai</u>rs
5 w<u>are</u>house

3C Put students in pairs to practise saying the sentences. Monitor and correct pronunciation of the target sounds as necessary. You may choose to play the recording first and ask students to repeat the sentences as a group before they practise in their pairs.

3A ▶ 4.4.2 Explain to students that they are going to watch another video call between members of the team at Sleek. You could tell them who is taking part in the call (William, Maria and Max), and refer them to page 6 of the Coursebook to remind them of each character's role at Sleek. Explain the activity: students first watch the video of the call without sound and think about what the people might be saying, then they should write the dialogue in pairs. Go through the conversation outline with them, checking understanding as you go along. Ask students to write the conversation, and encourage them to use phrases from the Speaking box. Monitor and offer help where necessary. If there is time, you could join pairs together into groups of four to compare their conversations.

3B ▶ 4.4.2 Play the video with sound for students to compare with their own conversation. When they have finished, ask each pair how similar their conversation was to the one in the video.

> **Model conversation**
> **William:** Hello, Max.
> **Max:** Hello, William?
> **William:** I can't hear you. Try unmuting your microphone.
> **Max:** Oh, sorry.
> **William:** That's better. I can hear you now.
> **Max:** Oh no! The connection isn't very good. Now the screen is frozen! Try turning your video off.
> **William:** Can you hear me?
> **Max:** Can you repeat that, please?
> **William:** You're breaking up!
> **Max:** Hang up! I'll call you back!
> **William:** OK. Max?
> **Max:** Hi, William.
> **William:** Ah, that's much better!

3C Students should do this in the same pairs as Exercise 3B. Get them to practise their conversation and if there is time, invite a few pairs to act it out for the rest of the class.

MyEnglishLab: Teacher's resources: extra activities; Extra speaking lessons; Additional interactive activities
Grammar reference: p.108 Making suggestions
Pronunciation bank: p.98 /ɪə/ and /eə/
Teacher's book: Resource bank Extra vocabulary practice p.139 Exercises 5 and 6; Photocopiable 4.4 p.119
Workbook: p.23 Exercises 1–3; p.47 Exercises 1–3

Business workshop
A business trip

> **GSE learning objectives**
> - Can extract key factual information such as prices, times and dates from short clear, simple announcements.
> - Can identify key information (e.g. places, times) from short audio recordings, if spoken slowly and clearly
> - Can understand short, simple emails on work-related topics.
> - Can answer simple questions on the phone, using fixed expressions.
> - Can discuss what to do and where to go, and make arrangements to meet.
> - Can write short, simple notes, emails and messages relating to everyday matters.

Introduction
Students read emails about a business trip.

1 Explain the activity and give students time to read the questions; check that they understand the meaning of *trade fair*. Students can complete the exercise individually or, in weaker classes, in pairs. Check answers with the class.

> **1** in Tokyo **2** next week **3** to help Karl with his presentation; to meet customers and make new contacts
> **4** Karl from the Seoul office and Alex

Arrangements
Students ask and answer questions about travel arrangements.

2 If you think your students will find this activity difficult, review the Communicative grammar section of Lesson 4.1 before you start. Explain to students that they are going to ask and answer questions about the arrangements for Alex's trip to Tokyo. Put them in pairs and give them time to read the questions and notes before they begin. When they have finished, check the answers with the class.

> **1** on Monday 4 April
> **2** having dinner with Ms Kimura
> **3** in the Hotel City Park for two nights
> **4** meeting Karl in the morning and practising the presentation
> **5** on Friday 8 April

A change in plans
Students listen to conversations about travel problems and write a text message explaining them, then listen to and roleplay an online meeting.

3A ◀) 4.06 Go through the instructions with students and ask or remind them who Karl is (an employee from the Seoul office – he's flying to Tokyo to attend the trade fair). Explain that he is now at the airport waiting for his flight to Tokyo, but has a problem. Students listen to the recording and note down what the problem is. Check the answer with the class.

> His flight is cancelled.

3B ◀) 4.07 Explain that Karl is now speaking to an airline employee to try and reschedule his flight. Students listen and note when he is now arriving. Check the answer with the class.

> at 12 o'clock midday on Tuesday

3C If you think your students will find this activity difficult, review the Reading and Writing sections of Lesson 4.2 before you start. Explain the writing task and give students 3–5 minutes to write their message while you monitor and help with vocabulary where necessary. When they have finished, ask students to compare their messages in pairs. Ask a few students to share their messages with the class.

Teacher's notes

> **Model answer**
> Hi, Alex. My flight to Tokyo is cancelled. I won't be there tomorrow morning! We need to change the time of our meeting. I'm staying in a hotel tonight and flying to Tokyo tomorrow. I'm arriving at midday.

3D Give students time to read Alex's message and answer the question, then check the answer with the class.

> Alex wants to have an online meeting when Karl gets to the hotel. They need to arrange a new time to practise their presentation and Alex has some new information.

4A 🔊 4.08 Explain that Karl is now at his hotel and is having an online meeting with Alex. Tell them that they are going to hear the first part of the meeting. Play the recording, twice if necessary, then check answers with the class.

> 1 Alex can't hear Karl. 2 Karl can't see Alex. The screen is frozen.

4B If you think your students will find this activity difficult, review the Grammar box in Lesson 4.4 before you start. Explain the activity and get students to write their suggestions individually. Elicit students' ideas.

> **Possible answers**
> 1 Try unmuting your microphone.
> 2 Try turning off your video, Karl.

4C Explain that students are going to roleplay the rest of Alex and Karl's call. Put them in pairs, direct them to the relevant pages and give them time to read their information. When they are ready, ask them to roleplay the call in their pairs. If necessary, let them listen to the first part of the call again. During the roleplay, monitor and note down any errors, but do not interrupt the meetings. When pairs have finished, have a brief feedback session, highlighting any points you noted while monitoring. If there is time, you could also invite a few pairs to act out their calls for the rest of the class.

> **Model answer**
> **Alex:** That's much better! I can hear you now. We need to arrange a meeting about our presentation.
> **Karl:** Yes, we need to practise. I'm arriving on Tuesday at midday. Are you available on Tuesday afternoon?
> **Alex:** Sorry, I'm meeting customers on Tuesday afternoon. How about Tuesday evening?
> **Karl:** Sorry, I can't. I'm attending a networking event. Can we meet on Wednesday morning after breakfast?
> **Alex:** I'm not available then. I'm meeting customers. How about Wednesday afternoon?
> **Karl:** I can't, I'm afraid. I'm attending a talk. How about Wednesday evening?
> **Alex:** Wednesday evening is good. How about after dinner?

An update

Students write text messages giving updates.

5 Explain that Karl has now arrived in Tokyo and is messaging Karl with an update. Ask students to complete the text messages individually, then to compare answers in pairs before class feedback.

> **Karl:** I'm waiting for my flight to Tokyo. I'm having breakfast and planning our presentation. I'm also arranging meetings with customers.
> **Alex:** I'm at the hotel. I'm having breakfast and writing emails. I'm also writing some of our presentation. Let me know when you arrive.

Grammar reference ◀ 4

4.1

> **1** 1 I'm going 2 She isn't staying 3 We're visiting
> 4 They aren't renting 5 I'm not meeting 6 He's flying
> 7 She's booking 8 They're starting
> **2** 1 Is 2 flying 3 isn't 4 Are 5 renting 6 are
> 7 Am 8 staying 9 aren't 10 am 11 going 12 are
> 13 meeting 14 'm meeting

4.2

> **1** 1 'll/will phone 2 'll/will do 3 'll/will open
> 4 'll/will help 5 'll/will send 6 'll/will get 7 'll/will be 8 won't be, 'll/will open

4.3

> **1** 1 'm 2 isn't 3 're 4 Are, am 5 Is, isn't 6 are they
> 7 aren't 8 's

4.4

> **1** 1 hanging 2 turning 3 turning 4 adding 5 calling
> 6 unmuting

Review ◀ 4

> **1** 1 book 2 stay at 3 goes by 4 rent 5 book
> 6 go by
> **2** 1 cancelled, arrived, late
> 2 departed, changed, delayed
> 3 platform, security, gate
> 4 cancelled, stopped, arrived
> **3** 1 are, flying 2 Are, meeting 3 am 4 are, staying
> 5 Is, meeting 6 is 7 is, getting 8 are going
> 9 Is, visiting 10 is
> **4** 2 Everything's going well here.
> 3 It isn't / It's not going well today.
> 4 Is Gerard writing a report?
> 5 No, he isn't.
> 6 Are they giving a presentation?
> 7 Yes, they are.
> 8 What is Lisa doing at the moment?
> 9 She's preparing the price list.
> **5** 1 c 2 a 3 d 4 b 5 b 6 d/c 7 a 8 c/d 9 d 10 c
> 11 a 12 b

Organising 5

Unit overview

	CLASSWORK		FURTHER WORK
5.1 **Trade shows and exhibitions**	Lead-in	Students talk about corporate events.	**MyEnglishLab:** Teacher's resources: extra activities; Additional interactive activities
	Vocabulary	Students look at vocabulary related to organising events.	**Grammar reference:** p.108 Talking about intentions
	Communicative grammar	Students study and practise *be going to* for intentions.	**Pronunciation bank:** p.99 /æ/, /e/ and /eɪ/
	Video	Students watch a video about Graduate Fashion Week.	**Teacher's book:** Resource bank Extra vocabulary practice p.140 Exercises 1 and 2; Photocopiable 5.1 p.120
	Task	Students talk about their plans for a trade show.	**Workbook:** p.24 Exercises 1 and 2; p.25 Exercises 1 and 2; p.48 Exercises 1-3
5.2 **Phoning about a conference**	Lead-in	Students read about a hotel conference centre.	**MyEnglishLab:** Teacher's resources: extra activities; Additional interactive activities
	Vocabulary	Students look at useful phrases for taking and leaving phone messages and making simple arrangements on the phone.	**Teacher's book:** Resource bank Extra vocabulary practice p.140 Exercise 3
	Listening	Students listen to phone calls about a conference.	
	Speaking	Students roleplay phone calls in which they take and leave phone messages, and make simple arrangements.	**Workbook:** p.24 Exercises 3 and 4; p.26 Exercises 1-4
5.3 **Invitations**	Lead-in	Students talk about when and how they write/send invitations.	**MyEnglishLab:** Teacher's resources: extra activities; Additional interactive activities
	Reading	Students read invitations and responses to invitations.	**Grammar reference:** p.109 Invitations with *would* and *want*
	Communicative grammar	Students study and practise *would* and *want* for invitations.	**Pronunciation bank:** p.99 /θ/ and /ð/ vs. /s/, /z/, /f/, /v/, /t/, /d/
	Writing	Students write messages inviting and responding to invitations.	**Workbook:** p.25 Exercises 3 and 4; p.27 Exercises 1-4; p.48 Exercises 1-3
5.4 **Work skills:** Socialising with clients	Lead-in	Students discuss socialising with colleagues.	**MyEnglishLab:** Teacher's resources: extra activities; Extra speaking lessons; Additional interactive activities
	Video	Students watch a video of people socialising in a work environment.	**Teacher's book:** Resource bank Extra vocabulary practice p.140 Exercises 4 and 5; Photocopiable 5.4 p.121
	Speaking	Students look at useful language for making small talk in a work environment.	**Workbook:** p.28 Exercises 1-3
Business workshop: The conference	Speaking	Students practise making simple arrangements on the phone and making small talk at a conference.	
	Writing	Students write an email responding to an invitation.	

Teacher's notes

Unit vocabulary list

Active vocabulary

5.1
exhibition badge	attend a trade fair
exhibition brochures	design a brochure
exhibition centre	launch an app
exhibition hall	meet clients
exhibition stand	provide freebies
	set up a stand

5.2
How can I help you?
I'm sorry, (s)he's not available right now.
Can I take a message?
Can you tell him/her (John/Tomas/Hinata) called?
Can you spell your name for me, please?
It's about the (conference/meeting) next (week/month).
Sorry, could you say that again, please?
Can I have your phone number?
So, that's (00 44 xxxxx xxxxxx).
I'll give her your message.

Passive vocabulary

5.1
awards	sponsors
business conference	technology exhibition
entry cost	tourism fair
motor show	

5.3
invitation	book (a table)
invite (*verb*)	factory
(be) free	tour

5.4
had	boring
flew	comfortable
saw	delicious
was/were	socialise
went	trade fair
	traffic

Teacher's notes

5.1 Trade shows and exhibitions

GSE learning objectives

- Can understand short, simple texts about everyday activities.
- Can express personal plans and intentions for the future using 'going to'.
- Can talk about plans for the near future in a simple way.
- Can identify simple information in a short video, provided that the visual supports this information and the delivery is slow and clear.
- Can get the gist of short, simple stories if told slowly and clearly.

Lead-in

Students talk about corporate events.

1A Draw students' attention to the title of the lesson and explain or elicit the meanings of *trade show* and *exhibition*. Ask if students can think of any famous ones (see examples in in the Notes box below). With stronger classes, ask students to cover the words in the box and elicit the events shown in the photos, then look at the rest of the words in the box with them. Otherwise, look at the events in the box with the class and check understanding, then elicit which events are in the photos.

A technology exhibition **B** motor show

Notes

- CES (Computer Electronics Show): an annual trade show hosting presentations of new products and technologies in the consumer electronics industry. It is held in Las Vegas, Nevada, USA.
- Chelsea Flower Show: a garden show held annually in the grounds of the Royal Hospital Chelsea in Chelsea, London, UK.
- London Fashion Week: a clothing trade show, one of the biggest in the world, held twice a year in London, UK.
- ITB (Internationale Tourismus Börse) Berlin: one of the world's largest tourism trade shows, held annually in Berlin, Germany.
- MICAM (Mostra Internazionale Calzature Concerie Affini e Macchinari) Milano: an international exhibition of the footwear industry held twice a year in Milan, Italy.

1B Put students in pairs or small groups to discuss the questions. When they have finished, nominate a few students to share their answers with the class. If students do attend specific events (conferences, shows, exhibitions, trade fairs) or would like to attend certain events, ask a few questions to find out more: *Which ones? When/Where do the events take place? Why do you (want to) attend these events?*

Vocabulary: Organising an exhibition

Students look at vocabulary related to organising events.

2 Draw students' attention to the mind map and check understanding of the words. Ask students to label the photos individually, then check answers with the class. You may also want to point out that in American English, an *exhibition stand* is a *booth*; a *free gift* (or *freebie*) is a *giveaway*.

2 exhibition brochures **3** exhibition centre **4** exhibition hall **5** exhibition stand

Pronunciation bank
p.99: /æ/, /e/ and /eɪ/

1 🔊 P5.01 🔊 P5.02 🔊 P5.03 Write the word *apple* on the board and explain that it begins with the sound /æ/. This example may also give students a hint on how /æ/ is actually produced: your lips are stretched out as if you were taking a bite of an apple, and the tongue is low at the front of the mouth. Play recording P5.01 and ask students to repeat the words with vowel /æ/. Point out that /æ/ is usually spelt with the letter *a*. Next, write the word *ten* on the board and explain that it contains the sound /e/. Demonstrate both vowels /æ/ and /e/ for students to notice the difference in the mouth position: when we pronounce /e/, our lips are loosely spread and the tongue is placed higher.

Play recording P5.02 and ask students to repeat the words with /e/. Explain that /e/ is often spelt with the letter *e*, but there are exceptions, such as m*a*ny or inst*ea*d. Finally, write the word *name* on the board and explain that it contains the sound /eɪ/.

Play recording P5.03 and ask students to repeat. Point out that /eɪ/ is usually represented by the letters *ay*, *ai* or *a*. Less common spellings include *ea* (great) and *ey* (they).

2 🔊 P5.04 This exercise presents two groups of minimal pairs: the first with words that vary by the vowels /æ/ and /e/, and the other one with words that differ in /e/ and /eɪ/. Play the recording and get students to repeat as a group or individually. The recording presents one minimal pair from each group at a time. For speakers of languages with a smaller vowel system, the difference between /æ/ and /e/ may be particularly hard to perceive.

3A-C 🔊 P5.05 Follow the same procedure for all three activities: explain the exercise and play the recording, twice if necessary. Get students to compare answers in pairs, then check answers with the class.

3A **1** attractive **2** stand **3** relax **4** platform **5** app
3B **1** event **2** fresh **3** hotel **4** met **5** special
3C **1** trade **2** cake **3** great **4** station **5** page

3D Put students in pairs to practise saying the sentences in Exercise 3A. If necessary, play recording P5.05 again, and get them to repeat the sentences before they practise on their own. During the activity, monitor and correct pronunciation as necessary.

Teacher's notes

3A Draw students' attention to the email and explain that it is about plans for an upcoming trade fair. Give them time to read the statements first, and check that they understand *visitors* and *exhibitors*. You may also want to pre-teach *freebies*, which students will see in the email. Ask them to complete the exercise individually, then check answers with the class. If students ask about *going to*, explain its meaning but do not go into detail about its form and use yet – tell them that they will look at it in more detail in the exercises that follow.

> **1** T **2** F **3** T **4** F

3B Explain the activity and go through the words in the box with students before they begin. Ask them to complete the exercise individually and then, if there is time, to compare answers in pairs. Check answers with the class, clarifying meanings as necessary. As an extension, you could ask students to think of more collocations with verbs 1–6, and provide some from the answer key.

> **1** a trade fair **2** a brochure **3** an app **4** clients
> **5** freebies **6** a stand

> **Other verb + noun collocations**
> **1** attend: a conference / a meeting / an exhibition
> **2** design: a poster / an advert / a website
> **3** launch: a new product / campaign / company
> **4** meet: people / friends
> **5** provide: information / brochures / free coffee / a (special) cake
> **6** set up: a room

4 Explain the activity and give students time to read the questions and answers first, and ask you about any unknown vocabulary. Check that they understand *rest/coffee/lunch break*, *badge*, *square metres*, *details* and *competition*. With weaker classes, do the first item as an example with the class. Students should complete the exercise individually and if there is time, compare answers in pairs before class feedback. As an extension, you could ask students to practise saying the questions and answers in pairs.

> **1** e **2** b **3** a **4** c **5** f **6** d

Extra activities 5.1

A This activity provides further practice of the vocabulary from the lesson. Ask students to complete it individually, then check answers with the class.

> **1** stand **2** exhibitors **3** badge **4** launch
> **5** provide **6** brochure **7** trade **8** attend **9** hall
> **10** exhibition

Communicative grammar: Talking about intentions

Students study and practise *be going to* for intentions.

> **Talking about intentions**
>
> Write on the board: *We're going to launch our new app*. Ask: *Is this the past, present or future?* (the future) Is it a plan or a prediction? (a plan). Explain that we use *be going to* in this way to talk about intentions, i.e. things that we have planned. This is slightly different to the use of the Present Continuous for future arrangements, which we use when the arrangement is fixed (e.g. in *I'm flying to London tomorrow*, we already know exactly when we will be travelling and have already bought a ticket). The difference is quite subtle, however, so there is no need to mention this unless students bring it up. Go through the examples in the Grammar box with the class and point out the form: *am/is/are going to* + infinitive. You may also wish to point out that in short answers, we only use the verb *be* (e.g. *Are you going to … ? Yes, I am. / No, I'm not.*). Refer students to the Grammar reference on pages 108–109 and go through it with them, clarifying any points as necessary. Students could then do the extra grammar activity there, in class or as homework.
> **Grammar reference answer key:** page 75

5 Ask students to complete the sentences individually, referring to the Grammar reference if they need help. Check answers with the class.

> **1** 're/are going to set
> **2** is not / isn't going to attend
> **3** 'm/am going to phone
> **4** 're/are going to have
> **5** aren't / are not going to launch
> **6** is not / isn't going to provide

6A Explain the activity and point out that the first word is given in each item. Get students to complete the exercise individually, and then to compare answers in pairs before class feedback.

> **1** How big is the exhibition hall going to be?
> **2** Are we going to provide any freebies?
> **3** When are we going to set up the stand?
> **4** Are we going to launch any new products?
> **5** Why are they going to change the brochures?

6B Give students time to read the sentences before they begin, and check that they understand *give away* and *attractive*. Ask them to complete the exercise individually, then check answers with the class. When they have finished, you could ask them to practise the questions and answers in pairs. If time is short, you could also do this as a whole-class activity, eliciting the correct answer for each question as you go.

> **1** e **2** c **3** a **4** b **5** d

Extra activities 5.1

B This activity provides further practice of *be going to*. Ask students to complete it individually and remind them that they can refer to the Grammar reference if they need help. Check answers with the class.

1 'm going to start
2 are going to attend
3 aren't going to provide
4 are, going to set up
5 isn't going to send
6 's going to launch
7 are going to be
8 Is, going to design

Video

Students watch a video about Graduate Fashion Week.

7A ▶ 5.1.1 Tell students that they are going to watch a video about Graduate Fashion Week and teach or elicit the meaning of *graduate*. Give them time to read the questions so that they know what to listen for, then play the video introduction (0:00–0:21) and elicit the answer.

Graduate Fashion Week is an exhibition that shows the best work by fashion students (from around the world). It takes place in London.

7B ▶ 5.1.1 Go through the words in the box with students and check that they understand each one. You may also wish to pre-teach the following words from the video: *run* (for an event), *attend, lanyard, catwalk, section, gala, award*. Play the full video, then check answers with the class.

awards, badges, brochures, cafés, exhibition hall (not directly referred to, but the narrator mentions the space used), stands, sponsors (the video mentions sponsor stands)

7C Give students a minute to read the sentences and ask any questions they have about vocabulary. Play the video, twice if necessary, then check answers with the class. In stronger classes, you could play the video a third time and ask students to correct the false statements.

1 T 2 F 3 F 4 F 5 T 6 T

Task

Students talk about their plans for a trade show.

8 Put students in pairs and direct them to page 128. Explain the first activity and go through the list with them, clarifying meanings as necessary. Start by letting students decide, in their pairs, what kind of event they are going to attend. It could be one related to their actual industry or, for pre-service students, their field of study. Then ask them to work individually to choose the six things they intend to do at the event – tell them that they should not show their list to their partner. Move on to the second activity and give students time to complete their diary. Again, tell them that they should not let their partner see it. When they are ready, introduce the final step: explain that in their pairs, students are going to tell their partner about what they intend to do at the event, and answer any questions their partner asks. Look at the example with them and before they begin, give them 1–2 minutes to think about what they are going to say, and what questions they could ask their partner. Remind them to use *going to* to talk about their intentions and encourage them to try to use vocabulary from the lesson. During the activity, monitor and note down any problems, but do not interrupt students' conversations – go through these points in a brief feedback session at the end.

MyEnglishLab: Teacher's resources: extra activities; Additional interactive activities
Grammar reference: p.108 Talking about intentions
Pronunciation bank: p.99 /æ/, /e/ and /eɪ/
Teacher's book: Resource bank Extra vocabulary practice p.140 Exercises 1 and 2; Photocopiable 5.1 p.120
Workbook: p.24 Exercises 1 and 2; p.25 Exercises 1 and 2; p.48 Exercises 1–3

5.2 Phoning about a conference

GSE learning objectives

- Can extract key factual information such as prices, times and dates from a recorded phone message.
- Can understand the main information in a work-related phone message.
- Can introduce themselves on the phone and close a simple call.
- Can answer simple questions on the phone using fixed expressions.
- Can take simple phone messages using fixed expressions.
- Can leave simple phone messages using fixed expressions.

Lead-in

Students read about a hotel conference centre.

1 Draw students' attention to the webpage and photo, and elicit what students can see / what the webpage is about (a conference centre). Give students time to read the information and answer the question. Check the answer with the class, clarifying meanings as necessary. Ask students if they would normally expect these services and equipment to be available at a conference centre, and if there is anything else they would expect.

data projector, screen, sound system (in large conference rooms), free Wi-Fi, free water, pens and paper

Teacher's notes

Vocabulary: Leaving a message

Students look at useful phrases for taking and leaving phone messages and making simple arrangements on the phone.

2 🔊 5.01 Tell students that they are going to hear a client phoning the conference centre they read about in Exercise 1. Explain the activity and give students time to read the message before they listen – encourage them to think about what type of information is missing from each gap (name, date, etc.). Play the recording, then check answers with the class.

> **1** Hinata **2** conference **3** 25th and 26th January
> **4** (0044) 3584 751 059

3A Explain to students that they are going to look at some useful expressions from the recording for taking and leaving phone messages. Draw their attention to the sentences and point out that the first letter of each missing word is given. Students can work in pairs to complete the expressions or complete them individually and then compare their answers in pairs. Reassure them that they do not need to worry if they cannot complete all the expressions – explain that you will look at them together later. Do not confirm the answers yet – students will check them in the next exercise.

3B 🔊 5.02 Play the recording for students to check their answers, then go through them with the class, clarifying meanings as necessary. As an extension, you could use the recording to drill the expressions, as a whole class and individually, and then get students to practise the conversation in pairs, using the audioscript on page 134 of the Coursebook.

> **1** help **2** sorry **3** take **4** tell **5** spell **6** about
> **7** could **8** have **9** that's **10** give

Listening: Organising a conference

Students listen to phone calls about a conference.

4A 🔊 5.03 Explain to students that Mary Duffy, the Conference Centre Manager, is now calling Ms Nakamura about the conference. Read through the list of topics with students, so they know what to listen for, then play the recording and check answers with the class.

> **1** d **2** b **3** a **4** c

4B 🔊 5.03 Explain the activity, give students time to read the questions before they listen, and check that they understand *confirm* in question 3. Ask students to make notes in answer to the questions while listening, then play the recording and check answers with the class.

> **1** between 120 and 130
> **2** between 48 and 55
> **3** on Friday
> **4** a list of names and total number (of conference participants and hotel guests)
> **5** an assistant (from the conference centre team)
> **6** morning break 11 a.m., lunch 1 p.m., afternoon break 3.30 p.m.

Extra activities 5.2

A This activity provides further practice of the expressions in Exercise 3A. Ask students to complete it individually and if there is time, get them to compare answers in pairs before checking with the class.

> **1** I'll give her your message.
> **2** How can I help you?
> **3** I'm sorry, she's not available right now.
> **4** How many participants are there going to be?
> **5** Can I take a message?
> **6** We'll confirm the details tomorrow.
> **7** Can you send me the list of participants?
> **8** What equipment are you going to need?
> **9** I'll send all the details today.
> **10** Hello, can I speak to Mike Williams?

B Again, ask students to complete the exercise individually. In stronger classes, you could ask them to cover the box and complete as many of the gaps as they can, then look at it to check/complete their answers. Check answers with the class. As an extension, you could put students in pairs to practise the conversation.

> **1** help **2** this **3** about **4** take **5** tell **6** spell
> **7** have **8** could **9** that's **10** give

Speaking

Students roleplay phone calls in which they take and leave phone messages, and make simple arrangements.

5 Explain to students that they are going to roleplay phone calls in which they take and leave phone messages. Start with phone call 1. Put students in pairs, assign roles A and B and explain: Student A is a client, and is phoning a conference centre about a conference they are going to attend. Student B represents the conference centre and is going to answer the phone. Refer students to their relevant pages and give them time to read and complete the information about phone call 1, while you monitor and offer help as necessary. Give students time to think about what they are going to say, reminding them that they can refer to Exercise 3A and audioscript 5.02 on page 134 if they need help. Students then roleplay the phone call. Monitor while they do this and make notes on any points to highlight during feedback. When they have finished, ask them to swap roles and repeat the procedure for phone call 2. Finally, have a brief feedback session, highlighting any points you noted while monitoring.

6 Keep students in the same pairs as Exercise 5 for this activity. Tell them that they are going to roleplay two more phone calls about the events they talked about in Exercise 5 – this time, the clients are going to speak to the managers and make arrangements for each event. Start with phone call 1. Direct students to their relevant information and give them time to read it. Go through the conversation outline with them, then give them time to prepare for their phone calls while you monitor and offer help as necessary. Again, remind them that they should use phrases from Exercise 3A and also that they can refer to audioscript 5.03 on page 134 if they need help. During the roleplay, monitor and make notes on any points

Teacher's notes

to highlight during feedback. Follow the same procedure for phone call 2, then if there is time, invite a few pairs to act out their conversations for the class. Finally, have a brief feedback session highlighting any points you noted during the roleplays.

MyEnglishLab: Teacher's resources: extra activities; Additional interactive activities

Teacher's book: Resource bank Extra vocabulary practice p.140 Exercise 3

Workbook: p.24 Exercises 3 and 4; p.26 Exercises 1–4

5.3 > Invitations

GSE learning objectives

- Can understand short, simple messages about when and where to meet.
- Can make requests and offers with 'would like to' + verbs in the infinitive.
- Can use language related to inviting.
- Can use language related to accepting or refusing.
- Can write a simple email accepting a work-related invitation.
- Can write a simple email issuing a work-related invitation.
- Can write short, simple notes, emails and messages relating to everyday matters.

Lead-in

Students talk about when and how they write/send invitations.

1 You could introduce the topic by asking the following questions and eliciting a few answers around the class: *When was the last time someone invited you somewhere? How were you invited (e.g. email, social media, a phone call)?* Then draw students' attention to the example messages next to Exercise 1 and elicit what the medium might be (a messaging app / text messages). Students could discuss the questions in pairs or small groups or, if you are short of time, as a whole class. If they work in pairs/groups, elicit answers from a few students at the end, and have a brief class discussion, feeding in ideas from the answer key where relevant.

Possible answers

Students may think of examples of inviting friends and family informally to meet for drinks, meals, sports events, trips to the shops, etc. In more formal work contexts they may send invitations to clients, suppliers and colleagues in other departments they do not know so well. They may start to mention the differences in their own informal and formal writing styles, e.g. use of abbreviations, emojis and spelling mistakes in quick, informal writing and the more formal, fuller forms and language use in more formal writing.

Reading

Students read invitations and responses to invitations.

2 Ask students to read the messages quickly and answer the questions individually, then check answers with the class.

The invitation is to join Carl for lunch.
Four people can attend. (A. Tanaka, Elisabeth Fischer, Sakura, Carl)
Carl's message: four, 1 p.m. / one/1 o'clock

3 Explain that Carl is now looking to invite people to dinner with him, so he sends an email. Ask students to read his email and the responses, then answer the questions – they could do this individually or, in weaker classes, in pairs. Check answers with the class, encouraging students to give reasons for their answer to question 1.

1 No, it appears not, because he writes *'We look forward to meeting you'* at the end of the email.
2 For a sales presentation.
3 He invites the clients to join him and Danielle for dinner at a French restaurant on 29th March after the sales presentation.
4 Oliver says 'yes' to the invitation but Emma says she can't come because she has a flight that evening.

Communicative grammar: Invitations with *would* and *want*

Students study and practise *would* and *want* for invitations.

Invitations with *would* and *want*

Ask students to look back at the messages and emails in Exercises 2 and 3, and find the phrases in bold. Elicit which are invitations and which are responses, and whether each one is formal or informal. Explain that in invitations, want is informal and would like is more formal, though the meaning is the same. Go through the Grammar box with the class, pointing out the different function of each group of phrases, and answer any questions students may have. Then refer them to the Grammar reference on page 109 and go through it with them. Students could then do the extra grammar activities there, in class or as homework.
Grammar reference answer key: page 75

> ### Pronunciation bank
> **p.99: /θ/ and /ð/ vs. /s/, /z/, /f/, /v/, /t/, /d/**
>
> **1** ◆) P5.06 ◆) P5.07 Explain to students that *th* mostly represents the sounds /θ/ and /ð/. For reference, /θ/ is an unvoiced consonant (the vocal cords do not vibrate), whereas /ð/ is a voiced consonant (the vocal cords vibrate), but they are both articulated in the same way by lightly touching the upper teeth with the tip of the tongue and blowing air through the mouth. The tip of the tongue is behind the teeth but visible. Sticking the tongue out a little may help students produce the sound. Play the recordings and get students to repeat the words as a group and then individually. You could then put them in pairs and ask them to take turns repeating two words at a time, one with /θ/ and one with /ð/.

Teacher's notes

2A 🔊 P5.08 The sounds /θ/ and /ð/ may present a challenge to those students who do not use them in their native languages. Learners often substitute /t/, /f/ or /s/ for /θ/, and /d/, /v/ or /z/ for /ð/ because of certain phonological features that these consonants have in common. The exercise is intended to make students aware that in some cases, replacing /θ/ and /ð/ with other consonants results in a change of meaning. Play the recording and ask students to underline the words they hear, then check answers with the class. If necessary, play the recording again during feedback, pausing after each item for students to hear the word again.

> **1** thing **2** free **3** three **4** mouth **5** day
> **6** clothing

2B 🔊 P5.09 Play the recording and ask students to repeat the minimal pairs as a group and then individually.

3A 🔊 P5.10 Explain the activity and play the recording, pausing after each item for students to write the word and think about its pronunciation. Check answers with the class.

> **1** both /θ/ **2** Thursday /θ/ **3** within /ð/
> **4** weather /ð/ **5** north /θ/ **6** brothers /ð/

3B 🔊 P5.10 Put students in pairs to practise saying the sentences in Exercise 3A. Before they begin, draw their attention to the words with the letters *th* in red and blue, which represent the target sounds /θ/ and /ð/ respectively. This should serve as a reminder that there are other instances of /θ/ and /ð/ in the sentences apart from the words students put in the gaps. You may also wish to play the recording again and get students to repeat the sentences as a group before they practise on their own. During the activity, monitor and correct pronunciation as necessary.

4A 🔊 5.04 Ask students to choose the correct option in each phrase and then decide if it is formal or informal, using the Grammar box to help them. When they are ready, play the recording for them to check their answers, then go through them with the class.

> **1** like **2** Do **3** Thank **4** I'd **5** like **6** but **7** very
> **8** us

4B Students could do this individually or, in weaker classes, in pairs. Explain the activity and if necessary, do the first item as an example with the class. If they do the exercise individually, get them to compare answers in pairs before class feedback. As an extension, you could ask students which of the sentences in Exercise 4A are a) inviting, b) saying 'yes' to invitations or c) saying 'no' to invitations (see answers in brackets in the answer key below).

> **1** F (inviting) **2** I (inviting) **3** F (saying 'yes') **4** I (saying 'yes') **5** F (saying 'no') **6** I (saying 'no') **7** F (saying 'no')
> **8** I (inviting)

5 Explain the activity and ask students to read each email/message quickly before attempting the exercise, and think about what type of word is needed in each gap. Ask them to complete the exercise individually, then check answers with the class.

> **1** like **2** join **3** Would **4** much **5** invitation **6** love
> **7** very **8** because **9** want **10** invitation

> The messages are about plans for a client's visit to the company. The plans include a meeting, lunch with senior managers and an invitation to tour the factory.

Extra activities 5.3

A/B These activities provide further practice of the expressions for inviting and responding to invitations. Ask students to complete both exercises individually, and remind them that they can refer to the Grammar box if they need help. If there is time, get them to compare answers in pairs before checking with the class.

> **A 1** Would you like to **join** us for lunch?
> **2** I am **sorry**, but I cannot come because I have a meeting in a few minutes.
> **3** Would they **like** to visit the factory?
> **4** Do you want **to** see the new brochure?
> **5** Thank you **for** the invitation. Yes, I would love to join you.
> **6** Do **you** want to walk to the conference centre?
> **7** Thanks for the invitation, **but** I'll take a taxi.
> **8** Thank you very **much** for the invitation, but I am not available today.
> **9** Sorry, but I have **other** plans.
> **10** I **would** like to join you, but I have an early flight.
> **B 1** F **2** F **3** F **4** I **5** F **6** I **7** I **8** F **9** I **10** F

Writing

Students write messages inviting and responding to invitations.

6 Explain to students that they are going to write and respond to invitations. Put them in groups of four, assign roles and ask them to look at their relevant pages. Give them time to read their information and before they begin, point out that all the invitations should be informal and in the form of social media messages. Encourage them to look at the model messages in Exercise 2 if they need help and remind them to use phrases from the Grammar box. Give them time to prepare, and offer help where necessary. When they are ready, ask them to write and respond to their messages. If students are comfortable doing so, they could exchange their messages via social media. Otherwise, they can just write them on paper. Monitor and check they are using the phrases correctly, and highlight any errors/difficulties in a brief feedback session at the end of the activity.

Model answers

Invitations

Student A: Hi everyone. I met my sales targets last month, so I'm going to celebrate tonight. Do you want to join me for dinner tonight at the French restaurant?

Teacher's notes

Student B: Hi everyone. As you know, our department is moving to London. Do you want to visit the new location next week?

Student C: Hi everyone. I'm celebrating my promotion with lunch at the French restaurant today. Do you want to join me?

Student D: Hello! It's my birthday today. Do you want to join me for cake and coffee in my office at 11 a.m.?

Replies

(See the Grammar box on page 53 of the Coursebook.)

7 Tell students that they are now going to write a more formal invitation, and direct them to page 118. Go through the information with them and point out that they need to use more formal language this time. Remind them that they can look at the model emails in Exercises 3 and 5, and that they should use phrases from the Grammar box. Give them time to plan their emails, while you go round and help with vocabulary where necessary. As an extension, students could exchange emails with a partner and write a reply, using the model emails in Exercise 3 to help them. They could do this in class or as homework.

> **Model answer**
>
> Dear Mr Murray,
>
> Senior management would like to invite you to see the production area and the warehouse at our head office. Would you like to have a tour of the company next Thursday morning before our meeting?
>
> I would also like to invite you to join me and my colleague, Carl Becker, for dinner on Thursday night at the Via Veneti Italian Restaurant at 8 p.m.
>
> We look forward to seeing you next week.
>
> Best regards,
>
> Juan

MyEnglishLab: Teacher's resources: extra activities; Additional interactive activities
Grammar reference: p.109 Invitations with *would* and *want*
Pronunciation bank: p.99 /θ/ and /ð/ vs. /s/, /z/, /f/, /v/, /t/, /d/
Workbook: p.25 Exercises 3 and 4; p.27 Exercises 1–4; p.48 Exercises 1–3

5.4 > Work skills
Socialising with clients

> **GSE learning objectives**
> - Can identify basic factual information in short, simple dialogues or narratives on familiar everyday topics, if spoken slowly and clearly.
> - Can follow short, simple social exchanges.
> - Can identify simple information in a short video, provided that the visual supports this information and the delivery is slow and clear.
> - Can understand simple, everyday conversations if conducted slowly and clearly.
> - Can express agreement using simple fixed expressions.
> - Can give simple opinions using basic fixed expressions.

Lead-in

Students discuss socialising with colleagues.

1A Before students do the activity, refer them to the lesson title *Socialising with clients* and check that they understand the meaning of *socialise*. Then put them in pairs to discuss the questions. As feedback, invite a few students to share their ideas with the class. You could then do a class vote for the most popular topics.

1B Ask students to discuss the questions in the same pairs as Exercise 1A, then get brief feedback from the class.

Video

Students watch a video of people socialising in a work environment.

2 ▶ 5.4.1 Tell students that they are going to watch a video of Max and Maria from Sleek meeting Julia, an external client. Remind students who Max and Maria are or refer them to page 6 of the Coursebook. Tell them that in the first part of the video, Max is talking to Julia. Give them time to read the sentences before they watch, then play the first part of the video (0:00–1:17) and check answers with the class.

> **1** Julia **2** this morning **3** great **4** lunch **5** doesn't know **6** in the conference hall

3 ▶ 5.4.1 Explain to students that they are now going to watch the second part of the video, where Max and Maria are talking to Julia. Go through the topics in the box with them, then play the second part (1:18–3:09) and check answers with the class.

> exhibitors, the city, the trade fair, the hotel

4 ▶ 5.4.1 Explain the activity and give students time to read the questions before they watch the video again. Ask them to make notes in answer to the questions while watching, then play the second part of the video and check answers with the class.

> **1** It's an important client.
> **2** She says there are some good presentations.
> **3** Maria saw a presentation about the impact of technology (on their industry).
> **4** It's comfortable and it's near a park.
> **5** It isn't near the city centre.
> **6** Get a taxi into the city, walk around the old town and have dinner.

5A Students could complete the exercise individually or, if you are short of time, you could do this as a whole-class activity, checking answers as you go.

> **1** c **2** b **3** d **4** a

5B Explain the activity, pointing out that all the verbs have irregular past forms, then ask students to complete the exercise individually. In weaker classes, you could let students refer to the Irregular verbs list on page 114. Check answers with the class.

> **1** hear, be **2** go **3** have **4** fly **5** see **6** be

> 73

> Teacher's notes

5C Explain the activity and look at the examples with the class. Students write their sentences individually, while you monitor and help with vocabulary where necessary. When they are ready, put them in pairs to share their sentences and then, as feedback, invite a few students to share any interesting information they found out about their partner with the class.

Speaking: Socialising with clients

Students look at useful language for making small talk in a work environment.

> **Socialising with clients**
>
> Tell students that they are going to look at useful phrases for socialising with clients, and point out the function of each group of phrases. Go through the Speaking box with the class, clarifying meanings and helping students with pronunciation as necessary. As an extension, you could put students in pairs and ask them to take turns to choose a question/opinion statement from the box for their partner to respond to with an appropriate expression.

> **Unit 5 Extra speaking lesson**
>
> This lesson gives further practice of speaking related to socialising with clients. To access the lesson go to MyEnglishLab > Extra speaking lessons.

> **Extra activities 5.4**
>
> **A/B** These activities provide further practice of the functional language from the Speaking box. They are both consolidation exercises, so students should complete them individually. If there is time, get students to compare answers in pairs before checking with the class.
>
> **A**
> 1 of 2 think 3 agree 4 very 5 right 6 like
> 7 It's 8 isn't 9 it's 10 hear
> **B**
> 1 a 2 b 3 b 4 a 5 b 6 a 7 a 8 b 9 a 10 a

6A Put students in pairs to match the questions and answers, then check answers with the class. If there is time, students could then practise asking and answering the questions in their pairs.

> 1 b 2 c 3 a 4 e 5 d

6B Students could do this in the same pairs as Exercise 6A or in new pairs. Give students time to write their responses first, while monitoring and offering help, correcting where necessary. Once you are confident their responses are correct, ask students to practise asking and answering the questions. In feedback, ask a few pairs to share their answers with the class.

7 Ask students to work individually and if there is time, get them to compare answers in pairs before class feedback. As an extension, they could practise the dialogue in pairs.

> 1 c 2 a 3 e 4 g 5 b 6 f 7 d

8 Explain to students that they are going to practise making small talk with a colleague – teach or elicit the meaning of *small talk*. Put them in pairs and go through the instructions with them. Point out that they should use phrases from the Speaking box, and encourage them to refer to the dialogue in Exercise 7 and the videoscript (page 131) if they need help. Give them time to prepare for their conversations and point out that they can use the ideas in the box or their own ideas. Weaker students could simply adapt parts of the dialogue in Exercise 7. During the activity, monitor and note down any errors/difficulties with the functional language; go over these in a brief feedback session at the end of the activity.

MyEnglishLab: Teacher's resources: extra activities; Extra speaking lessons; Additional interactive activities
Teacher's book: Resource bank Extra vocabulary practice p.140 Exercises 4 and 5; Photocopiable 5.4 p.121
Workbook: p.28 Exercises 1–3

Business workshop
The conference

> **GSE learning objectives**
> - Can talk about plans for the near future in a simple way.
> - Can make simple work-related arrangements on the phone.
> - Can write write a simple email issuing a work-related invitation.
> - Can make small talk using simple language, given a model.
> - Can give simple opinions using basic fixed expressions.

Introduction

Students read about an event.

1 Ask students to read the information and then answer the question – they could do this individually or in pairs. Check the answer with the class.

> It's an annual sales conference on 27th and 28th May at the Trent Hotel and Conference Centre, Nottingham.

Speaking

Students practise making simple arrangements on the phone.

2 If you think your students will find this activity difficult, review the phrases in Exercise 3A in Lesson 5.2 and look at audioscript 5.03 on page 134 with them before you start. Put students in pairs, explain the activity and direct them to their relevant information. Give them plenty of time to read it, and be on hand to offer help where necessary. When they are ready, ask them to roleplay their phone calls. During the roleplay, monitor and note down any errors/difficulties, but do not interrupt the phone calls. When pairs have finished, have a brief feedback session, highlighting any points you noted while monitoring.

Writing

Students write an email responding to an invitation.

3A Explain to students that the company is now emailing the sales staff about the conference, and look at the instructions with them. Ask them to complete the exercise individually and encourage them to read the whole email quickly before completing the gaps. Check answers with the class.

> 1 is going to take 2 are going to have 3 will send
> 4 like to invite 5 look forward 6 Best regards

3B If you think your students will find this activity difficult, review the Grammar box in Lesson 5.3 before you start. Ask students to write their replies individually, and remind them that they can refer back to the model emails in Lesson 5.3 if they need help. Monitor and check students' writing as they work, offering help where needed. As an extension, you could get students to compare their emails in pairs or small groups.

> **Model answers**
>
> **Saying yes**
> Thank you very much for the invitation. I would love to join the sales team for dinner at the hotel on 27th May.
> I look forward to seeing you at the conference.
> Best regards,
> Emma
>
> **Saying no**
> Thank you for the invitation but I am very sorry I cannot come to dinner with you on the 27th because I have a conference call with a client in Canada that evening.
> Best regards,
> Emma

Speaking

Students practise making small talk at a conference dinner.

4A Discuss the question as a class, and write students' ideas on the board so they can refer back to them as possible conversation starters in the next activity.

4B If you think your students will find this activity difficult, review the Speaking box in Lesson 5.4 before you start. Ask students to imagine that they are at the Hopkins sales conference dinner, put them in groups of three and direct them to their relevant pages. Give them a few minutes to read their role cards and think about what to say. Go round and help with vocabulary where necessary. When they are ready, students roleplay their conversations in their groups. You could then invite one or two stronger groups to act out their conversation for the class.

Grammar reference ◀ 5

5.1

> **1** 1 are going to attend
> 2 are not/aren't going to start
> 3 is/'s going to set up
> 4 Are they going to launch
> 5 is not/isn't going to provide
> 6 are we going to have
> 7 am/'m going to send
> 8 is not/isn't going to change

5.3

> **1** 1 like 2 sorry 3 Would 4 would 5 want 6 love
> 7 you 8 but 9 What 10 join

Review ◀ 5

> **1** 1 show 2 stand 3 Exhibitors 4 brochures 5 badge
> 6 attend 7 exhibition 8 launch
> **2** 1 How 2 about 3 I'm 4 take 5 phoned 6 spell
> 7 have 8 say 9 I'll
> **3** 1 c 2 b 3 b 4 a 5 c 6 c
> **4** 1 I *would like* to speak to the manager.
> 2 He *would like* to join us for the meeting.
> 3 We *would like* to order more computers.
> 4 A: *Would you like to* join us at the restaurant? B: Yes, I *would* / Yes, I *would love to*.
> 5 What time *would you like* to have lunch?
> 6 A: When *would you like* to see the factory? B: I *would like to* see it this afternoon.
> **5** 1 What do you think of the conference?
> 2 Do you like your hotel?
> 3 Did you enjoy the meal?
> 4 I think there are some very good new products.
> 5 The meeting was very interesting.
> 6 I like some of the exhibitors' stands.
> 7 The hotel is beautiful and it's near the town centre.
> 8 Yes, but it isn't near our office.
> 9 You're right, but it's a very popular product.
> 10 Did you see the local music show?
> 11 I want to visit the old city. I hear it's beautiful.
> 12 When did you arrive?

6 Products

Unit overview

		CLASSWORK	FURTHER WORK
6.1 Future products	Lead-in	Students discuss changes in how they use different products.	**MyEnglishLab:** Teacher's resources: extra activities; Additional interactive activities
	Vocabulary	Students look at vocabulary related to technology and the environment.	**Grammar reference:** p.110 Speculating about the future
	Video	Students watch a video about the future of business.	**Teacher's book:** Resource bank Extra vocabulary practice p.141 Exercise 1
	Communicative grammar	Students study and practise *will* and *might* for speculating about the future.	**Workbook:** p.29 Exercises 1 and 2; p.30 Exercises 1 and 2
	Task	Students practise speculating about the future.	
6.2 A problem with an order	Lead-in	Students discuss customer problems and customer services solutions.	**MyEnglishLab:** Teacher's resources: extra activities; Additional interactive activities
	Listening	Students listen to a customer phoning customer services.	**Pronunciation bank:** p.99 /ɑː/ and /ʌ/
	Vocabulary	Students look at useful language for making and responding to complaints.	**Teacher's book:** Resource bank Extra vocabulary practice p.141 Exercises 1 and 2
	Speaking	Students roleplay phone calls to customer services.	**Workbook:** p.29 Exercises 3 and 4; p.31 Exercises 1–3; p.32 Exercises 1–3; p.49 Exercises 1–3
6.3 The production process	Lead-in	Students complete an infographic showing a supply chain	**MyEnglishLab:** Teacher's resources: extra activities; Additional interactive activities
	Reading	Students read about ethical practices in the production process of a company.	**Grammar reference:** p.110 Describing production
	Communicative grammar	Students study and practise the Present Simple Passive.	**Pronunciation bank:** p.100 /uː/ and /ʊ/
	Writing	Students write a description for a company website.	**Teacher's book:** Resource bank Photocopiable 6.3 p.122
			Workbook: p.30 Exercises 3 and 4; p.49 Exercises 1–3
6.4 Work skills: Placing an order	Lead-in	Students learn key terms related to placing an order.	**MyEnglishLab:** Teacher's resources: extra activities; Extra speaking lessons; Additional interactive activities
	Video	Students watch a video of a client and manufacturer discussing an order.	**Teacher's book:** Resource bank Extra vocabulary practice p.141 Exercises 4 and 5; Photocopiable 6.4 p.123
	Speaking	Students look at useful language for placing orders.	**Workbook:** p.33 Exercises 1–3
Business workshop: Buy natural	Reading	Students read an extract from a company website about ethical products.	
	Speaking	Students practise placing an order, and making and responding to complaints.	

Teacher's notes

Unit vocabulary list

Active vocabulary

6.1
electric
energy
environment
machines
plastic
pollution
recycle
technology
packaging
renting
robots
sharing
smart technology

6.2
How can I help you?
There's a problem with the (laptops/photocopier).
I'm sorry to hear that.
Can I have your order number, please?
I'm very sorry about the mistake.
We'll change those for you.
Can I just check your (delivery) address?
It might take (3 or 4 days).
I understand this is important for you.
I'll talk to my manager.
Can I help you with anything else?
You're very welcome.

Thank you for your help.
Is there anything you can do about it?
We need it (fixed) as soon as possible.
When will (it / the technician) get here?

Passive vocabulary

6.3
clothes manufacturer
cotton farmer
cotton supplier
customer
distribution centre
retail store
designed
grown
made
paid
produced
sold
used

6.4
delivery date
payment terms
price
quantity
discount

> Teacher's notes

6.1 > Future products

GSE learning objectives

- Can use language related to environmental issues.
- Can use language related to machines and technology.
- Can recognise some basic fixed expressions to describe products or services, given help with vocabulary.
- Can identify key information in short, simple factual texts from the headings and pictures.
- Can use 'will' + infinitive for predictions about the future.
- Can make simple predictions about the future.
- Can identify simple information in a short video, provided that the visual supports this information and the delivery is slow and clear.
- Can follow the main points in a simple audio recording, if provided with written supporting material.

Lead-in

Students discuss changes in how they use different products.

1 Introduce the topic by talking about how you listen to music or watch films now, compared to 10/20 years ago (CDs, DVDs, etc.). Alternatively, you could bring in your latest phone and a previous one and compare them. Look at the examples with the class, then get students to discuss the question in pairs, small groups or as a whole class, depending on the time available and the size of your class. If students work in pairs or groups, elicit a few answers around the class as feedback.

Vocabulary: Technology and the environment

Students look at vocabulary related to technology and the environment.

2A Go through the words in the box with the class, clarifying meanings and modelling pronunciation as necessary. Point out that *plastic* is a high-frequency word both as a noun (e.g. *recycle plastic*) and as an adjective (e.g. *plastic bags*, *plastic bottles*). Ask students to complete the sentences individually, and then to compare answers in pairs. Do not confirm answers yet – students will check them in the next activity.

2B 🔊 6.01   Play the recording for students to check their answers to Exercise 2A, then go over them with the class.

> 1 energy   2 pollution   3 electric   4 environment
> 5 machines   6 technology   7 recycle   8 plastic

3 Put students in pairs or small groups to discuss the questions while you monitor and help them with any vocabulary they may need. For question 1, pre-service students could talk about their place of study instead. After 2–3 minutes, invite a few students to share their answers with the class.

Suggested answers

1 computer/laptop, mobile phone, coffee machine
2 paper, plastic, glass, tins
3 Students' own opinion and examples, e.g. electric car-share schemes have been introduced in many European cities.
4 Students' own opinion and examples, e.g. people might talk about the air quality in the town or city where they live.

4A Read the title and introduction to the text with the class and check that they understand *experts*. Elicit what products students think the text might discuss, then get them to complete the exercise individually. Check answers with the class. If students ask about the use of *will* and *might* in bold in the text, offer a quick explanation, but do not go into too much detail – tell them that they will look at both verbs in more detail later in the lesson.

> 1 B   2 C   3 A

4B Discuss the question with the class. You could include ideas from the following suggested answers.

Possible answers

Professional delivery drivers and taxis may be replaced by driverless cars, drones and lorries. Waiters and waitresses could be replaced by automated services. Many bank cashier jobs will disappear. All routine office tasks can be done by machines, e.g. customer service help desk for simple enquiries.

Extra activities 6.1

A This activity provides further practice of vocabulary from Exercise 2, so students should be able to do it individually, as consolidation. To help them, you could say that all the words they need to use are in the box in Exercise 2A; point out that they may need to change the form of some words. Check answers with the class, writing (or inviting students to write) the words on the board, so students can check their spelling.

> 1 machine   2 electric, pollution   3 technology, energy   4 plastic, environment   5 recycle

Communicative grammar: Speculating about the future

Students study and practise *will* and *might* for speculating about the future.

> **Speculating about the future**
>
> Go through the sentences with *will* in the Grammar box and explain that we use *will* for predictions – to say what we think will happen in the future. Point out that we often use *I think / I don't think* with *will*, since these are personal predictions (i.e. based on personal opinion). Then go through the sentences with *might* and explain that these are predictions we are less certain about (similar to *will + maybe* in meaning). Refer students to the article in Exercise 4A so they can look again at the target language in context – draw their attention to the words in bold in the text. Finally, refer students to the Grammar reference on page 110 and go through it with them, clarifying any points as necessary. Students could then do the extra grammar activity there, in class or as homework.
>
> **Grammar reference answer key:** page 85

5A Give students a minute to read through the sentences and answer any questions they may have about the vocabulary first. Then ask them to complete the exercise individually. Point out that there is more than one possible answer in each item – these are their own speculations about the future, so they can use *will* or *might* depending on what they think will happen. Pre-service students can make up the information for a company they want to work for or know about. During the activity, monitor and check students are using *will* and *might* correctly.

> 1 will / won't / might / might not be
> 2 will / won't / might / might not be
> 3 will / won't / might / might not move
> 4 will / won't / might / might not have
> 5 will / won't / might / might not do
> 6 will / won't / might / might not work
> 7 will / won't / might / might not buy
> 8 will / won't / might / might not use
> 9 will / won't / might / might not recycle

5B Put students in pairs to compare their ideas from Exercise 5A. When they have finished, ask a few students to share their ideas with the class and find out if others agree.

> **Extra activities 6.1**
>
> **B** This activity provides further practice of *will* and *might* for speculating about the future. Ask students to complete it individually and remind them that they can refer to the Grammar reference if they need help. Check answers with the class.
>
> > 1 There will be more electric trucks.
> > 2 I think robots will do more jobs.
> > 3 More people might work from home.
> > 4 Industries might recycle more materials.
> > 5 There won't be many shops.
> > 6 Companies might not use plastic.
> > 7 I don't think there will be many changes.
> > 8 Many jobs won't exist in the future.

Video

Students watch a video about the future of business.

6A ▶ 6.1.1 Explain that students are going to watch a video of different people making predictions about the future of business. You may want to pre-teach some or all of the following vocabulary from the video: *have an impact on something, exist, contactless credit card, in-store, reduce, waste, pollution, driverless/hybrid car*. Go through the topics in the table with students so that they know what to listen for, check understanding of any new words, then play the video and check answers with the class.

Apps	Kate, Lisa
Electric	Steve
Mobile phones	Leona, Lisa, Kate
Packaging	Leona
Pollution/Waste	Leona, Steve
Renting/Sharing	Steve, Kate
Robots	Leona, Lisa
Smart technology	Kate, Lisa, Leona (mentions paying for things by phone)

6B ▶ 6.1.1 Explain the activity, go through the words in the box with students, then put them in pairs to complete the sentences. Encourage them to read all the sentences quickly before they complete the gaps. When they are ready, play the video again for them to check their answers, then go over them with the class.

> 1 products 2 Cash 3 packaging 4 electric 5 share
> 6 cars 7 colour 8 recycled 9 rent 10 room 11 food
> 12 energy

6C Students could do this in the same pairs as Exercise 6B or in new pairs. Explain that they need to match each speaker from the video (Leona, Kate, Steve or Lisa) with the correct set of sentences in Exercise 6B, and then decide whether they agree or disagree with each speaker's ideas. Check the answers to the matching task, then give pairs 3–4 minutes to discuss. As feedback, invite students from different pairs to share their views with the class – encourage them to give reasons.

> 1 Leona 2 Steve 3 Kate 4 Lisa

Task

Students practise speculating about the future.

7A Explain the activity and give students a few minutes to write their predictions while you monitor and help as necessary. Fast-finishers can write more sentences.

7B Put students in pairs or small groups and give them 3–4 minutes to discuss their ideas. When they have finished, you could ask them to decide which of the ideas in their pair/group they think is most likely and share it with the class.

MyEnglishLab: Teacher's resources: extra activities; Additional interactive activities

Grammar reference: p.110 Speculating about the future

Teacher's book: Resource bank Extra vocabulary practice p.141 Exercise 1

Workbook: p.29 Exercises 1 and 2; p.30 Exercises 1 and 2

Teacher's notes

6.2 > A problem with an order

GSE learning objectives

- Can understand specific information in a short, simple phone call.
- Can understand simple work-related questions asked on phone calls.
- Can use language related to complaints and resolving complaints.
- Can talk about orders or deliveries using a few fixed expressions and given help with vocabulary.
- Can answer simple questions on the phone using fixed expressions.
- Can suggest possible solutions to a problem using simple language.

Lead-in

Students discuss customer problems and customer services solutions.

1A Introduce the topic by telling students about a time you had to call customer services (e.g. to query a bill, to fix a problem). Then put them in pairs or small groups to discuss the questions. When they have finished, ask a few students to share their experiences with the class. If time is short, you could also discuss the questions briefly with the whole class.

1B Give students time to read the sentences and clarify any vocabulary as necessary. Ask them to complete the matching task individually, and if there is time, get them to compare answers in pairs before checking with the class. During feedback, elicit any other solutions students can think of.

> **1** b **2** e **3** a **4** c **5** d

Listening: A problem with an order

Students listen to a customer phoning customer services.

2 🔊 6.02 Explain that students are going to listen to a customer phoning customer services, and draw attention to the form. Go through the headings on the form and check that they understand each one. If you think it will help your students, do some quick revision of numbers, spelling and how we say addresses and postcodes in English before students listen. For instance, get them to work in pairs and say all the numbers they see on the form. Revise the difference in pronunciation between *13* and *30*, *14* and *40*, *15* and *50*, etc. Then get them to spell out some of the key words on the form, e.g. company and street names. This will help prepare them for the listening task. Give students a minute to look at the form again before they listen, then play the recording, twice if necessary, and check answers with the class.

> **1** Patterson's **2** laptop **3** FT90087 **4** 14 **5** CR673
> **6** 13 **7** Northport **8** M19 5LH **9** Express **10** two

Vocabulary: Helping with a problem

Students look at useful language for making and responding to complaints.

3 🔊 6.02 Explain to students that these are some useful phrases for helping customers with a problem and responding to customer complaints. Stronger classes could complete the phrases from memory, then listen again to check/complete their answers. Otherwise, play the recording again for students to listen and complete the phrases, then check answers with the class, clarifying meanings as necessary. Students can then practise saying the phrases in pairs or, if you think they need help with the pronunciation of the phrases, you could drill them chorally and individually.

> **1** I help **2** problem with **3** sorry to **4** Can I
> **5** sorry about **6** change **7** check **8** might
> **9** understand **10** talk to **11** you with **12** welcome

> ### Pronunciation bank
> **p.99: /ɑː/ and /ʌ/**
>
> **1** 🔊 P6.01 🔊 P6.02 The vowel /ɑː/ is a long sound. It is pronounced with the mouth wide open and the tongue low and at the back of the mouth. By contrast, /ʌ/ is a short vowel. The mouth is not so wide open and the tongue is between the middle and the back of the mouth. Write the letter *R* and the verb *are* on the board. Model their pronunciation and explain that in standard British English, both are pronounced with a single sound: /ɑː/. Play recording P6.01 and get students to repeat as a group and then individually. Draw their attention to the spelling: the sound /ɑː/ is commonly represented by *ar* (*bar*) and *a* (*last*). Continue with the next sound: write the word *up* on the board, model its pronunciation and explain that it begins with the sound /ʌ/. Play recording P6.02 and get students to repeat as a group and then individually. Explain that /ʌ/ is often spelt with the letter *u*, but the sound can be represented by other spellings, including *o* (*some*), *ou* (*country*) and *oo* (*flood*).
>
> **2A** 🔊 P6.03 Explain to students that they are going to hear pairs of words and need to decide if they contain the same or different vowel sounds. Note that at this stage, it is not important for them to identify which sounds the words contain. Play the recording, then check answers with the class. During feedback, you could elicit or say which vowel sounds the words have. Note that because of first language interference, learners often read the letter *a* as /ʌ/, so words like *track* and *truck* are pronounced as homophones. You may wish to point out to students that in American English, the words *glass*, *half*, *last* and *can't* are all pronounced with /æ/. So are the words *answer* and *fast* presented in Exercise 1.
>
> > **1** different: /mɑːtʃ/, /mʌtʃ/ **2** different: /træk/, /trʌk/ **3** same: /rʌn/, /wʌn/ **4** different: /plæn/, /plɑːnt/ **5** same: /hɑːf/, /stɑːf/ **6** different: /pæk/, /pɑːk/ **7** different: /gæs/, /glɑːs/ **8** same: /kɑːnt/, /lɑːst/

2B 🔊 P6.03 Play the recording again and get students to repeat the pairs of words as a group and then individually.

3A/B 🔊 P6.04 Follow the same procedure for both activities: read the instructions and point out that students will have to identify two words in each sentence containing the target sound. Play the recording, twice if necessary, and get students to compare answers in pairs before class feedback.

> **3A**
> 1 aren't, cars 2 start, smart 3 department, target 4 passport, card
> **3B**
> 1 enough, buses 2 encourage, customers 3 discussed, production 4 refund, numbers

3C Put students in pairs to practise saying the sentences in Exercise 3A. If necessary, play recording P6.04 again, and get them to repeat the sentences before they practise on their own. During the activity, monitor and correct pronunciation as necessary.

4A/B Go through the phrases in the box with students, then ask them to complete the exercise individually and check answers with the class. After feedback, put students in pairs to practise the conversation.

> 1 There's a problem with the photocopier.
> 2 When will the technician get here?
> 3 We need it as soon as possible.
> 4 Is there anything you can do about it?
> 5 Thank you for your help.

Extra activities 6.2

A/B These activities provide further practice of the functional language from Exercises 3 and 4A. Ask students to complete them individually, and then to compare answers in pairs before class feedback. If there is time, they could practise the conversation in Exercise B in pairs.

> **A**
> 1 How can I help you?
> 2 I'm sorry to hear that.
> 3 I understand this is important for you.
> 4 We'll send a technician.
> 5 It might be Friday afternoon.
> 6 Someone might come tomorrow.
> 7 I'm very sorry about the mistake.
> 8 It might take three days.
> 9 I'll talk to my manager.
> 10 Can I help you with anything else?
> **B**
> 1 speaking 2 sorry to hear 3 might be
> 4 sorry about 5 understand 6 might come
> 7 very welcome

Speaking

Students roleplay phone calls to customer services.

5 Explain that students are going to roleplay two phone calls to customer services and put them in pairs. For extra support, you could put the phrases for the client role from Exercises 3 and 4A on one side of the board, and those for the customer services role on the other. Students can refer to these phrases during the first roleplay. For the second roleplay, you could remove the phrases, or words from the phrases, from the board so students have to rely more on their memory. Start with phone call 1. Direct students to their relevant pages and give them a few minutes to read the information and ask you any questions they may have. Remind them that they should use expressions from Exercises 3 and 4 (or the phrases on the board), and give them time to think about what to say while you monitor and offer help as necessary. When they are ready, ask them to begin their phone calls. During the roleplay, monitor and note down any errors/difficulties with the functional language, but do not interrupt students. Follow the same procedure for phone call 2, then have a brief feedback session, highlighting any points you noted while monitoring.

MyEnglishLab: Teacher's resources: extra activities; Additional interactive activities

Pronunciation bank: p.99 /ɑː/ and /ʌ/

Teacher's book: Resource bank Extra vocabulary practice p.141 Exercises 2 and 3

Workbook: p.29 Exercises 3 and 4; p.31 Exercises 1–3; p.32 Exercises 1–3; p.49 Exercises 1–3

6.3 ▶ The production process

GSE learning objectives

- Can understand simple details in simple informational texts (blogs, websites, catalogues, etc.).
- Can read a simple text and extract factual details.
- Can use the Present Simple Passive.
- Can write a description of a simple everyday process (e.g. a recipe).

Lead-in

Students complete an infographic showing a supply chain.

1 Go through the instructions with students and point out that the infographic represents the supply chain for cotton clothes – teach or elicit the meaning of *supply chain*. Go through the words in the box with students, then ask them to complete the exercise individually. Check answers with the class.

> 2 cotton supplier 3 clothes manufacturer
> 4 distribution centre 5 retail store 6 customer

Teacher's notes

Reading

Students read about ethical practices in the production process of a company.

2A Tell students that they are going to read a text about the supply chain of a company. Explain the task and point out that they should read the text quickly, in order to answer the question. Tell them not to worry about new words at this stage, as they will have a chance to read it again more carefully later. Give them 2–3 minutes to read the text and answer the question, and elicit the answer. If students do not arrive at the answer, use this as a learning point to clarify 'ethical' and what that involves. You can use examples from the text to help (e.g. farmers are paid a fair price, no dangerous chemicals are used, T-shirts are made from recycled packaging).

> It explains the company's environmental and ethical image. This is important to some consumers.

2B Explain the task and give students a minute to look at the questions. Ask them to read the text again more carefully and answer the questions, and encourage them to underline the parts of the text which give them the answers. Get them to compare answers in pairs, then check answers with the class. Clarify any unknown vocabulary as necessary, then teach the following verb + preposition collocations from the text and encourage students to record them in their vocabulary notebooks because they will need them later in the lesson:

- grow something **on** a farm
- pay a price **for** something
- make something **in** a country
- make something **from** a material
- produce something **to** the highest standards
- sell something all **over** the world.

If students ask about the passive forms in bold in the text, explain their meaning but do not go into detail about the use of the Present Simple Passive yet as students will look at it in more detail in the Communicative grammar section which follows.

> 1 (organic farms in) India
> 2 (our/the) creative team
> 3 (in) Morocco
> 4 It is made from recycled materials.

2C Go through the instruction with the class, and refer students to the verb forms in bold in the text. Explain that they are *past participles*, which we use in the Present Simple Passive – reassure students that they will look at passive forms in the next activity. Briefly explain that like the Past Simple form, some verbs form the past participle with the *-ed* ending, and others are irregular. You could briefly refer students to the Irregular verbs list on page 114 and explain that the past participle is the third form of the verb. Ask students to complete the exercise individually, then check answers with the class.

> design – are designed
> grow – is grown
> make – are made / is made
> pay – are paid
> produce – are produced
> sell – are sold
> use – are used

Communicative grammar: Describing production

Students study and practise the Present Simple Passive.

Describing production

Look at the examples in the Grammar box with students and ask them if they notice a pattern in the verb forms in bold. Explain or elicit that the Present Simple Passive is formed with the correct form of *be* + the past participle of the main verb. Explain that we use the Passive to describe products, processes and procedures. Refer students to the Grammar reference on page 110 and go through it with them, clarifying any points as necessary, then get them to do the extra grammar activities there, in class or as homework.

Grammar reference answer key: page 85

Pronunciation bank
p.100: /uː/ and /ʊ/

1 P6.05 P6.06 The vowel /uː/ is a long sound; the lips are pushed out lightly and rounded, while the tongue is high at the back of the mouth. The vowel /ʊ/ is quite similar to /uː/ but it is a short sound; the tongue is raised at the back of the mouth and the lips are rounded, but you do not push them out as for /uː/.

Write the letter *u* and the pronoun *you* on the board. Model their pronunciation and explain that they are both pronounced with the sound /uː/. Play recording P6.05 and get students to repeat as a group and then individually. Explain that the sound /uː/ is often represented by *u* (*music*), *ue* (*true*) or *oo* (*boot*). There are also some less common spellings such as *oe* (*shoe*), *ou* (*group*) and *ui* (*suit*). Continue with the next sound. Write the word *look*, model its pronunciation and explain that it contains the sound /ʊ/. Play recording P6.06 and get students to repeat as a group and then individually. Explain that /ʊ/ is often spelt with the letters *oo* (*foot*) or *u* (*put*), but there are also some less obvious spellings such as *o* (*woman*) and *ou* (*could*).

2A P6.07 Refer students to the words with *oo* in Exercise 1 and point out that in most words, the double *o* is pronounced either as /uː/ or /ʊ/. Unfortunately, the rules for reading *oo*, if any, are rather obscure, so it seems more reasonable to remember the pronunciation of individual words. Having said that, making some analogies (e.g. /ʊ/ is more common before *k*, e.g. *cook*, *book*, *took*) and highlighting some contrast (e.g. between *good* and *food*) may be helpful. Ask students to complete the exercise individually, then play the recording for them to check their answers. Pause after each item to confirm the answer and ask students which vowel sound, /uː/ or /ʊ/, the words contain.

> 1 same: /ʊ/   2 different: /gʊd/, /fuːd/
> 3 same: /uː/   4 same: /uː/

2B 🔊 P6.07 Play the recording again and ask students to repeat the pairs of words as a group and then individually.

3A 🔊 P6.08 Explain the activity and play the recording, pausing after each item for students to write the word and think about its pronunciation. Check answers with the class.

> 1 used /uː/ 2 popular /ʊ/ 3 through /uː/
> 4 booking /ʊ/ 5 news /uː/ 6 lose /uː/

3B Put students in pairs to practise saying the sentences in Exercise 3A. Before they begin, draw their attention to the words with the sounds /uː/ and /ʊ/, which are marked in red and blue, respectively. You may also wish to play the recording again and get students to repeat the sentences as a group before they practise on their own. During the activity, monitor and correct pronunciation as necessary.

3 Give students time to read the sentences, and check that they understand *wage* and *tablet sleeve*. Ask them to complete the exercise individually, referring to the Grammar reference and/or the Grammar box if they need help. Check answers with the class and write (or invite students to write) the passive forms on the board.

> 1 is made 2 are paid 3 are used 4 is grown
> 5 is designed 6 are sold

4 Again, ask students to work individually for this exercise, and if there is time, get them to compare answers in pairs before checking with the class. Write (or invite students to write) the answers on the board so students can check their spelling.

> 1 are made 2 are used 3 is produced 4 are given (also possible: is given) 5 is delivered 6 is bought

Extra activities 6.3

A This activity provides further practice of the Present Simple Passive. Before students complete the exercise, you may wish to check understanding of the following words from the text: *locate*, *own* (v), *lift* (n), *temperature*, *control* (v) and *voice*. To help students, you could tell them that all the verbs in brackets are regular. Ask them to complete the exercise individually, then check answers with the class.

> 1 is located 2 is owned 3 are supported 4 is used
> 5 is ordered 6 are scanned 7 is served
> 8 are controlled

B Explain the activity and point out that not all the sentences are in the Passive, so students should read them carefully in order to decide which form is correct. Ask them to complete the exercise individually, then check answers with the class.

> 1 is made 2 create 3 use 4 are paid
> 5 is not stored 6 do not use 7 are made 8 takes

Writing

Students write a description for a company website.

5 Go through the instructions with the class and explain that 'direct trade' is when coffee roasters and chocolate makers buy directly from the farmers of coffee or cocoa beans. It can also mean that a farmer or producer sells directly to the customer. Check understanding of the words in the diagram, then give students time to read the prompts and ask you about anything they do not understand. Teach or elicit the meanings of *quality*, *beans*, *speciality*, *guaranteed*, *minimum* and *headquarters*. Also explain that the adverbs *direct* and *directly* are synonymous, e.g. *sell direct/directly to*, *buy direct/directly from*. Look at the example with the class, then ask students to write their descriptions. Monitor and check they are using the Present Simple Passive correctly, and note down any common errors or difficulties. If there is time, put students in pairs to compare their descriptions before class feedback. Round off the activity by going over any points you noted while monitoring.

> We buy all our coffee direct from farmers in Colombia. We visit their farms every year. No dangerous chemicals are used to produce your coffee. We use quality beans in our speciality coffee. The farmers are paid a guaranteed minimum price for their/the coffee beans. The beans are delivered to a/the mill and then shipped to our headquarters. We roast and pack the beans here. We only sell our fresh coffee directly to you.

MyEnglishLab: Teacher's resources: extra activities; Additional interactive activities
Grammar reference: p.110 Describing production
Pronunciation bank: p.100 /uː/ and /ʊ/
Teacher's book: Resource bank Photocopiable 6.3 p.122
Workbook: p.30 Exercises 3 and 4; p.49 Exercises 1–3

6.4 ▶ Work skills
Placing an order

GSE learning objectives
- Can understand the main information in short, simple dialogues about familiar activities, if spoken slowly and clearly.
- Can use language related to business deals and agreements.
- Can conduct very simple business transactions using basic language.
- Can understand simple, factual information in a work-related video.

Lead-in

Students learn key terms related to placing an order.

1 As a brief warm-up, you could put students in pairs and ask them to make a list of things they need to think about when placing an order for something (e.g. delivery times, price, payment terms, quantity, possible discount). Give them 2–3 minutes to discuss in their pairs, then get brief feedback from the class. Introduce the exercise and go through the words in the box with the class, clarifying meanings as necessary. Get

Teacher's notes

students to match the terms with the extracts individually, then check answers with the class, and check understanding of any vocabulary in the extracts you think they might have difficulty with, e.g. *design* (n), *in stock*, *bank transfer*, *accept*. With weaker classes, you could also do this as a whole-class activity, checking answers and clarifying meanings as you go.

> 1 price 2 quantity 3 delivery date 4 payment terms

Video

Students watch a video of a client and manufacturer discussing an order.

2 ▶ 6.4.1 Tell students that they are going to watch a video of an external client placing an order with Sleek. Elicit or remind students what kind of company Sleek is (a clothes manufacturer). Go through points 1–6 with students and check that they understand each one, then play the video and check answers with the class.

> 1 b 2 e 3 d 4 a 5 c 6 f

3A ▶ 6.4.1 Explain the activity and give students time to read the notes before they watch the video again. Encourage them to think about what type of information is missing from each gap. To check answers, you could play the video more than once and tell students to ask you to pause when an answer is heard.

> 1 1,000 / one thousand 2 €2.50 / two euros fifty
> 3 €2,500 / two thousand five hundred euros 4 50/fifty
> 5 50/fifty 6 25th March / twenty-fifth March
> 7 10% / ten percent, €250 / two hundred and fifty euros

3B Answer the question as a class.

> €2,250

4 Explain to students that these are useful phrases for placing an order and ask them to complete the exercise individually. You could play the video again for students to check their answers and then go through them with the class. During feedback, check understanding of the phrases and clarify meanings as necessary.

> 1 price 2 How many 3 lower 4 How about
> 5 I'm afraid 6 Could we pay 7 When 8 Can you
> 9 Is there 10 think 11 OK 12 can

Speaking: Placing an order

Students look at useful language for placing orders.

> **Placing an order**
>
> Explain to students that they are going to look at some more useful phrases for placing an order. Go through the phrases in each category with them, checking understanding where necessary, and pointing out the function of each group of phrases.

Unit 6 Extra speaking lesson

This lesson gives further practice of speaking related to placing an order. To access the lesson go to MyEnglishLab > Extra speaking lessons.

Extra activities 6.4

A/B These activities provide further practice of the functional language in the Speaking box. Ask students to complete both exercises individually, and get them to compare answers in pairs before checking with the class. If there is time, you could get students to practise the exchanges in pairs.

> **A**
> 1 order 2 talk 3 deliver 4 give 5 about
> 6 pay 7 Can 8 take 9 there 10 pay
> **B**
> 1 e 2 c 3 i 4 g/h 5 h/g 6 a 7 b 8 d 9 f

5 Put students in pairs, explain the activity and direct them to their relevant pages. Give them time to read their information and prepare for their roleplay, while you monitor and offer help as necessary. Remind them to use phrases from the Speaking box, and to refer to videoscript 6.4.1 on page 131 for a model if they need to. During the roleplay, monitor and note down any errors/difficulties to go over during feedback, but do not interrupt students' conversations. For further practice, you could ask students to swap roles and repeat the activity, in the same or new pairs. At the end of the activity, get brief feedback from the class: *What did you find easy about placing/receiving the order? What did you find difficult? Did you use phrases from the Speaking box? What would you do differently next time?* Finally, go over any points you noted while monitoring.

MyEnglishLab: Teacher's resources: extra activities; Extra speaking lessons; Additional interactive activities

Teacher's book: Resource bank Extra vocabulary practice p.141 Exercises 4 and 5; Photocopiable 6.4 p.123

Workbook: p.33 Exercises 1–3

Business workshop

Buy natural

GSE learning objectives

- Can understand simple details in simple informational texts (blogs, websites, catalogues, etc.).
- Can read a simple text and extract factual details.
- Can use language related to business deals and agreements.
- Can use language related to complaints and resolving complaints.
- Can conduct very simple business transactions using basic language.
- Can talk about orders or deliveries using a few fixed expressions and given help with vocabulary.

Teacher's notes

Introduction

Students read an extract from a company website about ethical products.

1 Tell students that they are going to read an extract from an ethical company's website. Check that they remember what being ethical involves. Before they read, you may wish to pre-teach the following vocabulary from the text: *protect (somebody's skin or hair), natural/organic ingredients/products, plants, test something on animals, shampoo, shower gel, hair conditioner, face cream, packaging, recycle*. Ask students to complete the exercise individually and if there is time, get them to compare answers in pairs before class feedback. Encourage them to underline the parts of the text that led them to the answers. Check answers with the class and ask if students use any products like this themselves. Do they (or anyone they know) buy any organic personal care products or any other ethical consumers products (e.g. organic meat, 'green' detergents and cleaning products)? Do they think there is a market for these products in their country? As an extension, you could briefly review the Present Simple Passive from Lesson 6.3 by asking students to identify examples in the text (*are made, are not tested, no … are used, are made*).

> 1 It sells beauty products such as shampoo, shower gels, hair conditioners and face creams.
> 2 plants and organic ingredients
> 3 recycled paper and plastic
> 4 nature projects and environmental organisations

Speaking: Placing an order

Students practise placing an order.

2 If you think your students will find this activity difficult, review the Speaking section of Lesson 6.4 before you start. Tell students that they are going to roleplay placing an order with Natural, the company they read about in Exercise 1. Put them in pairs, direct them to their relevant information and give them plenty of time to read it and think about what they are going to say. Help where necessary, and remind students to use phrases from the Speaking box in Lesson 6.4 – you could elicit, drill and write some of the phrases on the board to help them. During the roleplay, monitor and note down any common errors or examples of good language use – go over these in a brief feedback session at the end.

Speaking: A problem with an order

Students practise making and responding to complaints.

3A Give students 1–2 minutes to read the email, and elicit the answer.

> The company delivered 200 bottles of shampoo and 200 of hair conditioner but the order was for 400 bottles of shampoo. The rest of the delivery was correct.

3B If you think your students will find this activity difficult, review the functional language in Exercises 3 and 4A of Lesson 6.2 before you start. You could put some of the phrases on the board for students to refer to during the activity. Explain to students that they are going to roleplay a phone call between the customer and Customer Services Agent at Natural, about a problem with the order they placed in Exercise 2. Put them in pairs and direct them to their relevant information. Give them time to read the instructions and make notes, and offer help where necessary. Remind them to use the phrases for making and responding to complaints from Lesson 6.2, and point out the examples for each role. When they are ready, students roleplay their phone calls. During the activity, monitor and note down any points to highlight during feedback, but do not interrupt students' phone calls. Highlight any points you note in a brief feedback session afterwards.

4A If you think your students will find this activity difficult, review the Communicative grammar section of Lesson 6.1 before you start. Go through the instructions and items in the box with students, look at the examples with them, then ask them to write their own predictions. Go round and help with vocabulary where necessary, and check students are forming their sentences correctly.

4B Put students in pairs to compare their ideas from Exercise 4A. When they have finished, ask a few students to share their predictions with the class and find out if others agree.

Grammar reference ◀ 6

6.1

> 1 Robots might work in offices.
> 2 I think many shops might disappear.
> 3 Many jobs won't exist in the future. / In the future many jobs won't exist.
> 4 I think most people will work from home.
> 5 There might not be many drivers.
> 6 I don't think there will be any petrol.
> 7 I think there will be more electric vehicles.

6.3

> 1 are grown 2 are used 3 makes 4 sell 5 are paid
> 6 is added 7 is produced 8 buy

Review 6

1.
   1 electric 2 pollution 3 recycle 4 technology
   5 energy 6 machine 7 plastic 8 environment

2.
   1 speaking 2 with 3 hear 4 When 5 might
   6 can't 7 about 8 possible 9 talk 10 for
   11 welcome

3.
   1 buy – active 2 are paid – passive 3 work – active
   4 visits – active 5 is sold – passive 6 are made – passive 7 are used – passive

4.
   1 There might not be any cash in the future.
   2 I think everyone will use their mobiles to pay for things.
   3 The weather might get hotter in the next few years.
   4 Children won't go to school. They will study by computer at home.
   5 I don't think there will be many shops. We will order everything online.
   6 There won't be many jobs in offices. Robots will do our work.
   7 I might not be in the same job two years from now.

5.
   1 I'd like to order 12,000 cotton shirts.
   2 How many white shirts do you want to order?
   3 Can we talk about price now?
   4 How about two dollars a shirt?
   5 Can you give us a lower price?
   6 Is there a discount for a large order?
   7 We'll pay by bank transfer.
   8 I'm afraid I can't agree to that.
   9 Could we pay 25 percent on signature and 75 percent on delivery?
   10 I'm afraid it's 50 percent on delivery.
   11 When can you deliver this order?
   12 What do you think?

Competition 7

Unit overview

	CLASSWORK		FURTHER WORK
7.1 **Should I upgrade?**	**Lead-in**	Students talk about products they like.	**MyEnglishLab:** Teacher's resources: extra activities; Additional interactive activities
	Vocabulary	Students look at vocabulary related to product qualities.	
	Listening	Students listen to two colleagues talking about using a product.	**Grammar reference:** p.111 Comparing (1): Comparatives
	Communicative grammar	Students study and practise comparative adjectives.	**Teacher's book:** Resource bank Extra vocabulary practice p.142 Exercise 1
	Video	Students watch a video comparing cars.	**Workbook:** p.34 Exercises 1 and 2; p.35 Exercises 1 and 2
	Task	Students compare products.	
7.2 **Services**	**Lead-in**	Students discuss types of services they and their companies use.	**MyEnglishLab:** Teacher's resources: extra activities; Additional interactive activities
	Vocabulary	Students look at vocabulary related to fees.	**Pronunciation bank:** p.100 /əʊ/ and /aʊ/
	Listening	Students listen to people discussing recruitment agencies.	**Teacher's book:** Resource bank Extra vocabulary practice p.142 Exercise 2
	Writing	Students write an advertisement for a courier agency.	**Workbook:** p.34 Exercises 3 and 4; p.36 Exercises 1–3; p.50 Exercises 1–3
7.3 **The best providers**	**Lead-in**	Students talk about choosing service providers.	**MyEnglishLab:** Teacher's resources: extra activities; Additional interactive activities
	Reading	Students read an email comparing services.	**Grammar reference:** p.111 Comparing (2): Superlatives
	Communicative grammar	Students study and practise superlative adjectives.	**Pronunciation bank:** p.100 /p/, /b/, /f/ and /v/
	Writing	Students write an email comparing services.	**Teacher's book:** Resource bank Photocopiable 7.3 p.124
			Workbook: p.35 Exercises 3 and 4; p.37 Exercises 1 and 2; p.50 Exercises 1–4
7.4 **Work skills:** Presentations	**Lead-in**	Students talk about giving presentations.	**MyEnglishLab:** Teacher's resources: extra activities; Extra speaking lessons; Additional interactive activities
	Video	Students watch a video of a presentation.	**Teacher's book:** Resource bank Extra vocabulary practice p.142 Exercises 3–5; Photocopiable 7.4 p.125
	Speaking	Students look at useful language for presentations.	**Workbook:** p.38 Exercises 1–4
Business workshop: The big contract	**Reading**	Students read about a trade show.	
	Speaking	Students give a presentation.	
	Writing	Students write an email comparing products and services.	

Teacher's notes

Unit vocabulary list

Active vocabulary

7.1
- design
- features
- product life
- speed
- unique selling point (USP)
- user experience
- value for money
- weight

7.2
- additional fee
- administration fee
- annual fee
- booking fee
- cancellation fee
- charge a fee
- fixed fee
- monthly fee
- pay a fee

Passive vocabulary

7.1
- battery (life)
- files
- load (verb)
- memory
- operating system
- battery (life)
- operating system
- software
- security (software)
- model
- top speed
- wheels

7.2
- advertising (service)
- cleaning (service)
- courier (service)
- financial (service)
- IT (service)]
- marketing (service)
- recruitment (service)
- tax (service)
- training (service)
- travel (service)

7.3
- energy provider
- internet provider
- mobile phone contract
- office cleaning service
- printer/photocopier contract

- easy to access
- friendly staff
- good/bad performance
- good service
- problem-solving
- quality of communication

- satisfied customers
- service reliability
- staff knowledge
- value for money

- Please find attached …
- Please find a summary below.
- If you have any questions, please let me know.
- Best regards,

7.4
- company history
- location
- prices
- products
- quality
- services
- unique selling point

Teacher's notes

7.1 Should I upgrade?

GSE learning objectives

- Can use language related to machines and technology.
- Can make simple, direct comparisons between two people or things using common adjectives.
- Can understand the general meaning of short, simple informational material and descriptions if there is visual support.
- Can identify simple information in a short video, provided that the visual supports this information and the delivery is slow and clear.
- Can discuss product features in a business setting using simple language.

Lead-in

Students talk about products they like.

1 Introduce the topic by telling students about a product you like from the list, using your own answers to the questions. Give students a few minutes to think about their answers and make notes while you monitor and provide help as necessary, then put students in pairs to share their answers. In feedback, ask a few students to tell the class about their or their partner's product.

Vocabulary: Product qualities

Students look at vocabulary related to product qualities.

2 Draw students' attention to the heading *Product qualities* and check that they understand its meaning. Explain that they are going to look at useful vocabulary to talk about product qualities. With weaker classes, you could do this as a whole-class activity, checking answers and clarifying meanings as you go. Alternatively, ask students to complete the matching task individually and clarify meanings during feedback.

> **a** speed **b** weight **c** product life **d** design **e** features
> **f** unique selling point (USP) **g** user experience
> **h** value for money

3A Draw students' attention to the advert and elicit what product it is for (a laptop). Ask students to read the advert quickly and answer the question. Reassure them that they do not need to worry about any unknown words for now, and encourage them to underline the parts of the text that give them the answers. Check answers with the class.

> **a** speed – yes ('loads three times faster')
> **b** weight – yes ('lighter')
> **c** product life – yes (battery)
> **d** design – no (But it could be argued that all the specifications taken together refer to how the product looks or works.)
> **e** features – yes (long battery, large memory, advanced security)
> **f** unique selling point – yes (longer battery life than other laptops)
> **g** user experience – yes ('files and programs load three times faster')
> **h** value for money – no (The text does not specifically mention this, but it might be argued the saving on security software offers value for money.)

3B Give students time to read the statements first, and check that they understand *easy to carry*, *power lead*, *hold*, *previous* and *security software*. Ask them to complete the exercise individually and, again, encourage them to underline the parts of the text which give them the answers. If there is time, get them to compare answers in pairs before class feedback. Note that the words in bold are examples of the target grammar in the Communicative grammar section that follows, but they should only be looked at as lexical items here. Explain their meanings if students ask about them, but do not go into detail about comparatives yet.

> **1** T ('lighter than other models so you can take it with you wherever you go')
> **2** F ('you can work without a power lead for up to twelve hours')
> **3** F ('files and programs load three times faster')
> **4** T ('PRO-TEC offer a discount on their software when you buy the new TP Pro')

4 Go through the questions with the class before they begin, and check that they understand *strengths and weaknesses*. Put students in pairs and give them 2–3 minutes to discuss the questions, then invite a few students to share their answers with the class.

Extra activities 7.1

A This activity provides further practice of the vocabulary in Exercise 2. Check that students understand *wide*, *spacious* and *light* in the descriptions, and ask them to complete the exercise individually. Check answers with the class.

> **1** c **2** d **3** e **4** a **5** b **6** h **7** f **8** g

Listening

Students listen to two colleagues talking about using a product.

5A 🔊 7.01 Explain that students are going to listen to two people talking about the laptop in the advert in Exercise 3. Go through the features in the box with them so that they know what to listen for, then play the recording and check answers with the class.

> battery life, memory, security software, speed

5B 🔊 7.01 Draw students' attention to the table and explain the activity. Point out that they should listen for each speaker's opinion on the product qualities in the table. Play the recording again, twice if necessary, then check answers with the class.

	Karim thinks the TP Pro is		Misako thinks the TP Pro is	
	Good	Bad	Good	Bad
Speed		✓		✓
Battery	✓		✓	
Size and weight	✓		✓	
Security		✓	✓	

Teacher's notes

Communicative grammar: Comparing (1): Comparatives

Students study and practise comparative adjectives.

> **Comparing (1): Comparatives**
> Tell students that they are going to look at how to compare things in English. Look at the first group of sentences in the Grammar box with them and point out the comparative forms in bold. Ask students if they notice a pattern in these forms and elicit or explain that the comparative of short adjectives is formed by adding *-er* to the adjective and often the word *than* after it. Point out the differences in spelling and reassure students that they are going to look at these in more detail later. Move on to the second group of sentences and, again, elicit or explain the pattern: for adjectives with two or more syllables, we use *more* before the adjective and *than* after it. Ask students to look at the last group of adjectives and explain that they are irregular and do not follow either of the patterns above; each adjective has its own comparative form. Refer students back to the advertisement in Exercise 3A so they can look again at the target language in context – point out the examples in bold. Finally, refer them to the Grammar reference on page 111 and go through it with them, paying particular attention to the spelling rules. Students could then do the extra grammar activities there, in class or as homework.
> **Grammar reference answer key:** page 98

6/7 Ask students to complete both exercises individually and if there is time, get them to compare answers in pairs before class feedback.

> **6** 1 This model goes faster than others.
> 2 My phone's bigger than my last one.
> 3 My new laptop is lighter.
> 4 The new car is more spacious than the old car.
> 5 The GTI model is more expensive than the standard car.
> 6 The features are more advanced than for other TVs.
> **7** 1 better 2 worse 3 cheaper 4 bigger

8 Explain that students are going to complete sentences comparing two cars. Give them time to read the sentences and teach or elicit the meaning of *powerful*, *engine* and *comfortable*, which students will also hear in the video later. Ask them to complete the sentences individually and remind them to pay special attention to the spelling – tell them that they can refer to the Grammar reference if they need help. Check answers with the class and write (or invite students to write) them on the board, to make sure students spell them correctly.

> 1 newer 2 more powerful 3 faster 4 more comfortable
> 5 heavier 6 bigger 7 cheaper 8 smaller

Extra activities 7.1

B This activity provides extra practice of comparative forms. Refer students to the table and explain that it compares two smartphones, ReTel Go and Waiwex P90. Ask them to write their sentences individually and if necessary, do the first item as an example with the class. If there is time, get them to compare answers in pairs before class feedback.

> 1 The ReTel Go is more expensive than the Waiwex P90.
> 2 The Waiwex P90 is cheaper than the ReTel Go.
> 3 The ReTel Go is smaller than the Waiwex P90.
> 4 The Waiwex P90 is bigger than the ReTel Go.
> 5 The ReTel Go is lighter than the Waiwex P90.
> 6 The Waiwex P90 is heavier than the ReTel Go.
> 7 The ReTel Go is slower than the Waiwex P90.
> 8 The Waiwex P90 is faster than the ReTel Go.

Video

Students watch a video comparing cars.

9 ▶ 7.1.1 Remind students of the sentences in Exercise 8, and explain that they refer to the two cars in the photos. Tell them that they are going to watch a video about these cars. Before students watch, you may wish to pre-teach the following vocabulary from the video: *per* (*hour*), *luggage*, *wheels*, *exciting*. Ask students to complete the exercise while watching, then play the video and check answers with the class.

> 1 T 2 F 3 F 4 T 5 F 6 F 7 T 8 T

10 ▶ 7.1.1 Explain the activity and give students time to read the text before they watch – encourage them to think about what types of words may go in each gap. Play the video for students to complete the text, then check answers with the class. In weaker classes, students may need to watch a second time to check/complete their answers.

> 1 5/five 2 sports 3 1950 4 2019 5 270 6 170
> 7 1,050 8 900 9 £78,000 10 1909 11 £39,000
> 12 exciting

Task

Students compare products.

11 Put students in pairs and tell them that they are going to ask and answer questions about different products. Refer them to their relevant pages and explain that they need to complete the questions they are going to ask their partner, and use the information in their table to answer their partner's questions. Give them time to complete the questions and be on hand to offer help where necessary. Check the answers with the class, but make sure they only give you the missing comparative forms so as not to give away too much information to their partners. Before they ask and answer their questions, give them a minute to look at the information in their table and check anything they do not understand with you. During the activity, monitor but do not interrupt students. If there are any points to highlight, go over them in a brief feedback session afterwards.

> Teacher's notes

> **Student A**
> **1** 1 GIT 250 2 GIT 200 3 GIT 250 4 GIT 200: better camera than any other model, advanced security software; GIT 250: longer battery life than any other model, larger memory than any other model 5 GIT 200
> **2** 1 lighter 2 more powerful 3 faster 4 N/A 5 more expensive
> **Student B**
> **1** 1 heavier 2 worse 3 thinner 4 N/A 5 cheaper
> **2** 1 Super K 2 Super S 3 Super S 4 Super K: large space for luggage, advanced safety features; Super S: advanced safety features, very comfortable for tall drivers 5 Super S

MyEnglishLab: Teacher's resources: extra activities; Additional interactive activities
Grammar reference: p.111 Comparing (1): Comparatives
Teacher's book: Resource bank Extra vocabulary practice p.142 Exercise 1
Workbook: p.34 Exercises 1 and 2; p.35 Exercises 1 and 2

7.2 > Services

> **GSE learning objectives**
> - Can understand information in advertisements for jobs and services.
> - Can make simple, direct comparisons between two people or things using common adjectives.
> - Can understand specific information in a short, simple phone call.
> - Can write a short, simple marketing document, describing products or services.

Lead-in

Students discuss types of services they and their companies use.

1 Go through the words in the box with the class and check that they understand each one. Introduce the topic by telling students about the services you use, then put them in pairs to discuss the services they use. As feedback, invite a few students to share their answers with the class.

Vocabulary: Fees

Students look at vocabulary related to fees.

2A Refer students to the heading *fees* and teach or elicit its meaning. Tell them that they are going to read adverts from three companies, and explain the activity. Give them a few minutes to read the adverts and match them to the services from Exercise 1 and then, if there is time, to compare answers in pairs. Check answers with the class.

> **1** recruitment **2** cleaning **3** travel

2B Students could do this individually and compare answers in pairs before class feedback. Check that they understand *worldwide* in the third option before they begin. Alternatively, you could do this as a quick, whole-class activity, checking answers as you go.

> **1** Office professionals **2** Best Clean UK
> **3** Cox & Co. Worldwide

2C Give students a few minutes to read the adverts again and answer the questions. Encourage them to underline the parts of the texts where they find the answers. Get them to compare answers in pairs, then check answers with the class.

> **1** Cox & Co. Worldwide **2** Office Professionals
> **3** Best Clean UK **4** Office Professionals **5** Best Clean UK Cox & Co. Worldwide

3A Draw students' attention to the spidergram and the phrases in bold in the texts, and explain the activity. Look at the example with them before they begin, then ask them to complete the spidergram individually or, in weaker classes, in pairs. While they are working, draw the spidergram on the board. Check answers with the class, writing (or inviting students to write) the words in the spidergram on the board.

> **1** includes **2** pay, charge **3** *additional*, (monthly or) annual / (any order) administration / booking / cancellation / fixed

3B With weaker classes, you could do this as a whole-class activity, checking answers and clarifying meanings as you go. Alternatively, get students to complete the task individually and clarify meanings during feedback. Encourage students to refer back to the adverts and look at the text around each word – this will help them work out their meanings. Be prepared to offer further examples if necessary.

> **1** charge **2** fixed **3** monthly **4** additional
> **5** cancellation **6** includes **7** administration **8** booking

> **Pronunciation bank**
> **p.100: /əʊ/ and /aʊ/**
>
> **1** ◀) P7.01 ◀) P7.02 The sounds /əʊ/ and /aʊ/ are diphthongs in which the vowel quality changes from /ə/ and /a/, respectively, towards the rounded position of /ʊ/. The sound /əʊ/ is used in British English. Its equivalent in American English is /oʊ/, in which the vowel quality changes from the rounded vowel /o/ towards /ʊ/. Write the word *go* on the board, model its pronunciation and explain that it ends with the sound /əʊ/. Play recording P7.01 and get students to repeat as a group and then individually. Explain that /əʊ/ is commonly represented by *o* (*no*), *oa* (*coat*) and *ow* (*below*). Words spelt with *ow* are presented in Exercise 2A. Continue with the next sound. Write the word *out* on the board, model its pronunciation and explain that it begins with the sound /aʊ/. Play recording P7.02 and get students to repeat as a group and then individually. Finally, explain that /aʊ/ is often spelt with the letters *ou* (*mouth*) and *ow* (*flower*).

Teacher's notes

2A ◆ P7.03 This exercise focusses on words with the letters *ow*. Point out that this spelling almost always represents either /əʊ/ or /aʊ/. There are no clear rules for which vowel to use, so learners are encouraged to remember the pronunciation of individual words. Explain the activity, play the recording and check answers with the class. During feedback, you could ask students which sound, /əʊ/ or /aʊ/, the words contain.

1 same: /aʊ/   2 different: /braʊn/, /snəʊ/
3 same: /aʊ/   4 same: /əʊ/   5 different: /nəʊ/, /haʊ/   6 same: /əʊ/

2B ◆ P7.03 Play the recording again and get students to repeat the pairs of words as a group and then individually.

3A ◆ P7.04 Explain the activity and play the recording, pausing after each item for students to write the word and think about its pronunciation. Check answers with the class.

1 vide**o** /əʊ/   2 l**oa**d /əʊ/   3 disc**ou**nt /aʊ/
4 with**ou**t /aʊ/   5 p**o**sters /əʊ/   6 s**ou**nd /aʊ/

3B Put students in pairs to practise saying the sentences in Exercise 3A. Before they begin, draw their attention to the words with the sounds /əʊ/ and /aʊ/, which are marked in red and blue, respectively. You may also wish to play the recording again and get students to repeat the sentences as a group before they practise on their own. During the activity, monitor and correct pronunciation as necessary.

3C Ask students to complete the sentences individually and before they begin, point out that they may need to change the form of some words. Check answers with the class.

1 charges   2 additional   3 fixed   4 includes   5 monthly
6 cancellation   7 booking   8 administration/fixed

Extra activities 7.2

A This activity provides further practice of the vocabulary in Exercise 3. Ask students to complete it individually, referring to the explanations in Exercise 3B if they need help, then check answers with the class.

1 b   2 d   3 h   4 c   5 e   6 g   7 f   8 a

Listening: Comparing recruitment agencies

Students listen to people discussing recruitment agencies.

4A Give students 1–2 minutes to think about their answers individually, while you monitor and help them with any vocabulary they may need. When they are ready, put them in pairs to share their ideas – encourage them to give reasons. In feedback, invite students from different pairs to share their answers with the class.

4B ◆ 7.02 Tell students that they are going to hear two colleagues talking about two recruitment agencies and explain the activity. To help them, you could write the names of the agencies on the board. Play the recording, then check the answer with the class.

They decide to use Jones if they are cheaper overall.

4C ◆ 7.02 Draw students' attention to the webpages and check understanding of *Speciality areas* in the headings. Give them time to read the information and ask you any vocabulary questions they may have, then play the recording and check answers with the class.

1 London   2 six   3 three   4 professional   5 interviews
6 10–15%   7 399   8 additional

4D Explain the activity and give students time to read the statements. Check that they understand (*wide*) *range*, *temporary* and *standard*, and give them time to complete the exercise individually. If there is time, get them to compare answers in pairs before checking with the class.

1 T   2 F   3 F   4 F   5 T

Writing

Students write an advertisement for a courier agency.

5 Tell students that they are going to write an advertisement for a new courier agency. Explain the task and give them time to look at the table and questions and ask you about any unknown words. Point out that they need to use full sentences, highlight the prompts for each item and remind them that they can refer to the advertisements in Exercise 2 if they need help. Give them plenty of time to prepare and write their advertisements, and encourage them to use vocabulary from the lesson. While they are writing, monitor and offer help as necessary. Depending on the time available, you could then put them in pairs to compare and check their adverts. Ask them to check if their partner has answered all the questions, written full sentences using the prompts and used vocabulary from the lesson – you could bullet these three points on the board for students to refer to while they check. Students could then write a second draft for homework.

Model answer

We provide local and national delivery of parcels and large and/or heavy items.

We offer same-day or next-day delivery. We charge a £22 fixed fee for same-day delivery.

We charge £10–20 for next-day delivery for items between 1 kg and 5 kg. Two-day delivery costs from £3 and 3–7-day delivery costs from £2.

Our fixed fees include collection and recorded delivery. We also offer contracts for a daily courier service.

We charge an administration fee for contract agreements.

There is a cancellation fee for cancellation of orders.

There is an additional fee for items over 5 kg.

Teacher's notes

MyEnglishLab: Teacher's resources: extra activities; Additional interactive activities

Pronunciation bank: p.100 /əʊ/ and /aʊ/

Teacher's book: Resource bank Extra vocabulary practice p.142 Exercise 2

Workbook: p.34 Exercises 3 and 4; p.36 Exercises 1–3; p.50 Exercises 1–3

7.3 The best providers

GSE learning objectives

- Can understand short, simple emails on work-related topics.
- Can form the superlative of regular adjectives with '-est'.
- Can form the superlative of longer regular adjectives with 'most'.
- Can form irregular superlatives of adjectives and adverbs such as 'best', 'worst'.
- Can use language related to aptitude, ability, knowledge and skills.
- Can make simple comparisons between people, places or things.

Lead-in

Students talk about choosing service providers.

1A Go through the services in the box with students and check that they understand each one. Put them in pairs and give them 2–3 minutes to discuss the question, then nominate a few students to share their answers with the class.

1B Go through the items in the box with students and check that they understand each one. Give them a minute to order the criteria individually, then get them to compare answers in pairs. As an extension, you could ask students to try and agree on an order, saying why they think particular items are more important than others. When they have finished, ask a few students to share their order with the class and find out if others agree.

Reading

Students read an email comparing services.

2 Explain the context and activity and go through the table with the class so that students know what information to look for in the email. Point out the *Strengths* and *Areas of improvement* lists in the email, and check that students understand both headings. Get them to complete the exercise individually, then check answers with the class. Students may not make the connection between 'the highest number of successful claims' (in the email) and 'service reliability', so you could elicit what makes an insurance company reliable before students start reading.

	Good performance	Bad performance
Service reliability	✓	
Staff knowledge	✓	
Satisfied customers (40–50 yrs)		✓
Time to answer calls		✓
Problem solving		✓
Value	✓	

3 Tell students that they are going to look at some useful phrases for business emails. You could do this as a whole-class activity, checking answers and clarifying meanings as you go. Alternatively, ask students to complete the exercise individually, and clarify meanings during class feedback.

1 b **2** d **3** a **4** c

Communicative grammar: Comparing (2): Superlatives

Students study and practise superlative adjectives.

Comparing (2): Superlatives

Look at the first group of sentences in the Grammar box with the class and elicit or explain the meaning of the adjectives in bold. Remind students of the comparative forms they looked at in Lesson 7.1, and explain that these forms are for comparing one thing with two or more things in the same group. Elicit or explain the pattern for short adjectives: we use *the* before the adjective and add the ending *-est* to it. Continue with the second group and, again, elicit or explain the pattern: we use *the most* before the adjective. Finally, look at the irregular adjectives with the class and explain that as with comparatives, the superlative form of these adjectives does not follow either of the patterns above. Refer students back to the email in Exercise 2 so they can look again at the target language in context – point out the superlative forms in bold. At this point you could also refer them to the Grammar reference on page 111 and go through it with them, paying particular attention to the spelling rules (which are similar to those for comparatives). Students can then do the extra grammar activities there, in class or as homework.

Grammar reference answer key: page 98

4A Look at the example with students and ask them to complete the rest of the sentences individually. Remind them that they can refer to the grammar box and/or the Grammar reference if they need help. Check answers with the class and write (or invite students to write) the superlative forms on the board so students can check their spelling.

1 the shortest **2** the cheapest **3** the most reliable
4 the most knowledgeable **5** the friendliest
6 the widest **7** the highest **8** the best

Teacher's notes

4B Explain the activity and if necessary, do the first item as an example with the class. Ask students to complete the exercise individually, then check answers with the class.

1 the most reliable 2 the best
3 the most knowledgeable 4 the lowest 5 the worst
6 the biggest

Extra activities 7.3

A/B These activities provide further practice of superlative adjectives. Students should complete them individually, as consolidation, and then if there is time, compare answers in pairs before class feedback.

A
1 most reliable 2 most knowledgeable 3 best
4 longest 5 friendliest 6 highest 7 most satisfied
8 quickest

B
1 We have the best customer service.
2 Our service is the most reliable.
3 We have the most knowledgeable staff.
4 We provide the best value for money.
5 We have the biggest number of hotels.
6 Our service is the cheapest.
7 Our customers are the most satisfied in the industry.
8 We have the highest levels of positive feedback.

Writing

Students write an email comparing services.

5 Go through the instructions with the class, and make sure students understand what they have to do. Remind them that they can refer to the model email in Exercise 2 if they need help. Encourage them to organise their email in the same way, using lists of *Strengths* and *Areas of improvement* when planning their answers. Also encourage them to use superlative adjectives and phrases from Exercise 3. Give them plenty of time to plan and write their emails, and monitor and offer help as necessary. In weaker classes, you could let students plan their emails in pairs.

Model answer

Dear …

Please find attached a copy of the customer satisfaction survey you asked me to perform.

We compared Travel Care and two other travel companies. Please find a summary below.

Strengths:

Travel Care has:
• the most knowledgeable staff.
• the friendliest staff.
• the best customer service.

Areas of improvement:

Travel Care has:
• the highest prices.
• the worst value for money.

Let me know if you have any questions.

Best regards,

Martina

Pronunciation bank
p.100: /p/, /b/, /f/ and /v/

1 🔊 P7.05 🔊 P7.06 🔊 P7.07 🔊 P7.08 The consonants /p/ and /b/ are plosives; the lips come together to form a complete closure, which is then released to let the compressed air escape. The sounds only differ in voicing: /p/ is unvoiced, while /b/ is voiced. The consonants /f/ and /v/ are fricatives; the air escapes through a narrow passage between the upper teeth and the lower lip. Again, the only difference between the sounds is that /f/ is unvoiced, while /v/ is voiced.

This exercise presents examples with the target sounds in the initial, medial and final positions in a word. Play recording P7.05 for the words with /p/, P7.06 for the words with /b/, P7.07 for the words with /f/ and P7.08 for the words with /v/. Ask students to repeat as a group. Note that /p/ is aspirated at the beginning of a word/syllable unless it is followed by /l/, /r/, /w/ or /j/, and it is slightly aspirated at the end of a word. Due to native language interference, some students may have a tendency to devoice /b/ and /v/ in the word-final position. For others, it may be challenging to pronounce the sounds /b/ and /v/.

2A 🔊 P7.09 Play the recording, then check answers with the class. If necessary, play the recording again during feedback for students to check their answers.

1 back 2 pin 3 view 4 save 5 fast 6 copy
7 vlog 8 best

2B 🔊 P7.10 Play the recording and get students to repeat as a group and then individually.

3 🔊 P7.11 Play the recording and ask students to repeat the phrases as a group and then individually. You could ask students which phrases are particularly difficult for them to pronounce, and help them articulate the sounds. For extra practice, you could then put them in pairs to practise saying the sentences, while you monitor and correct pronunciation of the target sounds as necessary.

MyEnglishLab: Teacher's resources: extra activities; Additional interactive activities
Grammar reference: p.111 Comparing (2): Superlatives
Pronunciation bank: p.100 /p/, /b/, /f/ and /v/
Teacher's book: Resource bank Photocopiable 7.3 p.124
Workbook: p.35 Exercises 3 and 4; p.37 Exercises 1 and 2; p.50 Exercises 1–4

Teacher's notes

7.4 Work skills
Presentations

> **GSE learning objectives**
> - Can use language related to products and goods.
> - Can identify simple information in a short video, provided that the visual supports this information and the delivery is slow and clear.
> - Can recognise a few key words or phrases in a simple presentation.
> - Can recognise some basic fixed expressions to describe products or services, given help with vocabulary.
> - Can use basic discourse markers to structure a short presentation.

Lead-in

Students talk about giving presentations.

1A Discuss the question as a class, asking students to raise their hand if they give presentations, then asking those who raise their hand how they feel about this. You could extend the discussion by asking students to think of a presentation they attended and tell the class what they liked / did not like about it.

1B Go through the instructions with students and check that they understand *potential* (*customers*). Go through the items in the box with them, then put them in pairs to discuss the question. When they have finished, ask a few students to share their ideas with the class and find out if others agree.

1C You could do this as a whole-class activity, checking answers as you go, or let students order the stages individually, then check answers with the class.

> **1** b **2** f **3** d **4** e **5** c **6** a

Video

Students watch a video of a presentation. 2A ▶ 7.4.1 Tell students that they are going to watch a video of an external client giving a presentation to a group at Sleek, in which they give an overview of a company and its products and services. Go through the questions with the class so they know what to listen for, and ask students to make notes in answer to the questions while watching. Play the video, then check answers with the class.

> **1** to introduce the company and its services
> **2** website building, online shops and payment systems / e-commerce services
> **3** Yes, they are.

2B ▶ 7.4.1 Give students time to read the sentences and answer any questions they have about vocabulary. When they are ready, play the video again, then check answers with the class.

> **1** F **2** T **3** T **4** T **5** T **6** T **7** F **8** T

3 ▶ 7.4.1 Explain the activity and tell students that these are all useful phrases for presentations. Play the video, then check answers with the class, clarifying meanings as necessary. With stronger classes, you could ask students to do the exercise first, then watch the video again to check/complete their answers.

> **1** morning **2** aim, introduce **3** tell **4** Finally **5** start
> **6** biggest **7** based **8** move **9** build **10** can **11** end
> **12** questions

Speaking: Presenting

Students look at useful language for presentations.

> **Presenting**
> Explain to students that they are going to look at useful phrases for presentations. Check understanding of the heading for each section and give students a minute to read the phrases, then go through them with the class, clarifying meanings as necessary. You may need to help students with the pronunciation of some words/phrases.

> **Unit 7 Extra speaking lesson**
> This lesson gives further practice of speaking related to presenting. To access the lesson go to MyEnglishLab > Extra speaking lessons.

> **Extra activities 7.4**
> **A/B** These activities provide further practice of the functional language from the Speaking box. Ask students to complete both exercises individually and if there is time, get them to compare answers in pairs before checking with the class.
>
> **A**
> **1** morning **2** aim **3** First **4** Then **5** Finally
> **B**
> **1** look **2** start **3** move **4** provider **5** can
> **6** based **7** Finally **8** questions

4 Go through the instructions with students and give them plenty of time to read the notes and write their presentations. Encourage them to use phrases from the Speaking box and while they are writing, monitor and offer help as necessary. When they are ready, put them in pairs or small groups to practise reading their presentations. In stronger classes, you could ask students to make brief notes on prompt cards and use those to give their presentations rather than reading them out.

Teacher's notes

Model answer

Good morning. I'm Sabine, the Sales Director of Force Sport Cars. Thank you for attending this presentation. The aim of today's presentation is to introduce our company and services. First, I'll tell you a bit more about the company history. Then I'll explain our products and services and how we can help you. Finally, we'll have a question and answer session at the end.

So let's start with more information about the company. Force Sport Cars is based in Spa, in Belgium, and we started the business in 1987. We started to fix motor racing engines at the beginning. Then we launched our own sports car in 1992 for public roads. Today we also provide a range of parts and hand-built engines for motor sport teams. This is our main business.

So let's move on to our main products: our engines. We can provide hand-built engines for your motor racing cars and motorcycles. Our high-performance engines are the most reliable in the industry. They are the quickest to build, they are the lightest, and they last the longest. This is why our customers think we provide the best engines for new racing teams.

Now, let's talk about our services. We can fix your motorsports cars and motorcycles. You can ship them to us and we can replace engines and other parts with our quality products. Our team have over thirty years' experience and are the best in the industry. We can make new engines and parts to meet your requirements.

So that's the end of my presentation. Does anyone have any questions?

5A Explain to students that they are going to give a presentation about a company at a trade show. They can either present information about their own company or invent the details. Go through the questions with them and check that they understand *across the world* in step 1. Encourage them to use the stages in Exercise 1C to organise their presentations and remind them to use phrases from the Speaking box. You could also let them refer to videoscript 7.4.1 on page 131 they need help. Allow plenty of preparation time and encourage students to make notes. Monitor and offer help where necessary.

5B Students now take turns to give their presentations in small groups. Point out that while listening to other students' presentations, they should write questions to ask the presenter at the end. It would be a good idea to set a time limit of around 3 minutes for each presentation, depending on how much time you have available. Make sure students factor in time for questions at the end of each presentation. During the activity, monitor and note down any points to highlight during feedback, but do not interrupt students' presentations – discuss any points as necessary at the end.

MyEnglishLab: Teacher's resources: extra activities; Extra speaking lessons; Additional interactive activities

Teacher's book: Resource bank Extra vocabulary practice p.142 Exercises 3–5; Photocopiable 7.4 p.125

Workbook: p.38 Exercises 1–4

Business workshop

The big contract

GSE learning objectives

- Can understand short, simple emails on work-related topics.
- Can make simple, direct comparisons between two people or things using common adjectives.
- Can use appropriate openings and endings in simple informal emails.
- Can write a simple email/letter in response to a request for information.
- Can use basic discourse markers to structure a short presentation.

Introduction

Students read about a trade show.

1 Explain to students that they are going to read an email about an international cruise show. Go through the advertisement with them and answer any vocabulary questions they have, then ask them to read the email and answer the question. Check the answer with the class.

to look at options for a new cruise ship

Presentations

Students give a presentation.

2 If you think your students will find this activity difficult, review the information on the stages of a presentation in Lesson 7.4, Exercise 1C before you start. Explain the activity and scenario to the class: they each work for a different cruise ship builder and are going to present their new ship at the cruise show they read about in Exercise 1. Put students in two groups, A and B, direct them to their relevant information and ask them to put the stages of their presentations in the correct order. When they have finished, check answers with the class by asking just for the letters relating to each stage, so as not to give away too much information at this stage. Students then practise reading their presentations in their groups (or to a partner within their group if it is large), as preparation for presenting to a partner from the other group in the next activity. Finally, they complete the table with information about their ship; point out that they should only complete *one* of the columns in the table, not both – they will complete the column about the other group's ship in the next activity. Monitor as they are doing this and offer help as necessary, but do not confirm answers yet.

Group A
1
1 d **2** c **3** a **4** e **5** b
Group B
1
1 c **2** a **3** e **4** d **5** b

Teacher's notes

3A/B If you think your students will find these activities difficult, review the Speaking box in Lesson 7.4 before you start. Put students in A/B pairs with a student from each group in Exercise 2. They should take it in turns to present their ship to their partner, who listens and completes the missing information in the table in Exercise 3A. During the activity, monitor and note down any points to highlight during feedback, but do not interrupt students' presentations. When they have finished, check answers with the class and go over any points you noted while monitoring.

Company	Seven Seas Ships	Saffron Ship Company	Delta Luxury Ships
Ship	The River Queen	The Star Sailor	The Cruise Star
Size	160 x 25 m	230 x 40 m	200 x 30 m
Decks	3	5	4
Rooms	95	150	110
Features	3 bars, 2 restaurants, swimming pool	5 bars, 3 restaurants, 3 swimming pools, dance floor	5 bars, 3 restaurants, 3 swimming pools
Build/ Delivery time	6 months	1 year	1 year 2 months
Estimated cost	$4.5 million	$5 million	$5.25 million

4 If you think your students will find this activity difficult, review the Communicative grammar sections of Lessons 7.1 and 7.3 before you start. Explain to students that they work for the cruise company in Exercise 1 and need to choose a cruise ship to buy. Go through the bullet points with them, then put them in pairs to compare the ships and decide which one is best. Monitor and make notes on any common errors with comparatives and superlatives. When they have finished, ask each group which ship they chose, find out if others agree and feed in information from the answer key – this will help them write their emails in Exercise 5. Note that no ship meets all the criteria – students have to compromise with some. Finally, go through any common errors you heard with the class.

> **Suggested answer**
> *The River Queen* is the smallest. *The Star Sailor* is the biggest.
> *The Cruise Star* takes the longest to build. *The River Queen* is the quickest to build.
> *The River Queen* is the cheapest. *The Cruise Star* is the most expensive.
> *The River Queen* is cheap and has three bars. It doesn't have enough restaurants, rooms or swimming pools. It has 95 rooms and we need 100 or more. It only has two restaurants and one swimming pool.
> *The Cruise Star* takes one year and two months to deliver – that is too long. *The Star Sailor* is quicker to build and deliver. *The Cruise Star* costs too much. Our budget is less than $5m.
> *The Star Sailor* is the best option. *The Star Sailor* is cheaper. It has all the bars restaurants and swimming pools we need. The problem is the build and delivery time and the cost.

Writing

Students write an email comparing products and services.

5A Explain to students that they are going to write an email reporting on their discussion and any decisions made in Exercise 4 but before they do, they are going to look at some useful phrases. You could do the activity with the whole class, checking answers as you go, or let students complete it individually and then check answers with the class.

> **1** E **2** M **3** M **4** B **5** E **6** B

5B Explain the writing task and look at the example opening with students. Remind them to a) think about the phrases in Exercise 5A and make sure their email has a clear beginning, middle and end, b) use comparatives and superlatives to explain their decision and c) make sure they include all the necessary information. If you think your students will find the writing task difficult, refer them back to the model email in Lesson 7.3, Exercise 2 and review the language in Exercise 3 in the same lesson before you start. Give students some time to plan their emails first – they could do this in pairs in weaker classes. During the writing task, monitor and be on hand to offer help where necessary.

> **Model answer**
> Hi David,
> Please find attached the analysis of three ships at the International Cruise Show. These were *The Star Sailor*, *The River Queen* and *The Cruise Star*. Here is a summary of the findings.
> I think our best option is *The Star Sailor*.
> Strengths
> • It's the biggest ship.
> • It has the most rooms.
> • It has more bars, restaurants and swimming pools than *The River Queen*.
> • The delivery time is shorter than *The Cruise Star*.
> • It's cheaper than *The Cruise Star*.
> Issues
> • It's more expensive than our budget.
> • The delivery time is one year. This is shorter than *The Cruise Star*, but longer than *The River Queen*.
> If you have any questions, let me know.
> Best regards,
> Hugo

Teacher's notes

Grammar reference ◀ 7

7.1

1 cheaper 2 smaller 3 longer 4 expensive 5 bigger
6 faster 7 brighter 8 easier

7.3

1 the most reliable 2 the friendliest 3 the most secure
4 the biggest 5 the lightest 6 the best 7 the worst
8 the most advanced

Review ◀ 7

1 1 design 2 life 3 features 4 speed 5 point 6 user
7 value 8 weight
2 1 charge 2 monthly 3 includes 4 administration
5 pay 6 booking 7 fixed 8 cancellation
3 1 more expensive 2 faster 3 bigger 4 easier
5 better 6 safer 7 noisier 8 more powerful
4 1 best 2 biggest 3 widest 4 friendliest 5 highest
6 worst 7 fastest 8 happiest
5 1 morning 2 aim 3 tell 4 First 5 talk about
6 start 7 move

Jobs 8

Unit overview

	CLASSWORK		FURTHER WORK
8.1 **Work experience**	**Lead-in**	Students talk about people they like working with.	**MyEnglishLab:** Teacher's resources: extra activities; Additional interactive activities
	Vocabulary	Students look at vocabulary related to skills and personal qualities.	**Grammar reference:** p.112 Talking about experiences
	Communicative grammar	Students study and practise the Present Perfect for experiences.	**Teacher's book:** Resource bank Extra vocabulary practice p.143 Exercise 1
	Video	Students watch a video of people talking about the skills and qualities they need for their job.	**Workbook:** p.39 Exercises 1 and 2; p.40 Exercises 1 and 2
	Task	Students practise the Present Perfect by talking about their experiences.	
8.2 **The best person for the job**	**Lead-in**	Students discuss advertising job vacancies.	**MyEnglishLab:** Teacher's resources: extra activities; Additional interactive activities
	Vocabulary	Students look at vocabulary related to job requirements.	**Pronunciation bank:** p.101 The vowel /ɒ/. The letter 'o' as /ɒ/, /əʊ/ and /ʌ/.
	Listening	Students listen to two managers discussing candidates for a job vacancy.	**Teacher's book:** Resource bank Extra vocabulary practice p.143 Exercise 2
	Speaking	Students describe and compare job candidates' skills and experience.	**Workbook:** p.39 Exercise 3; p.41 Exercises 1–3; p.51 Exercises 1–3
8.3 **Professional profiles**	**Lead-in**	Students discuss photos for different types of website.	**MyEnglishLab:** Teacher's resources: extra activities; Additional interactive activities
	Reading	Students read a profile for a professional website, then study and practise the Present Perfect and Past Simple.	**Grammar reference:** p.113 Talking about experiences and completed past events
	Writing	Students write an employee profile.	**Pronunciation bank:** p.101 Silent letters
			Teacher's book: Resource bank Photocopiable 8.3 p.126
			Workbook: p.40 Exercises 3 and 4; p.42 Exercises 1–3; p.51 Exercises 1–3
8.4 **Work skills:** A job interview	**Lead-in**	Students read and discuss a job advert.	**MyEnglishLab:** Teacher's resources: extra activities; Extra speaking lessons; Additional interactive activities
	Video	Students watch a video of a job interview.	**Teacher's book:** Resource bank Extra vocabulary practice p.143 Exercises 3–5; Photocopiable 8.4 p.127
	Speaking	Students look at useful language for job interviews.	**Workbook:** p.43 Exercises 1–4
Business workshop: The interviewer and the candidate	**Introduction**	Students read a job advertisement.	
	Speaking	Students look at common interview questions.	
	Roleplay	Students roleplay job interviews.	

Teacher's notes

Unit vocabulary list

Active vocabulary

8.1

analytical	language skills
communication skills	motivated
hard-working	organised
IT skills	team worker

8.2

useful skills/experience	advertisement
essential skills/experience	(choose) candidate(s)
	vacancy/vacancies
degree	
qualification(s)	

Passive vocabulary

8.1

calm	analytical skills
friendly	decisive
funny	positive attitude
intelligent	write well
polite	
reliable	

8.3

Profile	Location
Current job	Past positions
Full name	Qualifications
Job title	Skills summary

8.4

celebrate	motivate (staff)
challenges	reputation
meet/set goals	strengths

Teacher's notes

8.1 > Work experience

GSE learning objectives

- Can use language related to aptitude, ability, knowledge and skills.
- Can write simple sentences about personal skills.
- Can use the Present Perfect to refer to personal experiences in the past.
- Can ask questions using the Present Perfect with 'ever'.
- Can identify simple information in a short video, provided that the visual supports this information and the delivery is slow and clear.
- Can understand simple, factual information in a work-related video.
- Can describe skills and abilities using simple language.
- Can answer simple questions about work experience or education using simple language.

Lead-in

Students talk about people they like working with.

1 Go through the adjectives in the box with the class and check understanding first. Then introduce the discussion by telling the class about someone you like working with, using the adjectives in the box. Put students in pairs and give them 2–3 minutes to discuss their ideas, then ask a few students to share something interesting they found out from their partner with the class. You could also teach or elicit other adjectives which are near synonyms or antonyms of those in the box, e.g. *intelligent*, *clever*, *funny*, *humorous*.

Vocabulary: Skills and personal qualities

Students look at vocabulary related to skills and personal qualities.

2 Draw students' attention to the blog post and explain that it gives advice for job interviews. Ask them to complete the exercise individually and if there is time, get them to compare answers in pairs before checking with the class.

1 100 employers – to find out the top skills and qualities they want in staff
2 skills and personal qualities
3 give examples from other areas of their lives, e.g. university, interests, etc.

3 Explain the activity and before students begin, go through the examples in the table with them and check that they understand *assess*, *analyse*, 'can-do' attitude and *make an effort*. Ask them to complete the table individually, then check answers with the class, clarifying meanings as necessary. Alternatively, you could do this as a whole-class activity, checking answers and clarifying meanings as you go. As an extension, you could ask students which of the skills and personal qualities are important for their present or future profession.

1 organised   2 good communication skills
3 team worker   4 analytical   5 language skills
6 IT skills   7 motivated   8 hard-working

4 Give students time to read the sentences before they complete the exercise, and check that they understand *logical* and *achieve*. Complete the first item as an example by reading out the sentence and eliciting the correct skill/quality. Students then complete the rest of the exercise individually and compare answers in pairs before checking with the class. If you are short of time, this exercise can also be done as a whole-class activity, checking answers as you go.

a hard-working   b IT skills   c analytical
d good communication skills   e organised
f language skills   g motivated   h team worker

5 Refer students to the questionnaire on page 124 and look at the example with the class. Explain that they need to complete the rest of the questionnaire by ticking the correct box for each quality and then adding their own examples. To add more options for the degrees of ability in the table, you could add a third column headed *I'm OK at …* . Students complete the questionnaire for themselves while you monitor and offer help as necessary. When they have finished, put them in pairs to compare their answers, then invite different students to share their ratings and examples with the class. If you are short of time, you could also set the questionnaire for homework and discuss it in the next class.

Extra activities 8.1

A This activity provides extra practice of vocabulary related to skills and personal qualities. Ask students to complete it individually, then check answers with the class.

1 organised   2 analytical   3 hard-working
4 communication   5 IT skills   6 motivated
7 language   8 team worker

Communicative grammar: Talking about experiences

Students study and practise the Present Perfect for experiences.

Talking about experiences

Write on the board: *I've written sales reports.* and ask: *Do we know when I wrote them?* (No) *Is it important?* (No). Explain that these sentences are in the Present Perfect, the tense we use to describe experiences, then look at the examples in the Grammar box with the class. Ask students to look at the words in bold in the examples and try to work out how the Present Perfect is formed – elicit or give the pattern: *have/has* + past participle. Elicit how we form the past participle of regular verbs (with the *-ed* ending), and also that irregular verbs do not follow the *-ed* rule – they each have their own form. Refer students to the blog post in Exercise 2 so they can look again at the target language in context – draw their attention to the verb forms in bold in the text. You could then refer them to the Grammar reference on page 112 and go through it with them, clarifying any points as necessary. Students can then do the extra grammar activity there, in class or as homework.

Grammar reference answer key: page 109

101

> Teacher's notes

6 Ask students to complete the sentences individually. Remind them that they can refer to the Grammar reference on page 112 and the Irregular verbs list on page 114 if they need help. You might also ask them to use short forms where possible. Check answers with the class, inviting students to write the answers on the board, so they can check their spelling.

> 1 've/have worked 2 hasn't / has not had
> 3 hasn't / has not written 4 've/have given 5 used
> 6 've/have never presented

7A Again, ask students to work individually and if there is time, get them to compare answers in pairs before class feedback.

> 1 Have you ever managed a team?
> 2 How many companies have you worked for?
> 3 Have you ever lived in another country or region?
> 4 Have you worked in an international team before?
> 5 Have you ever written emails in English?
> 6 Where have you travelled for work?

7B Students could do this individually or you could do it as a whole-class activity, checking answers as you go. As an extension, you could get students to practise the questions and answers in pairs.

> 1 d 2 b 3 a 4 e 5 f 6 c

Extra activities 8.1

> **B** This activity provides further practice of the Present Perfect. Students should do it individually, as consolidation. If there is time, let them compare answers in pairs before class feedback.
>
> 1 b 2 b 3 a 4 a 5 b 6 b 7 a 8 a 9 b 10 a

Video

Students watch a video of people talking about the skills and qualities they need for their job.

8A ▶ 8.1.1 Tell students that they are going to watch people discussing the skills and qualities they need for their job. Play the introduction of the video (0:00–0:33), then elicit the answers.

> education company (James), advertising (Polly)

8B ▶ 8.1.1 Tell students that they are going to watch the complete video this time, and explain the activity. Point out that they may need to match some skills and qualities to more than one person. Go through the words in the box with the class and check that students remember what they mean. You may also wish to pre-teach the following vocabulary from the video: *own* (a business), *run* (a business), *require*, *work closely together*. Play the video, then check answers with the class.

> analytical skills – J; communication skills – J, P; decisive – D; organised – D; positive attitude – P; reliable – P; team worker – D (and by default, Polly (P), who doesn't mention it, but works for the same company as part of this team); write well – D

8C ▶ 8.1.1 Explain the activity and, to help students, tell them that they need to write *one* word in each gap. Give them time to read the text before they watch again, and encourage them to think about what type of information is needed in each gap (e.g. a number, a job, a place). Play the video, twice if necessary, then check answers with the class.

> 1 four/five 2 teacher 3 managed 4 two 5 2014, 2016 6 9/nine 7 Germany 8 3/three 9 television
> 10 8/eight 11 3/three 12 hard-working

Task

Students practise the Present Perfect by talking about their experiences.

9 Put students in pairs, explain the activity and look at the examples with them. Give pairs 3–4 minutes to ask and answer the questions while you monitor and note down any errors/difficulties with the Present Perfect and the vocabulary from the lesson. Go through any points you note in a brief feedback session at the end of the activity and if there is time, invite a few students to share anything interesting they found out about their partner with the class.

MyEnglishLab: Teacher's resources: extra activities; Additional interactive activities
Grammar reference: p.112 Talking about experiences
Teacher's book: Resource bank Extra vocabulary practice p.143 Exercise 1
Workbook: p.39 Exercises 1 and 2; p.40 Exercises 1 and 2

8.2 ▶ The best person for the job

GSE learning objectives

- Can use language related to job applications, hiring and firing.
- Can use language related to aptitude, ability, knowledge and skills.
- Can identify basic factual information in short, simple dialogues or narratives on familiar everyday topics, if spoken slowly and clearly.
- Can describe skills and abilities using simple language.
- Can make simple, direct comparisons between two people or things using common adjectives.
- Can answer simple questions about work experience or education using simple language.

Lead-in

Students discuss advertising job vacancies.

1 Go through the instructions with the class and check that they understand *advertise*, *advertisement* (and *advert/ad*) and *(job) vacancy*. Give students a minute to look at the job adverts, then discuss the question as a class, including information from the Notes below if necessary. Ask students about any specific job websites they know and/or have used.

> **Notes**
> Today there are thousands of job sites on the web. Well-known, global sites include Indeed.com, Dice.com for tech jobs, Google for Jobs, and LinkedIn. Companies usually advertise job opportunities online via job sites and their own company websites. Some companies will advertise through recruitment agencies. Job adverts in print newspapers are less common than in the past.

Vocabulary: Job requirements

Students look at vocabulary related to job requirements.

2A Explain to students that they are going to read an email about one of the job vacancies in Exercise 1. Go over the vocabulary in bold in the text, checking understanding and clarifying meanings where necessary. Get students to complete the exercise individually or, in weaker classes, in pairs, then check answers with the class. In feedback, you could go over the use of prepositions in these phrases: *have (three years') experience in, work in the chemical/pharmaceutical/etc. industry, work for a company, have a degree in, travel for work*. Put the phrases on the board and leave them there for students to refer to when they do Exercises 6A and 6B.

> He wants her to include the details about the 'essential' and 'useful' skills and experience in the advertisement for the Sales Manager vacancy. He also wants her to choose the best candidates for him to interview.

2B Discuss the question with the whole class.

> In this context, 'essential' skills are extremely important and necessary for the job – the skills that the candidate must have. 'Useful' skills are not essential to the job but can help. Useful skills are ones which are good to have. Sometimes these skills can overlap.

3 This activity looks at useful vocabulary from the email in Exercise 2A. Ask students to complete it individually and then compare answers in pairs if there is time. Check answers with the class, and be prepared to give further explanations/examples where necessary.

> **1** c **2** a **3** b **4** c **5** b **6** a **7** c **8** b

> **Extra activities 8.2**
>
> **A/B** These activities provide further practice of the vocabulary for job requirements. Ask students to complete both exercises individually, then to compare answers in pairs before class feedback. If there is time, you could put them in pairs to practise he questions and answers.
>
> **A**
> **1** qualifications **2** choose **3** candidates **4** degree **5** vacancies **6** languages **7** useful
> **B**
> **a** 4 **b** 6 **c** 1 **d** 7 **e** 2 **f** 3 **g** 5

Listening: Choosing job candidates

Students listen to two managers discussing candidates for a job vacancy.

4A 🔊 8.01 Explain to students that they are going to hear Dan and Elsa from Exercise 2 discussing candidates for the Sales Manager vacancy. Play the recording, then check the answer with the class.

> Dan and Elsa are both going to interview the candidates.

4B 🔊 8.01 Draw students' attention to the profiles, explain the activity and check that they understand *impression* in the first column. Give them time to look at the information in the table before they listen, and encourage them to think about what kind of information is missing from each gap. Play the recording, twice if necessary, then check answers with the class.

> **1** communication **2** three/3 **3** French **4** language **5** eight/8 **6** smaller **7** friendly **8** five/5 **9** basic

> **Pronunciation bank**
> **p.101: The vowel /ɒ/. The letter 'o' as /ɒ/, /əʊ/ and /ʌ/.**
>
> **1** 🔊 P8.01 The sound /ɒ/ is a short back vowel in which the lips are rounded and the tongue is low at the back of the mouth. Note that the sound /ɒ/ is not typically found in American English. The vowels /ɑː/, /ɔː/ and /ʌ/ are used instead. For example, *clock* is pronounced as /klɑːk/, *soft* as /sɔːft/ and *what* as /wʌt/.
>
> Write the word *on* on the board, model its pronunciation and explain that it begins with the sound /ɒ/. You may wish to tell students that it is usually spelt with the letter *o*, but there are exceptions, such as *a* (*watch*), *au* (*quantity*) and *ow* (*knowledge*). Play recording P8.01 and ask students to repeat as a group and then individually.

Teacher's notes

2A 🔊 P8.02 Write *home* and *come* on the board and remind students that the letter *o* can also represent the sounds /əʊ/ and /ʌ/. Refer students to the exercise and point out the letter *o* in bold in the words. Explain that in the first word in each pair, *o* is pronounced with /ɒ/. Students have to decide if the second word contains the same sound, /ɒ/, or a different sound (/əʊ/ or /ʌ/). Play the recording and check answers with the class.

> 1 different: /kɒst/, /məʊst/ 2 same: /ˈkɒlɪdʒ/, /ˈnɒlɪdʒ/ 3 different: /gɒn/, /dʌn/ 4 different: /ˈhɒlənd/, /ˈpəʊlənd/ 5 different: /lɒst/, /pəʊst/ 6 different: /sɒlv/, /səʊld/ 7 different: /ˈsɒri/, /ˈwʌri/ 8 different: /wɒnt/, /wəʊnt/

2B 🔊 P8.02 Play the recording again and get students to repeat as a group and then individually.

3A 🔊 P8.03 Explain the activity and if necessary, complete the first item as an example with the class. Point out that students only need to listen for the sound /ɒ/ – they do not need to decide which sound the rest of the letters *o* are pronounced as. To help them, you could say that they need to identify one word in each item. Play the recording, then check answers with the class.

> 1 pr**o**blems 2 econ**o**mics 3 l**o**t 4 **o**ffice 5 pr**o**ducts 6 m**o**del

3B 🔊 P8.03 Explain that students are going to listen to the same sentences and this time identify which of the letters *o* are pronounced as /əʊ/. Again, you could tell them that they need to circle one word per item. Play the recording, then check answers with the class.

> 1 m**o**tivated 2 s**o**cial 3 pr**o**gram 4 ph**o**t**o** 5 d**o**n't 6 kil**o**s

3C 🔊 P8.03 Explain to students that they now need to identify which of the letters *o* in the sentences are pronounced as /ʌ/. Play the recording, then check answers with the class.

> 1 c**o**mpany 2 L**o**ndon 3 m**o**ney 4 m**o**nth 5 c**o**lours 6 **o**ther

3D Put students in pairs to practise saying the sentences in Exercise 3A. You may wish to play the recording again and get students to repeat the sentences as a group before they practise on their own. During the activity, monitor and correct pronunciation as necessary.

5 Tell students that they are going to complete some sentences about the candidates in Exercise 4B using the Present Perfect. Look at the example with them, elicit how the Present Perfect is formed and write the pattern on the board for students to refer to if necessary: *positive: have/has + past participle; negative: haven't/hasn't + past participle*. Explain that in order to complete the sentences correctly (i.e. to decide which sentences are negative), students need to use the information in the table in Exercise 4B. You may also wish to ask them to use short forms where possible. Get them to complete the exercise individually and then to compare answers in pairs before class feedback.

> 2 hasn't / has not studied, 's/has studied 3 's/has lived, ('s/has) worked 4 hasn't / has not worked 5 's/has had 6 's/has travelled 7 have been, hasn't / has not 8 's/has worked, haven't / have not

Speaking

Students describe and compare job candidates' skills and experience.

6A Explain the activity and look at the example with students. Refer them to the words in bold in the text in Exercise 2A and also to the useful phrases on the board from the same exercise – encourage students to try and use them in their descriptions. Allow plenty of time for students to think about and write their answers. While they are writing, monitor and offer help as necessary.

6B Put students in pairs, explain the activity and look at the example with them. Give them time to compare their sentences from Exercise 6A and then to try and choose the best candidate. The important thing here is not who they choose, but that they are able to justify their choice. As feedback, invite students from different pairs to tell the class who they chose and why.

> **Notes**
>
> All the candidates have the essential sales manager skills and experience. Sam has experience in the chemical industry, knows a lot about the company and its products, has worked in Germany and speaks German, so some students might choose him for that reason. However, Isaac has more experience and manages a bigger team. He's also described as a team worker, which is an essential quality for the job. In addition, he has experience of working in European markets. Vicki has a technical knowledge of a chemistry, which is useful. She also has good communication skills, speaks good French and is happy to learn German.
>
> How well the three candidates do in their job interviews and their references will be crucial elements in the final decision.

MyEnglishLab: Teacher's resources: extra activities
Pronunciation bank: p.101 The vowel /ɒ/. The letter 'o' as /ɒ/, /əʊ/ and /ʌ/.
Teacher's book: Resource bank Extra vocabulary practice p.143 Exercise 2
Workbook: p.39 Exercise 3; p.41 Exercises 1–3; p.51 Exercises 1–3

8.3 Professional profiles

GSE learning objectives

- Can identify basic personal details about someone on website profiles, business cards, etc.
- Can use the Present Perfect to refer to personal experiences in the past.
- Can tell when to use the Past Simple and when to use the Present Perfect. (BrE)
- Can write simple sentences about personal skills.
- Can write a short online profile.
- Can write basic personal details for a website profile, business card, etc.

Lead-in

Students discuss photos for different types of website.

1 Discuss the questions as a class. Elicit their ideas and if desired, share some of the information from the Notes below in order to highlight the reasons for the answer. As an extension, and if students feel comfortable doing so, they could show the class photos of themselves that they use for their social media / professional website profiles.

> 1 A, B 2 C – it's a professional-looking face profile, has a simple background and is not a group photo, like B, or a casual photo photo where you can't see the full facial profile, like A.

> **Notes**
> A photo can be one of the most important elements of a professional profile. Research shows that having a photo makes a profile at least seven times more likely to be viewed. A good profile photo:
> - is a good quality photo.
> - is recent and professional-looking.
> - is *not* a selfie.
> - has a simple background.
> - is one where your face takes up most of the frame (a head shot or a head and shoulders shot).
> - is *not* a group photo – it shows only you, not your whole team.
> - is one where you have a friendly and warm expression – smile, but not too much, and aim to look professional!

Reading

Students read a profile for a professional website, then study and practise the Present Perfect and Past Simple.

2 Tell students that they are going to look at a profile for a professional website and refer them to the name and photo – ask them if they remember who Elsa is (an employee at Danotex Chemicals – students first saw her in Lesson 8.2). Go through the words in the box with students, clarifying meanings as necessary, then look at the example with them and ask them to complete the exercise individually. Check answers with the class.

> 2 Job title 3 Location 4 Skills summary
> 5 Current positions 6 Past jobs 7 Qualifications

Talking about experiences and completed past events

Go through the examples in the Grammar box with the class, and explain that we use the Present Perfect to talk about general experiences, when we do not know when something happened exactly (or it is not important), and the Past Simple when we know when something happened (or it is clear from the context). Refer students back to the examples in bold in the profile in Exercise 2. Go through each example with them and elicit whether it describes an experience or a completed past event. You could then refer students to the Grammar reference on page 113 and go through it with them, clarifying any points as necessary. Students can then do the extra grammar activities there, in class or as homework.

Grammar reference answer key: page 109

> **Pronunciation bank**
> **p.101: Silent letters**
>
> **1** ◀) P8.04 Play the recording and get students to repeat as a group. Ask them why they think some letters in the words are in green. Elicit or explain that the green letters are silent – they are not pronounced. Play the recording again and ask students to repeat the words individually.
>
> **2A** ◀) P8.05 Explain the activity and play the recording for students to listen and identify the silent letters. Get students to compare answers in pairs, then check them with the class. Note that some English speakers pronounce the word *often* with /t/.
>
> > 1 cu(p)board 2 ha(l)f 3 (k)nife 4 of(t)en
> > 5 (p)sychology 6 stron(g) 7 wou(l)d 8 (w)rote
>
> **2B** ◀) P8.05 Play the recording again and get students to repeat as a group and then individually.
>
> **3A** ◀) P8.06 This activity is best done in two stages. Explain to students that they are going to complete each sentence with one word, and that all the missing words contain silent letters, which they will need to identify later. Start by asking students to listen and just write the missing words – tell them not to worry about the silent letters for now. Check answers with the class, then play the recording a second time for students to identify the silent letters. To help them, you could tell them that one of the words contains two silent letters. Check answers with the class.
>
> > 1 ca**l**m 2 **k**new 3 ta**l**k 4 answ**e**r 5 **w**rong
> > 6 **h**ours
>
> **3B** ◀) P8.06 Play the recording again, then put students in pairs to practise saying the sentences. During the activity, monitor and correct pronunciation as necessary.

Teacher's notes

3 Ask students to complete the exercise individually. Remind them that before choosing an option for each item, they should think about whether the verb refers to a general experience or a completed past event with a specific time reference. Check answers with the class.

> 1 has worked, started 2 was, has had 3 studied, have designed 4 has been, went 5 have managed, worked

4/5 Both of these exercises practise the grammar from the lesson, and students should do them individually, as consolidation. Remind them that they can refer to the Grammar reference on page 113 if they need help. If there is time, get students to compare answers in pairs before class feedback. In feedback, write (or invite students to write) the answers on the board, so students can check their spelling.

> **4**
> 1 finished, spent 2 have written, started 3 has worked, produced 4 has organised, helped
> **5**
> 1 have worked 2 have managed 3 have motivated / motivated (use of 'and' means 'have' is not necessary)
> 4 have trained 5 was 6 interviewed 7 recruited
> 8 helped 9 had 10 prepared 11 analysed 12 wrote

Extra activities 8.3

A/B These activities provide further practice of the Present Perfect and Past Simple. Ask students to complete them individually, referring to the Grammar reference if they need help. Check answers with the class, clarifying any errors/difficulties as necessary.

> **A**
> 1 b 2 a 3 a 4 a 5 b 6 a 7 b 8 a
> **B**
> 1 f 2 a 3 d 4 c 5 b 6 e

Writing

Students write an employee profile.

6 Explain the writing task and read the two options with the class. Make it clear that this profile is five years in the future, so if students invent information, they should imagine themselves five years from now. Students should use a blank piece of paper with the categories given in the profile on page 83 – they should not write the information in the space provided in the Coursebook as it is not big enough for all the information they need to include. Encourage them to use the Present Perfect to describe general experience, the Present Simple to describe their present job and the Past Simple to talk about specific past events in companies they do not work for now. While students are writing, monitor and offer help as necessary. If there is no time to do the writing task in class, students could do it for homework, looking at online profiles of people with similar jobs to them.

Model answer

Jay Peters
Chemical Engineer
Antwerp, Belgium

Motivated, organised and analytical Chemical Engineer. I have worked on international project teams in the chemical industry. I am a team worker and have excellent IT, problem-solving and communication skills.

Experience

Senior Project Manager
Danotex Chemicals
Birmingham, UK
March 2019 – present date

I am responsible for special projects across the UK and Europe. I organise and lead project teams, motivate team members, write reports for senior managers and give presentations.

Project Manager
CUG Engineering Group
May 2017 to February 2019

I was responsible for engineering projects in the UK. I managed a team of engineers.

Education

Masters in Project Management
Drumford University
2019–2021

BSc Degree in Chemical Engineering
Drumford University
2015–2019

MyEnglishLab: Teacher's resources: extra activities; Additional interactive activities
Grammar reference: p.113 Talking about experiences and completed past events
Pronunciation bank: p.101 Silent letters
Teacher's book: Resource bank Photocopiable 8.3 p.126
Workbook: p.40 Exercises 3 and 4; p.42 Exercises 1–3; p.51 Exercises 1–3

8.4 Work skills

A job interview

GSE learning objectives

- Can identify simple information in a short video, provided that the visual supports this information and the delivery is slow and clear.
- Can understand the main information in short, simple dialogues about familiar activities, if spoken slowly and clearly.
- Can understand simple, factual information in a work-related video.
- Can answer simple questions and respond to simple statements in an interview.
- Can describe skills and abilities using simple language.

Teacher's notes

Lead-in
Students read and discuss a job advert.

1 Explain the activity, and give students 1-2 minutes to read the job advert and answer the question. Check answers with the class.

> skills: excellent communication skills; personal qualities: enthusiastic and motivated; experience: at least two years' customer service experience

Video
Students watch a video of a job interview.

2 ▶ 8.4.1 Before students watch the video, briefly explain the context: Matt Reece, HR Manager at Sleek, is interviewing Angela Davis, a candidate, for the job in Exercise 1. Go through the instructions with students, then play the beginning of the video (0:00–0:14) and elicit the answer.

> Team Leader in customer services for a retail company

3A ▶ 8.4.1 Give students time to read the statements before they watch, and check that they understand *deal with*, *stressful*, *bored* and *reputation*. You may also wish to pre-teach the following vocabulary from the video: *via*, *digital channel*, *adviser*, *set/meet goals*, *progress* (v), *opportunity*, *on-the-job training*. Play the video, then check answers with the class.

> **1** F **2** T **3** F **4** T **5** T **6** F **7** F **8** T

3B Tell students that they now have to correct the false sentences from Exercise 3A. If you think your students may remember some of the information, you could ask them to correct as many of the statements as they can before watching again, then play the video for them to check/complete their answers. Check answers with the class.

> 1 Angela's first job was as a ~~Personal Assistant (PA)~~ **shop assistant**.
> 3 She says ~~speaking~~ **listening** is the most important communication skill.
> 6 She says her job can sometimes be stressful when customers are ~~bored~~ **angry**.
> 7 She wants to work for the bank because it has an excellent reputation for ~~social media~~ **customer service**.

4A ▶ 8.4.1 Explain to students that these are the interview questions Matt asked Angela in the video. You could let them attempt the exercise without watching, then play the video for them to check/complete their answers. Alternatively, play the video and ask students to complete the questions while watching, then clarify meanings during feedback.

> **1** tell **2** strengths **3** helped **4** had **5** want **6** leave **7** see **8** questions

4B Put students in pairs and explain the activity. Give them 3-4 minutes for the matching task, and check the answers to it before students think about alternative answers to the questions. Allow another 3-4 minutes for the second part of the activity, then invite students from different pairs to share their ideas with the class.

> **1** c **2** d **3** e **4** h **5** a **6** g **7** b **8** f

Speaking: Job interviews
Students look at useful language for job interviews.

> ### Job interviews
> Draw students' attention to the heading Job interviews and explain that they are going to look at common interview questions as well as useful language for a candidate's answers to them. Give students 1-2 minutes to look at the phrases by themselves, then go through the Speaking box with them, clarifying meanings as necessary.

> ### Unit 8 Extra speaking lesson
> This lesson gives further practice of speaking related to job interviews. To access the lesson go to MyEnglishLab > Extra speaking lessons.

> ### Extra activities 8.4
> **A–C** These activities provide further practice of the functional language in the Speaking box. Students should complete them individually and then, if there is time, compare answers in pairs before checking with the class. As an extension, you could put students in pairs to practise the questions and responses in Exercises A and B.
>
> **A 1** started, moved **2** experience **3** set **4** good **5** done **6** problems **7** develop **8** reputation
> **B a** work **b** What **c** for **d** motivate **e** people **f** Where
> **C a** 1 **b** 2, 4, 5 **c** 8 **d** 3 **e** 6 **f** 7

5 Put students in pairs and tell them that they are going to roleplay two job interviews, taking turns to be the interviewer and the job candidate. Start with roleplay 1. Direct students to their relevant pages and give them time to read their information and ask you about anything they do not understand. Go through the conversation outline with them, and remind them that they need to use phrases from the Speaking box and also add ideas of their own. Allow some preparation time, during which you monitor and offer help as necessary. In weaker classes, you could let students prepare for their interviews in A–A and B–B pairs, then ask them to return to their original pairs for the roleplay. During the activity, monitor and note down any common errors/difficulties and examples of good language use to highlight during feedback. After the first interview, ask students to swap roles and follow the same procedure for roleplay 2. When pairs have finished, have a brief feedback session, highlighting any points you noted while monitoring.

Teacher's notes

MyEnglishLab: Teacher's resources: extra activities;
Extra speaking lessons; Additional interactive activities
Teacher's book: Resource bank Extra vocabulary practice p.143
Exercises 3–5; Photocopiable 8.4 p.127
Workbook: p.43 Exercises 1–4

Business workshop
The interviewer and the candidate

> **GSE learning objectives**
> - Can understand information in advertisements for jobs and services.
> - Can describe skills and abilities using simple language.
> - Can ask about someone's work experience or education using simple language.
> - Can answer simple questions and respond to simple statements in an interview.
> - Can answer simple questions about work experience or education using simple language.
> - Can make simple, direct comparisons between two people or things using common adjectives.
> - Can give simple reasons to explain preferences, given a model.

Introduction
Students read a job advertisement.

1 Draw students' attention to the title of the job advert and ask them what they think the job involves. Elicit a few ideas around the class, then tell them that they are going to check their ideas when they read the advert. Explain the activity and get students to complete it individually, then check answers with the class.

> **a** About our company   **b** Your role and responsibilities
> **c** Your skills and experience

Speaking
Students look at common interview questions.

2 If you think students will find this activity difficult, remind them of the difference between *essential* and *useful* skills from the Reading section of Lesson 8.2 and go through the words in the box with them. Draw their attention to the example and point out that they need to give reasons for their answers. Put them in pairs and give them 2–3 minutes to discuss the skills for the job, then elicit their ideas around the class. As an extension, you could ask students if they can think of any more useful/essential skills for the job.

> **Suggested answers**
> Essential skills:
> Previous management experience in transport operations
> IT skills – the Operations Manager needs to use software programs
> analytical – the person needs good problem-solving skills
> organised – the person needs to meet project deadlines
> communication skills – the person needs to manage and motivate managers and staff and deal with clients
> Useful skills:
> Language skills are not mentioned in the job advertisement
> hard-working, motivated, team worker – these are not obvious from the job advert but are always useful qualities to have

3 Ask students to match the question halves individually, then check answers with the class. Alternatively, do this as a quick, whole-class activity, checking answers as you go.

> **1** c   **2** d   **3** b   **4** a   **5** e

4 If you think students will find this activity difficult, review the Communicative grammar section of Lesson 8.1. Ask students to complete the questions individually, then check answers with the class. In feedback, write (or invite students to write) the answers on the board, so students can check their spelling.

> **1** Have you ever worked   **2** Have you managed
> **3** Have you ever dealt with   **4** Have you used   **5** Have you ever worked

Roleplay
Students roleplay job interviews.

5 Ask students what the vacancy in Exercise 1 was (Operations Manager for a global transport and logistics company), and ask them to imagine that they are candidates for it. Before referring them to their respective information, you may wish to check they understand some useful vocabulary from this and other units that is reviewed in the information profiles: *organised, busy, deal with clients, intern, provide admin support, enthusiastic, recruit, train, manage, responsible for, delivery, deliveries, have experience in, warehouse, dispatch, manufacturer, computer and problem-solving skills, work to deadlines, coordinate, assist*. Put students in groups of four, assign roles and direct them to their relevant pages to complete their profiles. Point out that they have to use the Present Perfect and remind them that they do not need to repeat the auxiliary *have* with verbs in the same sentence. Check answers with the class by eliciting the verb forms only for each candidate, so as not to give away too much information at this stage. After class feedback, give students time to read their completed profiles, in preparation for the roleplay in the next activity.

Teacher's notes

Candidate A
1 've/have worked 2 've/have organised
3 've/have managed
Candidate B
1 've/have had 2 've/have recruited 3 trained
4 managed
Candidate C
1 've/have planned 2 managed 3 've/have had
Candidate D
1 've/have organised 2 've/have worked

6 Remind students of the questions they can ask and answer from Exercises 3 and 4.

Elicit some examples of good answers to give. Also refer them to the job interview in Lesson 8.4 to identify some good answers. Elicit and model a few ideas as a whole class, e.g.

(Exercise 3)

1 I'm an Operations Manager. I work in the transport and courier industry. I've organised deliveries in the UK and Europe.
2 I'm (very organised) and I have excellent communication skills.
3 Because your company has an excellent reputation (in the transport and logistics industry).
4 Because I want to progress in my career/profession. / Because your company offers more opportunities.
5 I'd like to (manage international projects / work abroad / manage a department).

(Exercise 4)

1 Yes, I've worked with many big clients in this industry.
2 No, but I've managed a small team and am sure I can manage a bigger one. / Yes, I've had experience in managing and motivating a big team.
3 Yes, there have been some difficult clients. It's essential to listen to them and solve their problems.
4 Yes, I'm very familiar with Microsoft software. I've used Excel and Word.
5 Yes, I'm very organised and have worked on projects with deadlines many times.

Before students begin their roleplays, allow time for them to prepare for both roles. Ask them to choose five or six questions as interviewers. As interviewees, they should think about their possible answers to all questions because they do not know what they will be asked at the interview. Set a time limit for each interview, and ask students to begin. At the end of each interview, ask students to rotate roles and continue with the next one. At the end of the activity, stronger pairs could act out their interviews for the class.

7A Explain to students that they are now going to review the candidates they interviewed in the previous activity, in order to decide who should get the job. Put them in pairs and if necessary, refer them to their descriptions from Exercise 6A in Lesson 8.2 for a model answer. During the activity, monitor and offer help as necessary.

7B Students should do this activity in the same pairs as Exercise 7A. Explain the activity, look at the example with them and ask them to begin. Remind them that they should give reasons for their choices. As feedback, invite students from different pairs to tell the class which candidate they chose and why.

Grammar reference 8

8.1

1 1 've/have had 2 's/has changed 3 've/have never been 4 's/has gone 5 haven't / have not studied 6 haven't / have not written 7 hasn't / has not designed 8 haven't / have not had 9 Has (she) given 10 Has (he) bought 11 Have (they) ever delivered 12 Have (we) sold

8.3

1 Past Simple: a few days ago, five minutes ago, from 2016 to 2018, in 2017, in November, last month, last week, many times, three times, yesterday
Present Perfect: before, ever, many times, never, three times
(Note that some expressions can be used with either tense (*many times, three times*), e.g. *I've been to Italy three times / I went there three times when I was at University*. However, the most common use is with the Present Perfect, and you may want to encourage this use with your students, rather than with the Past Simple, which is more complex.)
2 1 ever written 2 written 3 did you write 4 wrote 5 did you write 6 wanted 7 ever travelled 8 have/'ve travelled 9 was 10 did you go 11 was 12 went 13 did you stay 14 did you do 15 visited 16 gave 17 had 18 Did you have

Review 8

1 1 c 2 b 3 c 4 b 5 a 6 b 7 a 8 b
2 1 candidates 2 essential 3 degree 4 choose 5 advertisements 6 useful 7 vacancy 8 qualifications
3 1 She's / She has written many emails and reports in English.
2 I've / I have never managed an international project.
3 Have you ever given presentations to clients?
4 He hasn't / has not had much experience (of) managing staff.
5 Has she ever been to Japan for business?
6 We've / We have worked with many large manufacturers.
4 1 've/have been 2 's/has taken 3 haven't / have not bought 4 've/have sent 5 's / has made 6 hasn't / has not gone
5 1 you been, went 2 she ever spoken, spoke 3 we had, had 4 they ever sold, sold
6 1 Can you tell me about your work experience?
2 I have excellent communication skills.
3 I'm good at motivating my team.
4 How have you motivated your staff?
5 Why do you want to work for our company?
6 Where do you see yourself in five years?
7 I've done a lot of staff training.

Resource bank — Photocopiables

Photocopiables

1.3	Grammar: Questions	112
1.4	Work skills: Talking about people and roles	113
2.1	Grammar: Things you can and can't count	114
2.4	Work skills: Making agreements	115
3.3	Grammar: Talking about the past (2)	116
3.4	Work skills: Talking about projects	117
4.3	Grammar: Things happening now	118
4.4	Work skills: Problems with teleconferencing	119
5.1	Grammar: Talking about intentions	120
5.4	Work skills: Socialising with clients	121
6.3	Grammar: Describing production	122
6.4	Work skills: Placing an order	123
7.3	Grammar: Comparing (2): superlatives	124
7.4	Work skills: Presenting	125
8.3	Grammar: Talking about experiences and past events	126
8.4	Work skills: Job interviews	127
	Photocopiables teacher's notes	128

Resource bank — Photocopiables

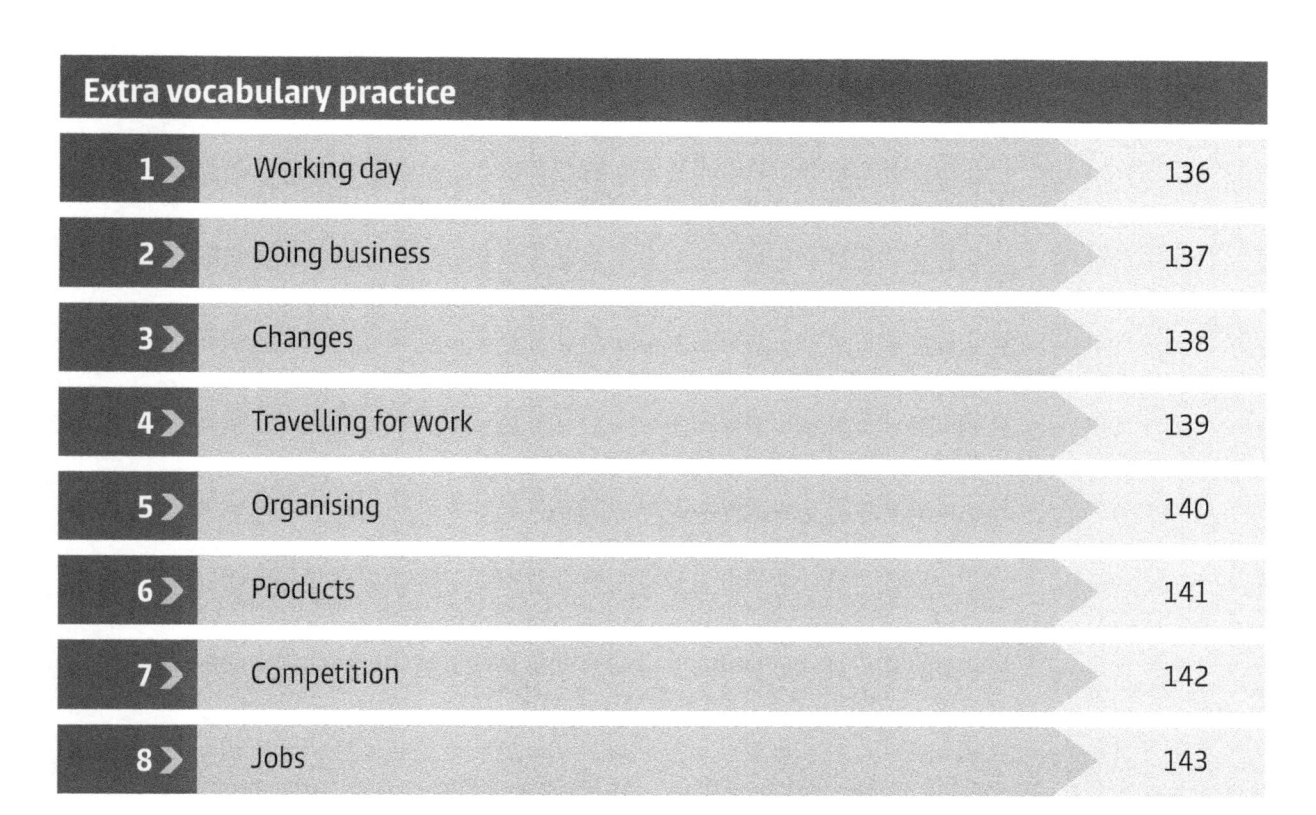

Extra vocabulary practice

1	Working day	136
2	Doing business	137
3	Changes	138
4	Travelling for work	139
5	Organising	140
6	Products	141
7	Competition	142
8	Jobs	143

1 Working day — Photocopiables

1.3 Grammar

1 Complete the questions with *is, are, do* or *does*.

1 What _____ your working hours?
2 How _____ you get to work?
3 Where _____ the meeting rooms?
4 _____ you eat in the canteen at work?
5 When _____ your day finish?
6 _____ your company have a car park?
7 Where _____ your desk?
8 When _____ your working day start?

2 Discuss the questions in Exercise 1 in pairs.

3 Work in groups of three. Divide the cards between you and take turns to turn over one card. When you have a question, the first person to answer it wins a point.

4 Choose four cards with question beginnings from Exercise 3. Use them to write your own questions about a partner's workplace.
Where is your office?

5 Ask and answer your questions from Exercise 4 in pairs. Give more information.
A: *Where is your office?*
B: *In the city centre. It's on Green Street.*

Where is	the gym?	When does	your day start?
Where	is the canteen?	How do	you get to work?
What time	do you usually have a break?	Does your company have	an area for relaxing?
Do you	use the gym?	Do you	work from home?
How long	is your lunch break?	Where do	you usually have lunch?
What	is your department?	What are	your working hours?

1 Working day — Photocopiables

1.4 ▶ Work skills

1 Complete the conversations with one word in each gap.

1. **A:** Ricardo, _____ is Alice. She _____ in the New York office.
   B: _____ to meet you.
   C: Nice to meet you, _____.
2. **A:** Tyler, _____ you know Khalil?
   B: Yes, I _____. Hi, Khalil!
3. **A:** Which department do you _____ in?
   B: I work _____ the Sales department.
4. **A:** What _____ you do?
   B: I _____ a Sales Assistant.
5. **A:** Do you travel _____ work a lot?
   B: No, I _____.

2 Complete the information on your card.

3 Work in pairs. Take turns to introduce yourself to each other.
A: Hi, I'm Aki. I'm a Sales Manager in the Warsaw office.
B: Nice to meet you.

4 Now work in groups of four. Introduce your partner to other members of the group.
A: Jan, do you know Aki? She works in the Warsaw office.
B: No, I don't. Nice to meet you, Aki.

Name: _____
Office: _____
Job: Sales Manager
Department: Sales
Activities:
- visit clients
- have sales meetings
- travel for work

Name: _____
Office: _____
Job: Digital Designer
Department: Design
Activities:
- do research
- go to meetings
- design websites

Name: _____
Office: _____
Job: Admin Assistant
Department: Shipping and Receiving
Activities:
- write emails
- answer the phone
- process orders

Name: _____
Office: _____
Job: Finance Officer
Department: Finance
Activities:
- analyse data
- write reports
- go to meetings

Name: _____
Office: _____
Job: Production Engineer
Department: Production
Activities:
- process orders
- travel for work
- write reports

Name: _____
Office: _____
Job: IT Specialist
Department: IT
Activities:
- solve staff computer problems
- go to meetings
- call customers

Name: _____
Office: _____
Job: Finance Officer
Department: Finance
Activities:
- analyse data
- write reports
- do research

Name: _____
Office: _____
Job: Sales Manager
Department: Sales
Activities:
- have meetings
- travel for work
- manage sales team

Name: _____
Office: _____
Job: Marketing Manager
Department: Marketing
Activities:
- travel for work
- have meetings
- analyse data

Name: _____
Office: _____
Job: Warehouse Manager
Department: Shipping and Receiving
Activities:
- process orders
- make calls
- write reports

Name: _____
Office: _____
Job: IT Specialist
Department: IT
Activities:
- analyse data
- go to meetings
- write reports

Name: _____
Office: _____
Job: Admin Assistant
Department: Marketing
Activities:
- go to meetings
- make calls
- write reports

Name: _____
Office: _____
Job: Sales Manager
Department: Sales
Activities:
- analyse sales data
- visit clients
- have sales meetings

Name: _____
Office: _____
Job: Finance Officer
Department: Finance
Activities:
- analyse data
- write reports
- go to meetings

Name: _____
Office: _____
Job: Digital Designer
Department: Design
Activities:
- do research
- go to meetings
- design marketing material

Name: _____
Office: _____
Job: Marketing Manager
Department: Marketing
Activities:
- travel for work
- have meetings
- analyse data

2 Doing business — Photocopiables

2.1 Grammar

1 Choose the correct option.
1. I usually have *a / some* pasta for lunch.
2. We don't have *a / any* gym at work/school.
3. My office/school is in *a / an* old building.
4. I write a lot *of / any* emails every day.
5. Not *many / much* people are in class today.
6. My school/company doesn't have *much / many* employees/teachers.
7. How *much / many* time do you have for lunch?
8. How *much / many* different products does your company (or a company you know well) sell?

2 Work in pairs. Tell your partner if sentences 1–6 in Exercise 1 are true for you. Then ask and answer questions 7 and 8.

3 Work in pairs. Read the instructions on your card and practise the conversations.

Student A

1
Student B is a supplier of office supplies and you are the customer. Your order is wrong. Phone Student B. Tell him/her what you have using the list below.
I have a / an / some / a lot of …

- an envelope
- not much paper
- a laptop
- some coffee
- not any pens
- some notebooks

2
You work for a food delivery company and Student B is your customer. He/She phones you because an order is wrong. Check what he/she has against the order below and decide if each item is correct or not.
How much/many … do you have?

- a lot of pasta
- two sandwiches
- a drink
- a lot of fries
- a lot of rice

Student B

1
You are a supplier of office supplies and Student A is your customer. He/She phones you because an order is wrong. Check what he/she has against the order below and decide if each item is correct or not.
How much/many … do you have?

- a lot of envelopes
- a lot of paper
- a laptop
- 100 pens
- some notebooks

2
Student A works for a food delivery company and you are the customer. Your order is wrong. Phone Student A. Tell him/her what you have using the list below.
I have a / an / some / a lot of …

- an orange
- some pasta
- ten sandwiches
- ten drinks
- a lot of fries
- not much rice

2 Doing business — Photocopiables

2.4 Work skills

1 Put the words in the correct order to make questions and responses.

1 do / days / how / cleaning service / a / many / need / you / the / ?
_____ CL

2 work / how about / we / before / coming / start / ?
_____

3 can't / I'm / we / sorry / no, / .
_____

4 there / are / offices / many / how / ?
_____

5 cleaner / the / time / what / come / want / you / do / to / ?
_____

6 fine / yes, / that's / .
_____

7 do / can / that / team / your / ?
_____

8 the / wash / can / coffee cups / cleaner / the / ?
_____

9 doesn't / no, / it / .
_____

10 can / we / yes, / .
_____

11 is / how / that / much / ?
_____

12 do / to / us / what / want / you / do / ?
_____

13 workers / there / many / how / are / ?
_____

14 Monday / next / about / how / ?
_____

15 start / when / your / can / team / ?
_____

16 price / include / the / does / cleaning products / ?
_____

2 Is each phrase in Exercise 1 a question for a cleaning company (CO), a question for a client (CL) or a response (R)?

3 Work in pairs. Write a conversation between a cleaning company and a client. Use as many of the phrases from Exercise 1 as possible.

4 Practise your conversation.

3 Changes — Photocopiables

3.3 Grammar

1 Complete the sentences with the Past Simple form of the verbs in brackets.

1. We _____ (have) a few problems with our email system last week.
2. I _____ (not send) you the email this morning, sorry.
3. It _____ (not be) a very good year.
4. Sharon _____ (buy) some advertising space in the magazine.
5. They _____ (meet) the clients yesterday.
6. We _____ (build) strong relationships with our suppliers this year.
7. Unfortunately, we _____ (not hit) our targets last month.
8. They _____ (win) a lot of new business last year.

Student A

2 Read the email about a company's performance last year. Was it a good year? Why? / Why not?

> **To:** All staff
> **From:** marvin.austin@crimcakes.co.uk
> **Subject:** Yearly summary
>
> Dear team,
>
> First, a very happy new year to you all! Thank you for all your hard work last year. Because of you, we grew ¹_____ from ten stores to fifteen. We also hit our sales target of 50% growth.
>
> We had a few problems with ²_____ at the start of the year, but then we went to some events and found a new one. We also built strong relationships with ³_____ at these events.
>
> We spent a lot of money on advertising, and bought ⁴_____ in the local media. Because of this, we made good progress with our plans and won a lot of new business in the ⁵_____ area.
>
> You were great last year. Well done, everyone!
>
> Best regards,
> Marvin Austin

3 Work in pairs. Take turns to ask questions to find out the missing information in your email.

Student B

2 Read the email about a company's performance last year. Was it a good year? Why? / Why not?

> **To:** All staff
> **From:** marvin.austin@crimcakes.co.uk
> **Subject:** Yearly summary
>
> Dear team,
>
> First, a very happy new year to you all! Thank you for all your hard work last year. Because of you, we grew our business from ten stores to fifteen. We also hit ¹_____ of 50% growth.
>
> We had a few problems with our supplier at the start of the year, but then we went to ²_____ and found a new one. We also built strong relationships with new clients at these events.
>
> We spent a lot of money on ³_____, and bought adverts in the local media. Because of this, we made good progress with ⁴_____ and won a lot of new business in the Green Hill area.
>
> You were ⁵_____ last year. Well done, everyone!
>
> Best regards,
> Marvin Austin

3 Work in pairs. Take turns to ask questions to find out the missing information in your email.

3 Changes — Photocopiables

3.4 ▸ Work skills

1 Match 1–6 with a–f to make questions about projects.

1	Why did	a	go well?
2	What went	b	well, in particular?
3	What didn't	c	to change?
4	How did	d	this happen?
5	What was	e	it go, generally?
6	What do we need	f	the problem?

2 Match these answers (a–f) to the questions (1–6) in Exercise 1.

a We didn't communicate the changes well.
b We made some mistakes with production.
c It was OK.
d We need to improve our design.
e The problem was with quality.
f We met some new clients.

3 Work in pairs or small groups. Take turns to turn over two cards at a time. When you have a match, keep that pair of cards.

4 Count your cards. The student with the most cards is the winner.

How did it go, generally?	What went well, in particular?	What didn't go well?
What was your experience?	What did you do?	What happened?
Why did this happen?	What was the problem?	What do we need to change?
It went well.	We met each deadline.	We had a problem with the design.
The teamwork was good.	We found a new supplier.	We didn't communicate the changes well.
We didn't meet the deadline.	We didn't hit our targets.	We need to make the process clearer.

4 Travelling for work — Photocopiables

4.3 Grammar

1 Complete the email with the Present Continuous form of the verbs in the box.

do   go   not have   manage   meet   prepare   start   write

Hi Paolo,
How are you? How ¹_____ things _____ in Rio? I ²_____ to let you know how things are here. As you know, we opened the new warehouse last week, and today we ³_____ work on our first major orders. We ⁴_____ any problems, and everything is going as planned.
Mika ⁵_____ the process and she ⁶_____ really well.
I ⁷_____ a new client this week, so right now I ⁸_____ for that. Things look good here.
Speak soon,
Gisele

2 Play the board game in small groups.

20 they / manage / the project well?	21 	22 I / not finalise / the sales figures	23 I'm not …	Finish
19 she / work / from home	18 Miss a turn.	17 you / try / to hire new staff	16 Go down to square 13!	15 
10 we / have / a sales meeting	11 Alex / talk / customers?	12 I'm …	13 Mike and Rita / deal / with the paperwork	14 Go up to square 27!
9 Go down to square 4!	8 My colleagues …	7 you / expect / a delivery?	6 	5 they / prepare / for a meeting
Start	1 Carlos / not work / today	2 My teacher …	3 Go up to square 11!	4 we / have / problems / with the design

118   Business Partner A2   © Pearson Education 2020

4 Travelling for work — Photocopiables

4.4 Work skills

1 Complete the conversations with the words in the box.

| adding | audio | connection | frozen | off | microphone | mute | repeat | sharing | up |

1 **A:** I can't hear you. Are you on _____?
   B: No. I think my _____ isn't working.
2 **A:** The screen is _____.
   B: Try turning _____ your video. Let's have a(n) _____ call.
3 **A:** Sorry, can you _____ that, please?
   B: Yes, I said …
   A: You're breaking _____. The internet _____ is slow.
4 **A:** I'm _____ Sergei to the call.
   B: OK. I'm _____ my screen. Can you see it?

2 Work in pairs. Practise the conversations in Exercise 1.

3 Work in groups. Take turns to pick up a card and read out the problem for other students to suggest solutions. The first student to suggest a solution wins the card. The student with the most cards at the end is the winner.

The connection isn't very good.	You're breaking up.	My camera isn't working.
My microphone isn't working.	I can't see you.	I can't hear you.
The screen is frozen.	I can't hear Diana.	My internet connection is slow.

Business Partner A2 © Pearson Education 2020 119

5 Organising — Photocopiables

5.1 Grammar

1 Write a sentence with *be going to* for each picture. Use the prompts and one of the verbs in the box.

change   launch   not be   not phone   provide   set up

1 they / a new product
   _____

2 he / a stand
   _____

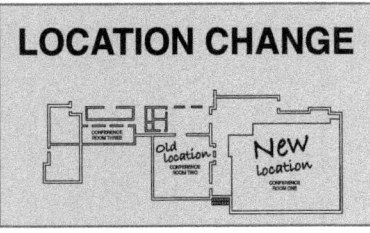

3 we / in the usual location
   _____

4 they / freebies
   _____

5 she / her boss
   _____

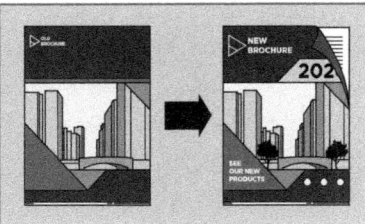

6 I / the brochures
   _____

2 Work in pairs. You are going to organise a stand at an upcoming conference to represent your company. Use the ideas below to plan what your stand is going to look like. Make notes.

- launch a product?
- free coffee?
- brochures?
- furniture?
- freebies?
- size of stand?
- technology/TVs?

We're going to …   *Our stand is going to …*   *There is/are going to be …*

3 Present your ideas to the class. Listen to other presentations and ask questions.

Are you going to … ?   *Is your stand going to be … ?*   *When/How/What are you going to … ?*

120   Business Partner A2   © Pearson Education 2020

5 Organising — Photocopiables

5.4 > Work skills

1 Put the conversations in the correct order.

1
- [ ] **B:** I think there are some very good presentations.
- [ ] **A:** Yes, I agree.
- [ ] **A:** How are you?
- [ ] **B:** Very well, thanks.
- [ ] **A:** What do you think of the conference?

2
- [ ] **B:** At the Central. And you?
- [ ] **B:** I flew here yesterday.
- [ ] **A:** Where are you staying?
- [ ] **A:** Hi! When did you arrive?
- [ ] **A:** At the Central, too!

3
- [ ] **B:** Yes, but it isn't near the city centre.
- [ ] **A:** You're right, but there was some useful information in it.
- [ ] **B:** Yes, you're right. What do you think of the hotel?
- [ ] **A:** Did you like the presentation?
- [ ] **A:** It's very comfortable.
- [ ] **B:** It was a bit boring.
- [ ] **A:** You're right, but it's easy to get there by taxi.

2 Work in pairs. Practise the conversations in Exercise 1.

3 Work in groups of three. Practise making small talk with clients. Follow the instructions below.

Student A Pick a white card and ask for Student B's opinion.

Student B Give your opinion.

Student C Pick a grey card and agree or disagree with Student B's opinion.

A: What do you think of … ? / Do you like the … ?
B: I think … / It's … but …
C: Yes, you're right. / Yes, but …

city centre?	your room?	trade fair?	food?
conference?	presentation?	hotel?	football match last night?
agree	agree	agree	agree
disagree	disagree	disagree	disagree

Business Partner A2 © Pearson Education 2020

6 Products — Photocopiables

6.3 Grammar

1 Rewrite the sentences in the Present Simple Passive.

1 People grow coffee in Brazil.
   Coffee _____.
2 We produce our T-shirts to the highest standard.
   Our T-shirts _____.
3 We don't test our products on animals.
   Our products _____.
4 We make our bags from recycled materials.
   Our bags _____.
5 We design the packaging in London.
   The packaging _____.
6 We pay the factory workers a fair price.
   The factory workers _____.

2 Work in pairs. What stages do you think are involved in the production of chocolate and magazines?

3 Work in pairs. Read the steps and complete the missing information.

Student A

Follow the steps below.

- Read your sentences to your partner, who will tell you which verb to use. Complete your sentences with the correct Present Simple active or passive form of the verbs.
- Listen to your partner's sentences and choose the best verb from the box below to complete each one.

Verbs for Student B:

| agree | create | decide | design |
| edit | select | send | write |

Chocolate production

1 Chocolate _____ from cocoa beans.
2 Farmers pick and _____ the cocoa beans to manufacturers.
3 The dirty cocoa beans _____.
4 The beans _____ at temperatures of 100–150°C.
5 Cocoa butter _____ from the cocoa.
6 The cocoa butter _____ again to create a liquid.
7 Other ingredients, such as sugar and milk, _____ to the cocoa butter to make different flavours.
8 The liquid chocolate _____ into chocolate bars.

Student A

Follow the steps below.

- Listen to your partner's sentences and choose the best verb from the box below to complete each one.
- Read your sentences to your partner, who will tell you which verb to use. Complete your sentences with the correct Present Simple active or passive form of the verbs.

Verbs for Student A:

| add | clean | heat | make (x2) |
| roast | sell | separate | |

Magazine production

1 A publication date _____ by the publisher and the printers.
2 A schedule of work _____.
3 The editorial team _____ on the topics for the magazine.
4 Writers research and _____ the material.
5 The content _____ by an editorial team.
6 Photos and artwork _____.
7 The magazine pages _____ by a special design team.
8 The magazine _____ to the printing company for printing.

6 Products — Photocopiables

6.4 Work skills

1 Choose the correct option to complete the conversations.

1

A: ¹*Could / Do* we talk about price now?
B: How ²*many / much* units do you want to order?
A: ³*We like / We'd like* 4,000. Is there a discount?
B: Sorry, but that's not possible. The price is €3 ⁴*for / per* unit.
A: How about for 5,000 units?
B: Hmm, I think we can ⁵*change / do* that. How about €2.75?
A: OK, that's better.

2

A: When can you ⁶*deliver / place* the order?
B: In two weeks.
A: OK, we'll pay 50% ⁷*for / on* signature, and 50% on delivery.
B: I'm afraid for new clients it's 75% on signature and 25% on delivery.
A: I'm afraid I can't agree ⁸*for / to* that.
B: How ⁹*about / many* 60/40?
A: Yes, I think that's ¹⁰*OK / right*.

2 Practise the conversations in Exercise 1 in pairs.

3 Read the information on your card and roleplay with a partner.

Student A

You are the director of a large language school. Use the information below to place an order for new books with Student B.

You want to buy new books for your students before the new term starts on 2 September, so that your teachers can plan their lessons before classes start. At the moment you have around 450 students, but this number might increase. Try to get as close as possible to the terms you want.

Price	€15 per book
Amount	450+
Delivery	15 August
Payment	by bank transfer on delivery

Student B

You are a publisher of language books. Use the information below to receive an order for new books from Student A.

Try to get as close as possible to the terms you want.

Price	€25 per book on orders below 750 €20 per book on orders over 750
Delivery	12 September
Payment	by bank transfer on signature

7 Competition — Photocopiables

7.3 Grammar

1 Find and correct one mistake with comparative or superlative adjectives in each sentence.

1. I like shopping there – they have most knowledgeable staff around.
2. Their products are the cheaper on the market.
3. The survey shows that people think they have the worse customer service.
4. The third option is the most good value for money.
5. It's official: we have the more satisfied customers in the industry!
6. They have most reliable service, in my experience.
7. Sales are the friendlier department in the company.
8. This company offers the most wide range of services.

2 Work in groups. Take turns to compare your internet service providers. The highest score each time wins.

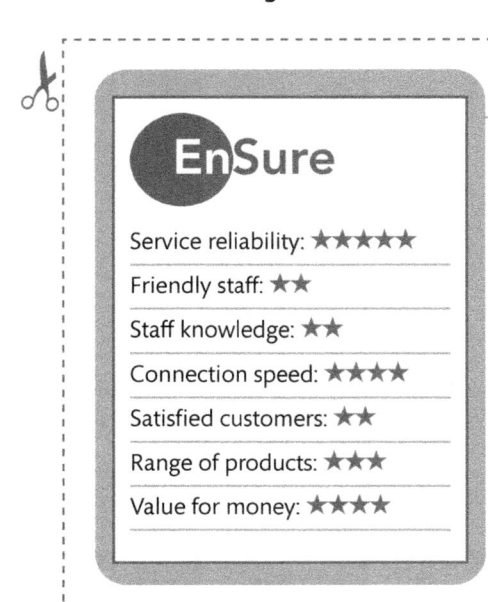

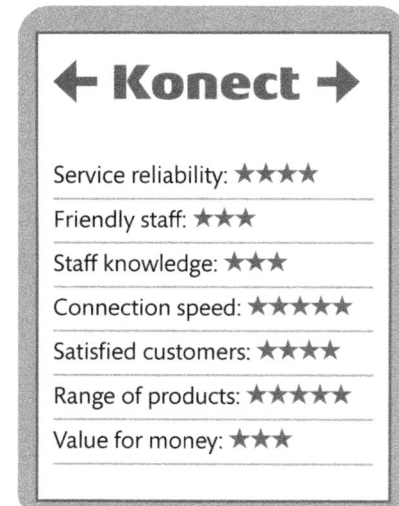

EnSure
- Service reliability: ★★★★★
- Friendly staff: ★★
- Staff knowledge: ★★
- Connection speed: ★★★★
- Satisfied customers: ★★
- Range of products: ★★★
- Value for money: ★★★★

SmarTech ✓
- Service reliability: ★★
- Friendly staff: ★★★★★
- Staff knowledge: ★★★★★
- Connection speed: ★★
- Satisfied customers: ★★★
- Range of products: ★★★★
- Value for money: ★★★★★

← Konect →
- Service reliability: ★★★★
- Friendly staff: ★★★
- Staff knowledge: ★★★
- Connection speed: ★★★★★
- Satisfied customers: ★★★★
- Range of products: ★★★★★
- Value for money: ★★★

VPQ
- Service reliability: ★★★
- Friendly staff: ★★★★
- Staff knowledge: ★★★★
- Connection speed: ★★★
- Satisfied customers: ★★★★★
- Range of products: ★★
- Value for money: ★★

7 Competition

Photocopiables

7.4 ▶ Work skills

1 Complete the sentences from presentations with the words in the box.

| about | aim | based | everyone | finally | have | move | provider |

1. So, good morning _____.
2. The _____ of today's presentation is to tell you about our new product.
3. Let's _____ on to our main products and services.
4. I'll talk _____ what we do and where we operate.
5. We _____ offices in every major European capital.
6. We're _____ in Tokyo.
7. We're the main _____ of insurance services in the country.
8. _____, I can answer your questions at the end.

2 Imagine you work for a company that you know well and/or would like to work for. Use the questions to prepare a short presentation about it.

Company history
- How old is your company?
- Where are you based?
- What do you do?
- How big is your company?

Products and services
- What are your main products and services?
- What else can you do?
- Where can you deliver?

3 Work in pairs. Practise 'speed-presenting' using your cards and the information from Exercise 2. Follow these steps.
- Student A, turn over a card and complete the sentence(s) on it with information about your company.
- Turn over another card and do the same. Continue until your teacher asks you to stop.
- Give Student B as much information about your company as you can.
- Move on to the next Student B and do the same.
- Continue until the time is up or until you are back in your original seat.

4 Swap roles and repeat the activity in Exercise 3.

I'm … , an employee at …	The aim of today's presentation is to …	Let's start with …	Let's move on to …
First, … Then, … Finally, …	I'll tell you about …	I'll explain …	I'll talk about …
We are the … provider of …	We're based in …	We have offices in …	We provide a range …
We can …	We'll …	Now let's talk about …	We can …

8 Jobs — Photocopiables

8.3 Grammar

1 Choose the correct option to complete the conversations.

1. **A:** *Did you ever manage / Have you ever managed* a team?
   B: Yes, when I *worked / have worked* at Hawson's, from 2015 to 2018.
2. **A:** *Did he go / Has he been* to Japan?
   B: Yes, he *went / 's been* there many times.
   A: When *was / has been* the last time he went?
   B: Last year, I think.
3. **A:** I *worked / 've worked* for many different companies like this.
   B: When *did you start / have you started* working here?
   A: Three years ago.
4. **A:** Tell me about your experience.
   B: Well, I *was / 've been* a Project Manager with Veronex from 2010 to 2019, then I *started / 've started* working here.
   A: I see. *Did you work / Have you worked* anywhere else in the same type of position?

2 Use the prompts below to create questions about past experiences.

1 give / a presentation	Details:
2 design / a website	Details:
3 organise / an event	Details:
4 manage / an international team	Details:
5 miss / an important deadline	Details:
6 have / a job interview	Details:
7 write / a professional profile	Details:
8 write / a report in English	Details:
9 lead / a meeting	Details:
10 use / a job website	Details:

3 Ask people in the class if they have done the things in Exercise 2. Find people who answer 'Yes' and write complete sentences in the first column of the table with their name, e.g. *Juan has given a presentation*. Then find out more information and write notes in the second column.

A: Have you ever … ?   **B:** Yes, I have. I …   **C:** When did you … ?

8 Jobs — Photocopiables

8.4 Work skills

1 Complete the questions with the words in the box. There are three words you do not need.

| had   helped   leader   main   problems   questions   sessions   staff   why   work |

1 Can you tell me about your _____ experience?
2 What are your _____ strengths?
3 How have you _____ to motivate staff?
4 Have you ever organised training _____?
5 Have you ever _____ problems with difficult people?
6 _____ do you want to work for our company?
7 Do you have any _____ for me?

2 Match the answers (a–g) to the questions (1–7) in Exercise 1.
a Yes, I've done a lot of staff training and given presentations.
b I started in sales, then I moved into marketing.
c Yes, I had a member of my team who always missed deadlines.
d Yes, how many people are in each team?
e Your organisation has an excellent reputation.
f I have excellent IT skills.
g I've always set goals with staff.

3 Think about your own answers to the questions in Exercise 1 and make notes.

4 Work in pairs. Take turns to interview your partner using the questions in Exercise 1. Follow the instructions on your card.

Student A

Interview Student B for the job of Project Manager. Every time he/she says one of the words below, cross it out.

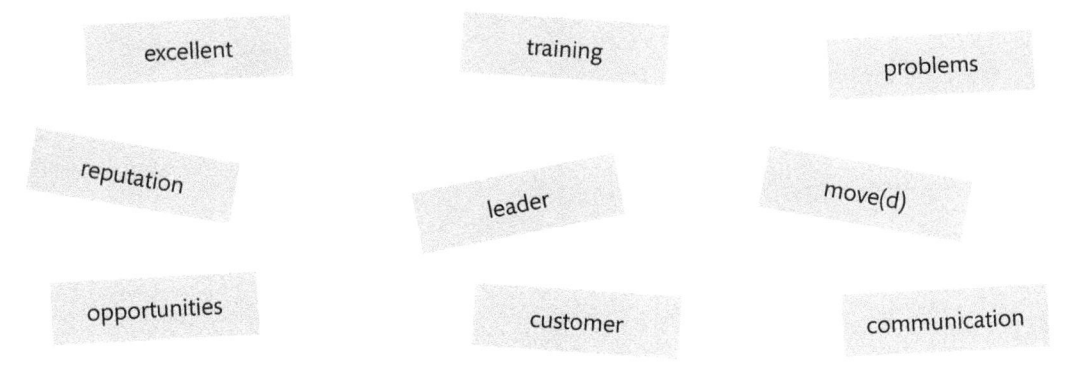

excellent   training   problems
reputation   leader   move(d)
opportunities   customer   communication

Student B

Interview Student A for the job of Team Leader. Every time he/she says one of the words below, cross it out.

staff   goals   motivate
experience   good   strengths
skills   presentation(s)   company

Business Partner A2 © Pearson Education 2020

Photocopiables teacher's notes

1.3 ❯ Grammar

- Tell students that they are going to practise forming questions.
- Give everyone a copy of Exercises 1–5.
- Ask students to complete the questions in Exercise 1 individually and if there is time, get them to compare answers in pairs before class feedback.
- Check answers with the class.
- Move on to Exercise 2. Put students in pairs to ask and answer the questions. Pre-service students can talk about a company they know well or would like to work for.
- When they have finished, ask a few students to share their answers with the class.
- Introduce Exercise 3. Put students in groups of three and give each group a set of cards. Ask students to deal out the cards equally and to keep the cards in front of them, face-down, without looking at them. Students take turns to turn over a card and place it face-up in front of them, until the two halves of a question appear (this can be combined from any two of the cards face-up). If no question appears after the first round, students keep laying a card face-up on top of the previous one in front of them. As soon as a question appears, the first student to provide a logical answer takes those two cards and wins a point.
- Play continues until all the cards have been turned over. The player with the most points wins.
- Move on to Exercise 4. Ask each group to turn over and spread out the cards with the question beginnings. Students choose four cards each and, individually, write a question for each one. Monitor and check they are forming their questions correctly, and offer help where needed.
- When students are ready, move on to Exercise 5. Put them in pairs and ask them to ask and answer their questions from Exercise 4.

1
1 are **2** do **3** are **4** Do **5** does **6** Does **7** is **8** does

1.4 ❯ Work skills

- Tell students that they are going to practise talking about people and roles.
- Give everyone a copy of Exercises 1–4.
- Ask students to complete the conversations in Exercise 1 individually. Point out that only one word is missing from each gap.
- Get students to compare answers in pairs, then check answers with the class. If there is time, you could put students in pairs to practise the conversations.
- Move on to Exercise 2. Give each student a role card, and ask them to complete the *Name* and *Office* sections individually. Tell them that they can invent the information if they prefer, and explain that for *Office*, they need to write the city they work in. If there are more students than cards in your class, some cards can be duplicated.
- Introduce Exercise 3. Put students in pairs and ask them to practise introducing themselves to each other, asking and answering about their job, where they work, which department they are in and what they do. You may wish to go over the useful language in the Speaking box on page 15 of the Coursebook first.
- For Exercise 4, join pairs together into groups of four and ask students to introduce their partner to the other group members, telling them what they can remember about their roles. Monitor and make notes on any common errors/examples of good language to highlight during feedback.
- When they have finished, ask a few students to introduce people from their group to the class.
- Have a brief feedback session, highlighting any points you noted while monitoring.

1
1 this, works, Nice, too **2** do, do **3** work, in **4** do, am/'m
5 for, don't / do not

2.1 Grammar

- Tell students that they are going to practise talking about things you can and can't count.
- Give everyone a copy of Exercises 1–3.
- Ask students to complete Exercise 1 individually.
- Check answers with the class.
- Move on to Exercise 2. Put students in pairs to discuss which sentences from Exercise 1 (1–6) are true for them. If they are not true, they should change them to make them true. Students also ask and answer questions 7 and 8.
- When they have finished, ask a few students to share their answers with the class.
- Introduce Exercise 3. Keep students in the same pairs and give a set of cards to each pair. Give them time to read the instructions and think about what they are going to say. Go round and offer help where necessary.
- When they are ready, students roleplay conversations 1 and 2 in their pairs. Monitor and check they are forming the questions and answers correctly, and make notes on any common errors/examples of good language to highlight during feedback.
- When they have finished, ask pairs which parts of each order were correct.
- Have a brief feedback session, highlighting any points you noted while monitoring.

1
1 some 2 a 3 an 4 a lot of 5 many 6 many
7 much 8 many

3
1 Correct: a laptop, some notebooks
2 Correct: a lot of fries

2.4 Work skills

- Tell students that they are going to practise making agreements.
- Give everyone their own copy of the worksheet.
- Ask students to complete Exercise 1 individually and if there is time, get them to compare answers in pairs before class feedback.
- Check answers with the class.
- Move on to Exercise 2. Get students to complete it individually or, in weaker classes, in pairs, then check answers with the class.
- Introduce Exercise 3. Put students in pairs to write a conversation for a meeting between a cleaning company and a potential client. Encourage them to use as many of the questions and responses from Exercise 1 as they can, and to invent others where necessary. Go round and offer help where necessary.
- When students are ready, move on to Exercise 4, asking them to practise their conversations in their pairs. If there is time, they could swap roles and practise again.
- Choose two or three pairs to perform their conversations for the class.
- Find out who managed to use the most phrases in their conversations.

1/2
1 How many days do you need the cleaning service? CL
2 How about coming before we start work? CL
3 No, we can't. I'm sorry. / No, I'm sorry. We can't. R
4 How many offices are there? CL
5 What time do you want the cleaner to come? CL
6 Yes, that's fine. R
7 Can your team do that? CO
8 Can the cleaner wash the coffee cups? CO
9 No, it doesn't. R
10 Yes, we can. R
11 How much is that? CO
12 What do you want us to do? CL
13 How many workers are there? CO
14 How about next Monday? CL
15 When can your team start? CO
16 Does the price include cleaning products? CO

> **Photocopiables teacher's notes**

3.3 > Grammar

- Tell students that they are going to practise talking about the past.
- Give everyone a copy of Exercise 1.
- Read the instructions for Exercise 1 and ask students to complete it individually.
- Check answers with the class.
- Move on to Exercise 2. Put students in pairs and give them their respective copies of Exercises 2–3. Make sure they do not show them to each other at this stage.
- Give students 1–2 minutes to read their emails quickly (ignoring the gaps) and answer the question.
- Check the answer with the class.
- Introduce Exercise 3. Explain the activity and if necessary, do the first item in each email as an example. With stronger classes, students can do this as an oral activity, coming up with the necessary questions as they go along. Otherwise, ask students to write the questions for each gap first. Monitor while they are writing, checking they are forming their questions correctly, and offer help where necessary.
- When they are ready, students take turns to ask and answer their questions in order to complete the missing information in their emails. Go round and offer help where necessary.
- When students have finished, ask them to show each other their emails and check their answers.

1
1 had **2** didn't / did not send **3** was not / wasn't
4 bought **5** met **6** built **7** did not / didn't hit **8** won
2
Yes; they grew their business, hit their targets and won a lot of new business.
3
Student A
1 Q: What did we grow?
   A: the business
2 Q: What did we have (a few) problems with?
   A: our supplier
3 Q: Who did we build strong relationships with (at the events)?
   A: new clients
4 Q: What did we buy?
   A: adverts
5 Q: Where / In which area did we win a lot of new business?
   A: Green Hill
Student B
1 Q: What did we hit?
   A: our sales target
2 Q: Where did we go?
   A: some events
3 Q: What did we spend a lot of money on?
   A: advertising
4 Q: What did we make good progress with?
   A: our plans
5 Q: What were we/you last year?
   A: great

3.4 > Work skills

- Tell students that they are going to practise talking about projects.
- Give everyone a copy of Exercises 1–4.
- Ask students to complete Exercise 1 individually and if there is time, get them to compare answers in pairs before class feedback.
- Check answers with the class.
- Move on to Exercise 2. Students could do it individually or, if you are short of time, you could do it as a whole-class activity, checking answers as you go.
- As an extension, students could test each other in pairs: they cover the questions in Exercise 1 and take turns to point at a response for their partner to remember the question. Alternatively, they can practise the questions and answers in pairs.
- Put students in pairs or small groups and introduce Exercise 3. Give each pair/group a set of question (shaded) and response (white) cards, and ask them to lay them out on the table face down, in two groups: questions and responses.
- Students take turns to turn over one card from each group. If they match, the student who turned them over keeps them. If they don't, the student turns them over again, keeping them in the same place. Students need to try and remember where the cards are in order to make matching pairs.
- Monitor and be on hand to check/adjudicate if students have doubts.
- For Exercise 4, ask students to count up the pairs of cards they have. The student in each pair/group with the most cards wins.

1
1 d **2** b **3** a **4** e **5** f **6** c
2
1 a **2** f **3** b **4** c **5** e **6** d

4.3 ▶ Grammar

- Tell students that they are going to practise using the Present Continuous to talk about things happening now.
- Give everyone their own copy of the worksheet.
- Introduce Exercise 1 and ask students to complete it individually.
- Check answers with the class.
- Move on to Exercise 2. Tell students that they are going to play a game, put them in groups of three or four and ask each group to use one copy of the board. They will also need one dice per group and a counter for each player. If you do not have these, ask each student to use a small piece of paper with their name on as a counter. Instead of a dice, they can use a coin. Each turn, they toss the coin and if it lands on 'heads', they move one square; if it lands on 'tails', they move two squares.
- Students take turns to move and make sentences using the Present Continuous. When they land on a square with prompts (e.g. square 1), they need to use them to form a correct sentence. If they land on a square with a sentence starter (e.g. square 2), they need to say a true sentence about that person/people. If they land on a square with a picture (e.g. square 6), they need to say a sentence about that picture. If students land on a square with an arrow (e.g. square 3), they move up or down to the square indicated, without having to say a sentence.
- Monitor and help/adjudicate where necessary.
- The first player to reach the 'Finish' square wins.

1
1 are (things) going   2 am/'m writing   3 are/'re starting
4 are not / aren't having   5 is/'s managing   6 is/'s doing
7 am/'m meeting   8 am/'m preparing

2
1 Carlos isn't / is not working today.
4 We're / are having problems with the design.
5 They're / are preparing for a meeting.
6 She's / is repairing/mending/fixing a/the computer.
7 Are you expecting a delivery?
10 We're / are having a sales meeting.
11 Is Alex talking to customers?
13 Mike and Rita are dealing with the paperwork.
15 They're / are having/drinking coffee/tea. / They're / are talking/chatting. / They're / are having a meeting.
17 You're /are trying to hire new staff.
19 She's / is working from home.
20 Are they managing the project well?
21 He's / is giving a presentation. / He's / is describing a graph/chart. / He's / is presenting (sales figures).
22 I'm not / am not finalising the sales figures.

4.4 ▶ Work skills

- Tell students that they are going to practise talking about problems with teleconferencing.
- Give everyone a copy of Exercises 1-3.
- Ask students to complete Exercise 1 individually.
- Check answers with the class.
- Put students in pairs for Exercise 2, and ask them to practise the conversations. When they have finished, you could ask them to swap roles and practise again.
- Introduce Exercise 3. Put students in small groups and give each group a set of cards in a pile face down. Students take turns to pick up a card and read out the problem on it. The first student in the group to give a logical solution wins the card.
- Monitor and help/adjudicate where necessary.
- The student with the most cards at the end wins.

1
1 mute, microphone   2 frozen, off, audio
3 repeat, up, connection   4 adding, sharing

5.1 Grammar

- Tell students that they are going to practise talking about intentions.
- Give everyone their own copy of the worksheet.
- Introduce Exercise 1. With weaker classes, elicit the first sentence as an example and write it on the board. You could also match the verbs in the box to the pictures before students write their sentences. Otherwise, ask students to work individually to write the sentences and if there is time, get them to compare answers in pairs before class feedback.
- Check answers with the class.
- Move on to Exercise 2. Put students in pairs and ask them to imagine they work together in the same company. Ask them to decide what type of company it is. Then explain that they have been asked to design their company's stand for an upcoming conference.
- Students use the prompts to discuss and plan what they are going to include in the stand, what it will look like, etc. Go round and help with vocabulary where necessary, and encourage students to make notes.
- For Exercise 3, ask each pair to present their stand to the rest of the class. Encourage other students to listen and make notes in order to ask any questions they have at the end.
- You could finish by holding a class vote for the best stand.

1
1 They're / are going to launch a new product.
2 He's / is going to set up a stand.
3 We aren't / are not going to be in the usual location.
4 They're / are going to provide freebies.
5 She isn't / is not going to phone her boss.
6 I'm / am going to change the brochures.

5.4 Work skills

- Tell students that they are going to practise making small talk.
- Give everyone a copy of Exercises 1–3.
- Ask students to complete Exercise 1 individually. With weaker classes, you could give them the first line of each conversation.
- Check answers with the class.
- Put students in pairs for Exercise 2, and ask them to practise the conversations. When they have finished, you could get them to swap roles and practise them again.
- Introduce Exercise 3. Put students in groups of three (A, B and C). Give each group a set of cards and ask them to place them face-down in two piles in the middle of the group. Student A starts by picking a card from the pile with questions (white cards) and asking for Student B's opinion. Student B then responds. Student C takes a card from the other pile (grey cards) and agrees or disagrees with Student B's opinion. It is then Student B's turn to take a card from the first pile, then Student C's, etc.
- If a student uses their card correctly, they keep it. If not, it is returned to the bottom of the pile.
- Look at the example with students before they begin. During the activity, monitor and help/adjudicate where necessary.
- The activity ends when all the cards are used. The student with the most cards wins.

1
1 A: How are you?
   B: Very well, thanks.
   A: What do you think of the conference?
   B: I think there are some very good presentations.
   A: Yes, I agree.
2 A: Hi! When did you arrive?
   B: I flew here yesterday.
   A: Where are you staying?
   B: At the Central. You?
   A: At the Central, too!
3 A: Did you like the presentation?
   B: It was a bit boring.
   A: You're right, but there was some useful information in it.
   B: Yes, you're right. What do you think of the hotel?
   A: It's very comfortable.
   B: Yes, but it isn't near the city centre.
   A: You're right, but it's easy to get there by taxi.

6.3 Grammar

- Tell students that they are going to practise talking about the stages of a production process using the Present Simple Passive.
- Give everyone a copy of Exercises 1 and 2.
- Focus attention on Exercise 1 and ask students to complete it individually.
- Check answers with the class.
- Move on to Exercise 2. Put students in pairs and ask them to think about the different stages involved in each process. Tell them not to worry if they cannot think of all the stages, just to think of what is involved. Go round and help with ideas (see answer key below) and vocabulary where necessary. If you think your students will struggle to come up with ideas, or if time is short, this could be done as a whole-class activity.
- Put students in pairs for Exercise 3, and give each pair a set of cards. Give students time to read the sentences and ask any questions they have about vocabulary. Explain that they each have a set of sentences to complete and their partner has the missing verbs. Look at the instructions with them and point out that they have to use the passive or active form of the verbs. You could ask students to work individually first, to think what the missing verbs might be. Point out that they should ignore the verbs in the box below their sentences at this stage – these verbs complete their partner's sentences, not their own. If necessary, complete the first item for each student as an example with the class. During the activity, monitor and offer help where necessary.
- When they have finished, ask students to show each other their sentences and check their answers.
- Check answers with the class.

1
1 Coffee is grown in Brazil.
2 Our T-shirts are produced to the highest standard.
3 Our products aren't / are not tested on animals.
4 Our bags are made from recycled materials.
5 The packaging is designed in London.
6 The factory workers are paid a fair price.

2
Possible answers
Chocolate: cocoa beans are grown, picked, sold, made into chocolate, packaged
Magazines: articles are planned, written, edited; photos are taken; the magazine is designed, printed

3
Student A
1 is made   2 sell   3 are cleaned   4 are roasted
5 is separated   6 is heated   7 are added   8 is made
Student B
1 is agreed   2 is created   3 decide(s)   4 write   5 is edited
6 are selected   7 are designed   8 is sent

6.4 Work skills

- Tell students that they are going to practise placing an order.
- Give everyone a copy of Exercises 1 and 2.
- Ask students to complete Exercise 1 individually and if there is time, get them to compare answers in pairs before class feedback.
- Check answers with the class.
- Put students in pairs for Exercise 2, and ask them to practise the conversations. When they have finished, they could swap roles and practise them again.
- For Exercise 3, put students in new pairs and give each student their card. Give them plenty of time to read their information and think about what 'deals' they could make. Go round and offer help where necessary. Explain that students probably won't be able to get exactly what they want, so they should be prepared to be flexible.
- When they are ready, students begin their conversations. You could remind them of the phrases in the Speaking box and the conversation flow chart on page 65 of the Coursebook to help them.
- Monitor and make notes on any common errors/ examples of good language to highlight during feedback.
- Have a brief feedback session, highlighting any points you noted while monitoring.
- If your students need more practice, you could put them in new pairs and ask them to swap roles and repeat the activity.

1
1 Could   2 many   3 We'd like   4 per   5 do   6 deliver
7 on   8 to   9 about   10 right

7.3 ▶ Grammar

- Tell students that they are going to practise comparing things.
- Give everyone a copy of Exercises 1 and 2.
- Ask students to complete Exercise 1 individually and if there is time, get them to compare answers in pairs before class feedback.
- Check answers with the class, writing (or inviting students to write) the correct forms on the board so students can check their spelling.
- Move on to Exercise 2. Put students in groups of three or four and give each group a set of cards. Ask students to take one card each and explain that it gives information about their internet service provider.
- The first player starts by picking a category and telling the group how many stars it has for that category (e.g. Friendly staff: five stars). The other players then take turns to tell the group about the same category, using a comparative form, e.g. *My company is better value for money than SmarTech.*
- Students then say which company has the highest value in that category using a superlative form e.g. *EnSure has the most reliable service.* Whoever has that card wins the round. Ask students to keep a record of who wins each round. The student who wins most rounds wins the game.
- Before students start the game, point out that they should use different adjectives to talk about each category; you could go through the categories with them and elicit how they can change each one using adjectives (*service reliability: (most) reliable service; staff knowledge: (most) knowledgeable staff, range of products: (widest range); connection speed: fast(est) connection,* etc.). During the game, monitor and make notes on any common errors/examples of good language to highlight during feedback.
- When they have finished, you could ask a few students to shuffle the cards and play again, in the same or new groups.
- Have a brief feedback session, highlighting any points you noted while monitoring.

1
1 I like shopping there – they have **the** most knowledgeable staff around.
2 Their products are the **cheapest** on the market.
3 The survey shows that people think they have the **worst** customer service.
4 The third option is the **best** value for money.
5 It's official: we have the **most** satisfied customers in the industry!
6 They have **the** most reliable service, in my experience.
7 Sales are the **friendliest** department in the company.
8 This company offers the **widest** range of services.

7.4 ▶ Work skills

- Tell students that they are going to practise presenting.
- Give everyone a copy of Exercises 1–4.
- Ask students to complete Exercise 1 individually and if there is time, get them to compare answers in pairs before class feedback.
- Check answers with the class.
- Move on to Exercise 2. Ask students to work individually to think of answers to the questions about a company they know well and/or would like to work for and make notes.
- Introduce Exercise 3. Put students in pairs and give a set of cards to each pair, in a pile face down. Explain that they are going to practise 'speed presenting'. Student Bs sit with the cards, and Student As turn over a card and complete the sentence on it with information about their company from Exercise 2. After 1–2 minutes, clap your hands loudly and explain that Student As should move clockwise round the class to the next Student B. Repeat for as long as time allows, or until Student As arrive back in their original position.
- For Exercise 4, students swap roles and repeat the activity, with Student Bs 'speed-presenting'.
- During the activity, monitor and make notes on any common errors/examples of good language to highlight during feedback.
- Have a brief feedback session, highlighting any points you noted while monitoring.

1
1 everyone 2 aim 3 move 4 about 5 have 6 based
7 provider 8 Finally

8.3 ▶ Grammar

- Tell students that they are going to practise talking about experiences and completed past events.
- Give everyone their own copy of the worksheet.
- Ask students to complete Exercise 1 individually.
- Check answers with the class, and elicit that we use the Present Perfect when talking about experiences in general, but we need to use the Past Simple when a specific date or specific details are mentioned. (The first conversation in Exercise 1 provides a good example.)
- Move on to Exercise 2. Explain the activity and tell students that if they cannot fit writing a question in or next to the table, they can write their questions in their notebook. Ask students to complete the exercise individually. Monitor and help where necessary.
- Check answers with the class.
- Introduce Exercise 3. Tell students that they need to walk around the class, asking questions to find someone who each sentence is true for. If possible, ask them to try and find a different person for each sentence. Demonstrate by asking the question for sentence 1 around the class until someone says *Yes*. With weaker classes, elicit the question they need to ask for each sentence, i.e. *Have you ever given a presentation? Have you ever designed a website?*, etc.
- Tell students that when they find someone who answers *Yes*, they need to write a sentence about that person. Point to the example sentence in the instructions for Exercise 3. Then, they need to ask follow-up questions using the Past Simple to find out more details, e.g. *When/Where/Why did you … ?* Demonstrate with the student who answered *Yes* in your previous demonstration, and look at the example with the class.
- Ask students to stand up and walk around the class, asking and answering the questions. Monitor and check they are using the Present Perfect and Past Simple correctly, and make notes on any common errors/examples of good language to highlight during feedback.
- When they have finished, students could compare their information in pairs.
- You could also ask a few students to share anything interesting they found out with the class.
- Have a brief feedback session, highlighting any points you noted while monitoring.

1
1 Have you ever managed, worked
2 Has he been, 's been, was   **3** 've worked, did you start
4 was, started, Have you worked
2
1 … has given a presentation.
2 … has designed a website.
3 … has organised an event.
4 … has managed an international team.
5 … has missed an important deadline.
6 … has had a job interview.
7 … has written a professional profile.
8 … has written a report in English.
9 … has led a meeting.
10 … has used a job website.

8.4 ▶ Work skills

- Tell students that they are going to practise asking and answering job interview questions.
- Give everyone a copy of Exercises 1–4.
- Ask students to complete Exercise 1 individually and if there is time, get them to compare answers in pairs before class feedback.
- Check answers with the class.
- Introduce Exercise 2, and ask students to complete it individually.
- Check answers with the class. You could then put students in pairs and get them to practise the questions and responses.
- Move on to Exercise 3. Give students time to think about their own answers to the questions in Exercise 1 and make notes. They can either answer as themselves or, if they do not have work experience, they could invent their answers. Monitor and offer help with ideas and vocabulary.
- In Exercise 4, students play 'Job Interview Bingo'. Put them in pairs, give them their respective role cards and explain the activity: Student A interviews Student B first, using the questions in Exercise 1, and crosses out any words from the list which Student B uses, in the style of 'Bingo'. When they have finished, students swap roles and repeat. During the activity, monitor and make notes on any common errors/examples of good language to highlight during feedback.
- When students have finished, ask them to count up how many words from the list their partner used and award a point for each one. The student with the most points wins.
- Have a brief feedback session, highlighting any points you noted while monitoring.

1
1 work **2** main **3** helped **4** sessions **5** had **6** Why
7 questions
The words *leader*, *problems* and *staff* are not needed.
2
1 b **2** f **3** g **4** a **5** c **6** e **7** d

1 ▶ Working day — Extra vocabulary practice

1 Choose the correct word.
1 Elena *calls / goes / reports* customers on the phone every day.
2 I need to *do / go / call* to meetings with different customers.
3 We'd like to *book / make / write* a meeting room for tomorrow.
4 Felix *answers / reports / processes* all the orders for the company.
5 Anastasia *calls / calculates / makes* all the costs for each project.
6 Aleks *makes / does / works* research to find new projects.

2 Choose the correct word.
1 I *never / always* travel for work. I work in this office every day.
2 Our Sales Manager *often / never* visits clients in other countries – two or three times a month.
3 I *sometimes / usually* travel with the Sales Manager – but nine times out of ten, it's me and a Sales Assistant.
4 Clients *often / rarely* visit our offices. Our offices are small, so we visit our clients.
5 The manager is great because she *rarely / always* helps us with problems.

3 Complete the dialogue with words from the box.

| agenda   brief   budget |
| calculate   presentation |
| update |

A: Now, the first thing for me to do is send out the ¹_____ for tomorrow's meeting. I think the first item is an introduction to the project.
B: That's right. Then we can discuss what work we need to do and create the ²_____ for that work.
A: Good. I also have a(n) ³_____ from the Project Manager in China. So, we also need a(n) ⁴_____ meeting to ⁵_____ the production costs and then decide the final budget.
B: I agree. Then I can prepare the ⁶_____ for the meeting with the senior executives next week.

4 Complete the emails with phrases from the box.

| afraid   available |
| change   good |
| how about   see you |
| shall   that's fine   we can |

Hi Felix
I need to ¹_____ the date of our meeting. I have a client meeting then. Are you ²_____ on Friday afternoon at 4 p.m.?
Best regards,
Sandra

Hi Sandra
Sorry, I'm ³_____ I'm busy then.
⁴_____ Friday morning?
Best regards,
Felix

Hi Felix
Friday morning at 11 is ⁵_____.
⁶_____ we meet in my office?
Sandra

Hi Sandra
Yes, ⁷_____. Perhaps ⁸_____ go to lunch after that. ⁹_____ then.
Felix

5 Complete the dialogue with one word in each gap.

Jan: Hello, Marek. ¹_____ is Bella from Italy.
Marek: Hello, Bella. Nice to ²_____ you.
Bella: You, too.
Jan: Bella ³_____ in the Rome office.
Marek: Which ⁴_____ do you work in?
Bella: Marketing.
Marek: What do you ⁵_____?
Bella: I'm responsible for social media.

Marek: ⁶_____ is your manager?
Bella: Italo Benino.
Marek: I know him. ⁷_____ is he?
Bella: He's fine.
Marek: Do you ⁸_____ Pierina Scarlatti?
Bella: Yes, I do. She's ⁹_____ IT specialist.
Marek: Do you ¹⁰_____ for work a lot?
Bella: Not very much. I spend most of the time in Rome.

2 Doing business — Extra vocabulary practice

1 Complete the text with the correct form of a word from the box.

deliveries   delivers   delivery   orders   supplier   supplies

Haklan Furniture is a furniture [1]_____. It [2]_____ more than one thousand office and home furniture products. Kurt is a driver for the company. He [3]_____ products from the warehouse to the customers. He makes [4]_____ six days a week to private customers and seven days a week to large shops. There is no [5]_____ charge for [6]_____ over £1,000.

2 Complete the dialogue with one word in each gap.

M = Melanie   GS = Graham Sands

M: Haklan Furniture. Good morning. Melanie [1]_____. How can I [2]_____ you?
GS: Morning! This is Graham Sands from SND Stores. I'd [3]_____ to order some office tables.
M: Of course. Do you [4]_____ the product reference number?
GS: Yes, it's XK 00-72-345.
M: Thanks. That's the grey colour, isn't it?
GS: That's right. And how [5]_____ are they?
M: They're £175 per table.
GS: How much does delivery [6]_____?
M: It's free. How [7]_____ tables do you need?

3 Put sentences a–g in the correct order to complete the dialogue from Exercise 2.

GS: We need eight tables.
M: [1]_____
GS: [2]_____
M: [3]_____
GS: [4]_____
M: [5]_____
GS: [6]_____
M: You're welcome. Can I help you with anything else?

a £1,400, OK. And can you deliver them tomorrow?
b That's fine. I'd like to order those now, please.
c Thank you for your help.
d Eight. OK, so that's £1,400 in total.
e I'm very sorry, we can't. They're not in stock, but we can deliver them on Saturday. Is that OK?
f Great. I'll put your order on the system.

4 Match these question halves.

1 What do you want
2 How about
3 How many
4 What time do
5 How much
6 Does the price
7 When can you
8 Is there

a coming before 7 a.m.?
b time do the chefs need?
c include materials?
d a place for the materials?
e you want us to come?
f start?
g workers are there?
h the staff to do, exactly?

5 Match the answers (a–h) with questions 1–8 from Exercise 4.

a How about 5.30 p.m.?
b No, it doesn't. There's an extra charge for those.
c We can't. I'm sorry.
d How about next week?
e Cook and serve the food, provide drinks, clear the tables and wash the dishes.
f Yes, there is a room on the first floor.
g It's usually five workers for a house this size.
h About five hours.

3 Changes — Extra vocabulary practice

1 Complete the text with verbs from the box. Use the verbs in the form they appear in the box. There is one extra verb.

change   create   expand
hire   launch   move
open   produce   start

You do not always need a lot of money to ¹_____ a company. My company is now very successful so we need a bigger factory. We now plan to ²_____ the factory from Germany to Vietnam. We ³_____ metal parts for old cars and we ⁴_____ a new product in two months. I plan to ⁵_____ our market and to ⁶_____ sales offices in China and Malaysia. This means we have to ⁷_____ new staff. We also plan to ⁸_____ a new company this year.

2 Complete the email with phrases from the box

best wishes
to all staff
please do the following
we thank you for your help

1 _____
Next week we start work in our new offices. In preparation for this, on Friday
2 _____:
• put everything from your desk in a box.
• write your name on the box and leave it on the desk.
• check the plan attached and find your new workspace.
3 _____
4 _____
Tetsuo

3 Complete the email with one word in each gap.

¹_____ employees
As you know we move offices next week. Before you leave on Friday, can you please ²_____ these instructions:
• don't leave anything in your desk.
• put everything in the company boxes.
Over the weekend, we will take them to the new offices.
We ³_____ your cooperation.
⁴_____
Ruth

A: Morning. ¹*How / Where* did the project go, generally?
B: Not very ²*OK / well*. We ³*had / got* some problems.

A: ⁶*What / How* was the problem?
B: We ⁷*not / didn't* have enough staff.

A: Really? What ⁴*happened / went*?
B: We ⁵*made / did* some mistakes with planning.

A: I see. What do we need to ⁸*make / change*?
B: Well, we need to ⁹*improve / communicate* the project planning process.

4 Choose the correct word.

5 Complete the dialogue with one word in each gap.
A: What was your experience of the last factory project?
B: ¹_____ was OK, I'm happy to say.
A: Good, so tell me, what ²_____ well, in particular?
B: The construction of the building was quick.
A: What didn't ³_____ well?
B: ⁴_____ was a delay with the equipment we ordered.
A: What did you ⁵_____?
B: We found another supplier, but we still didn't meet the first deadline.

4 Travelling for work — Extra vocabulary practice

Box: airport book bus customs delayed passport rent stay

1 Complete the email with words from the box.

Hi Gina,

Sorry I didn't have time to meet you at the [1]_____ yesterday. Unfortunately, the flight to Melbourne was [2]_____ for seven hours, so I was very tired when I finally got to Australia. It also took a long time to go through [3]_____ control. Then I was stopped at [4]_____ and the officer opened both my suitcases. I decided to go to the hotel by [5]_____. I was too tired to drive but I know we need to [6]_____ a car for the rest of the trip. I'll arrange it when you arrive here tomorrow.

It was a good idea to [7]_____ the Ace Grand Hotel for the trip. I didn't want to [8]_____ in an apartment like last time.

Best wishes,
Karl

2 Choose the correct word.

Ray missed his flight [1]*control / connection* to Manchester because of the bad weather. When he got to [2]*departures / arrivals* there were no other flights that day. They were all [3]*stopped / cancelled* so he had to go by [4]*coach / train*. But it took all night because it [5]*departed / stopped* at every station. When Ray got to Manchester, he took a [6]*coach / taxi* to save time and go straight to the offices.

3 Put the letters in bold in the correct order to make words about the airport.

1 D **PETARREU** S   2 T **AMINER** L   3 A **VRILA** RS   4 B **GAGAG** E

4 Complete the travel itinerary.

- 28th September: fly to Beijing; meet Ms Chen at [1]a _ _ _ _ _ _ _.
- 28th September: [2]s _ _ _ at the Three Bridges Hotel in Beijing for three nights.
- 1st October: take the train to Shanghai and meet Mr. Kelly on the [3]p _ _ _ _ _ _ _.
- 1st October: stay at the company's [4]a _ _ _ _ _ _ _ _ for four nights.
- 2nd October: [5]r _ _ _ a car for two days to attend the conference on 3–4 October.
- 5th October: take return [6]f _ _ _ _ _ to London.

Mark, can you [7]b _ _ _ my train ticket from Beijing to Shanghai, please? Also, from Shanghai to London, do you know where my flight [8]c _ _ _ _ _ _ _ _ is?

5A Complete the conversation with phrases from the box. There is one extra phrase.

Box: are frozen I'm here I'm sharing it's working on mute see turning you there working

Elsa: Good morning everyone. Are [1]_____?
Khaled: Yes, [2]_____.
Carla: Me, too.
Elsa: Can you [3]_____ me?
Carla: Sorry, I can't see you.
Elsa: My camera isn't [4]_____. Just a moment. Is that better?
Everyone: Yes, [5]_____ now.
Elsa: Hans, [6]_____ you there? I can't hear you.
Hans: Oh sorry, Elsa. I was [7]_____. Can you hear me now?
Elsa: Yes. OK, let's start then.
Hans: Oh no! The screen is [8]_____.
Elsa: Try [9]_____ off your video.

5B Complete the rest of dialogue with one word in each gap.

Elsa: Let's have a(n) [1]_____ call, then. Khaled, please give us an update on the work.
Khaled: Sorry, can you [2]_____ that? The [3]_____ isn't very good, you're [4]_____ up. My internet is very slow.
Elsa: [5]_____ up and I'll call you all [6]_____.

5 › Organising — Extra vocabulary practice

1 Complete the paragraph with verbs from the box. There is one extra verb.

attend   design   launch
meet   provide   receive
set

As you know, trade fairs are a good opportunity to ¹_____ clients. I'm happy to announce that we're going to ²_____ the Chicago Trade Fair again this year. We're planning to ³_____ the new app for our services there. We need to ⁴_____ up a large stand this year because we have more products. We are also going to ⁵_____ a new brochure for the fair. And of course, as usual, we're going to ⁶_____ our visitors with drinks, snacks and some freebies.

2 Complete the words which collocate with *exhibition*.

1 Each employee needs to have an exhibition b_____ to wear on their jackets.
2 We have a large exhibition s_____ this year, so we can show more products.
3 The new exhibition c_____ in the town can hold over 5,000 visitors.
4 The exhibition b_____ has photographs and information about all our products.
5 This year, our stand is in the main exhibition h_____ and not one of the smaller rooms.

3 Complete the dialogue with phrases from the box.

can I help   can I take   for me   give her   I have your
it's about   not available   you say that

A: Good morning! How ¹_____ you?
B: I'd like to speak to Ms Garten.
A: Ms Garten? I'm sorry she's ²_____ right now. She's in a meeting. ³_____ a message
B: Yes, can you tell her that Axel Pfeiffer called from the German office? ⁴_____ the trade fair in Poland next month.
A: OK, the trade fair in Poland next month. Can you spell your name ⁵_____, please?
B: It's P-F-E-I-F-F-E-R.
A: Sorry, can ⁶_____ again?
B: Yes, of course. It's P-F-E-I-F-F-E-R.
A: OK, thank you, Mr Pfeiffer. Can ⁷_____ phone number?
B: She has my number.
A: OK. I'll ⁸_____ your message.

4 Choose the correct word.

A: What do you think of the conference?
B: I think it's ¹*little / a bit* boring.
A: Really? I ²*think / like* some of the stands.
B: Yes, I ³*agree / think*. Some of them are interesting.
A: Do you ⁴*enjoy / like* the hotel?
B: It's comfortable and near the trade centre.
A: You're ⁵*agree / right*, but it's noisy.
B: Yes, that's true, but it's not too bad. Did you ⁶*enjoy / think* the meal last night?
A: I thought it was delicious.

5 Choose the correct option.

1 I thought the exhibition was very interesting.
   a That's right.   b Yes, but it isn't boring.   c Yes, I agree.
2 Do you like the conference centre?
   a Yes, I agree.   b Yes, but it isn't near the city centre.   c Yes, you're right.
3 What do you think of the new app?
   a I like it.   b I think so.   c I agree.

6 Products — Extra vocabulary practice

1 Complete the words.
1 Our **e _ _ _ _ y** bill is expensive. We're paying too much for gas and electricity.
2 There is a lot of **p _ _ _ _ _ _ _ n** in this city, mainly from the cars.
3 To help protect sea life, the beach café is only going to sell drinks in glass bottles now, not **p _ _ _ _ _ c** ones.
4 Protecting the **e _ _ _ _ _ _ _ _ _ t** is very important for the future of the world.
5 We **r _ _ _ _ _ e** all the office paper, so we put it in a bin for paper only.
6 More and more factory **m _ _ _ _ _ _ s** are replacing human work.
7 I'm going to buy an **e _ _ _ _ _ _ c** car. They don't use petrol.
8 Digital **t _ _ _ _ _ _ _ _ y**, such as phones, laptops and watches, improves every year.

2 Complete the dialogue.
A: How can I ¹_____ you?
B: There's a ²_____ with the desks you delivered. Two of them are the wrong colour.
A: I'm sorry to ³_____ that. Can I have your order ⁴_____, please?
B: Of course. It's GH 4513.
A: I'm very ⁵_____ about the mistake. We'll change them for you.
B: Great, thanks.
A: Can I just check your delivery ⁶_____?
B: Unit 5, Harley Industrial Park. How long will it take? We need the desks as soon as possible.

3 Put the words in italics in the correct order.
A: (*days / take / it / three / might / .*) ¹_____ That's Friday. Is that OK for you?
B: (*manager / to / I'll / my / talk / .*) ²_____ I know he wants to set up the new office on Thursday.
A: (*important / this / I / is / understand*) ³_____ for you. Let me check with the Warehouse Manager. ... Hello? The Warehouse Manager says we can deliver them to you by 10 a.m. on Thursday. Is that OK?
B: Thanks. That's great.
A: (*else / with / you / anything / help*) Can I ⁴_____?
B: No. It's just the desks. (*you / help / your / thank / for / .*) ⁵_____
A: You're very welcome.

4 Put the dialogue in the correct order.
a We'll pay by bank transfer. I'll confirm my order by email.
b We'd like 1,000. Is there a discount?
c Monday next week.
d Well, the price is $10 each, and there's a 10% discount on orders of 1,000 or more.
e Sure. How many lamps do you want to order?
f Monday ... I think that's OK.
g We'd like to order some desk lamps, please.
h Great. And how will you pay?
i That's fine. So $9,000 in total. And when can you deliver the order?

1 _g_ 2 _____ 3 _____ 4 _____ 5 _____ 6 _____ 7 _____ 8 _____ 9 _____

5 Choose the correct word.
1 I'm *afraid / worry* that delivery usually takes four weeks.
2 Can you give us a *signature / discount* on the order? It's quite expensive.
3 I'll *confirm / deliver* the date by email.
4 How many desks do you want to *deliver / order* from us?
5 Could we pay 25% on *order / signature* and 75% on delivery?
6 We're very sorry about the *mistake / discount*. We'll send the correct goods immediately.

7 Competition — Extra vocabulary practice

1 Choose the correct word.
1 The *weight / speed / feature* of this printer is much faster than the other printer.
2 We want to give our customers a great user *point / life / experience* when they use our product.
3 The unique selling *point / value / feature* is that it is very light and very fast.
4 Our customers tell us that what they really want is *point / value / speed* for money – a good product for a good price.
5 The adverts highlight the important *features / life / experiences* of the new printer.
6 We've spent a lot of money on the *life / design / weight* of this product so that it looks good.
7 Customers complain that the product *life / speed / feature* of their phones is too short.
8 The total *speed / experience / weight* of the new product is less than 400 grams.

2 Complete the sentences.

> additional
> administration
> booking
> cancellation
> charge
> include
> fixed
> monthly

1 To maintain your Current Bank Account, there will be a(n) _____ fee of £10, paid at the start of every month.
2 After the original payment, customers can still upgrade the model of their hire car at any time, for a(n) _____ fee.
3 Customers who want to leave Calls4UMobile before the end their contract will have to pay a(n) _____ fee.
4 Our trainers' fees _____ three full days' training sessions, training materials and access to our online training blog.
5 All hotel reservations made by credit card will include a(n) _____ fee of £3.50.
6 Our three-day training programme is available for a(n) _____ fee of £5,000. We do not offer training for hourly rates.
7 The airline will _____ a fee for any requests to change flight details.
8 There is a(n) _____ fee of £25 to process your driver's application form.

3 Complete the presentation with one word in each gap.

Good afternoon, everyone. I'm Sonny Dharwan, the CEO of IKFServ. Thank you for ¹_____ this presentation. The ²_____ of today's presentation is to introduce my company to you.
First I'll ³_____ you about the history of the company. Then I'll ⁴_____ what we can do for your organisation. Then I'll ⁵_____ about our future plans. At the end, we'll have a ⁶_____ and answer ⁷_____.
So, OK, let's start …

4 Complete the text with words from the box. There are two extra words.

> based   offer   offices   provide   provider   qualities   started   supplied

The company ¹_____ in 2006. We are now the biggest ²_____ of technical help in the country. We're ³_____ in Germany and have ⁴_____ in India and China. We can ⁵_____ IT support twenty-four hours a day. We also ⁶_____ our customers with technology product solutions, including software.

5 Match the sentence halves.
1 We offer a wide
2 I'd like to talk
3 Let's move
4 Let's start
5 We can offer

a our services for a fee of $1,000 per month.
b about the new design.
c on to the services we provide.
d range of office furniture.
e with the history of our company.

8 Jobs — Extra vocabulary practice

1 Complete the text with words from the box.

analytical
communication
IT
language
motivated
organised
team-worker

My manager says I deal with customers really well, so I definitely have good ¹_____ skills. I enjoy working with other people on projects and believe that I am a good ²_____. I like to work with ³_____ people who don't miss deadlines. I have good ⁴_____ skills and speak Chinese, English and Spanish. I also like solving problems by looking at information so I can say that I'm ⁵_____. However, sometimes I have difficulty with some computer software, so my ⁶_____ skills are not so good. I think I am ⁷_____ because I always do my best.

2 Complete the words.

Marketing Manager Required

Job ¹A_____
We have an exciting ²v_____ in our marketing department for someone with the right skills and experience.
³E_____ skills and experience: • at least two-years' marketing experience • good design experience
⁴U_____ skills and experience: • can speak Spanish • a ⁵d_____ in Marketing
We will ⁶c_____ the ⁷c_____ for interview by Friday 14 October.

3 Choose the correct words to complete the dialogue.

A: Can you ¹*explain / tell* me about your work experience?
B: At the moment, I ²*work / became* as a designer in the Marketing department of the company.
A: Have you always worked in the Marketing department?
B: No, I ³*started / was* as an Admin Assistant in office facilities. I ⁴*made / became* a Designer in marketing after I completed a part-time degree.
A: I can see you also have a professional ⁵*organisation / qualification* in Marketing. When did you ⁶*move / become* to the Marketing department?
B: Three years ago.

4 Complete the questions with the phrases from the box.

organised training sessions
had problems with difficult staff
want to work for our company
helped to motivate your team
what are your main strengths

A: So, ¹_____?
B: I'm very hard-working. I don't stop until I've completed each task.
A: And how have you ²_____?
B: I always discuss new ideas with them and let them contribute to projects.
A: Have you ever ³_____?
B: Of course. I've done a lot of staff training and given presentations.
A: Have you ever ⁴_____?
B: Yes. That's normal for a team leader or manager.
A: Why do you ⁵_____?
B: Because I believe it's the best in this industry.

5 Complete the text with the words in the box.

analyse
candidates
communication
experience
motivate
opportunity
qualifications
reputation
strengths

I had an interview this morning. The company has a really good ¹_____ for career development and everyone wants to work there. It can offer me the ²_____ to develop my management skills. I think I have all the right ³_____ for the job – especially my degree and industry training. I told them that my ⁴_____ are working with other people and my ability to ⁵_____ information. There were four other ⁶_____ for the job and we had to work together as a team to solve some problems. We chose a leader, but his ⁷_____ skills weren't very good and we didn't understand what he wanted us to do. So, he found it difficult to ⁸_____ us. In the end I used my team-leader ⁹_____ to organise everyone to finish the task.

Business Partner A2   © Pearson Education 2020

Extra vocabulary practice Answer key

Unit 1

1 1 calls 2 go 3 book 4 processes 5 calculates 6 does
2 1 never 2 often 3 sometimes 4 rarely 5 always
3 1 agenda 2 brief 3 update 4 budget 5 calculate
   6 presentation
4 1 change 2 available 3 afraid 4 How about 5 good 6 Shall 7 that's fine 8 we can 9 See you
5 1 This 2 meet 3 works 4 department/office 5 do
   6 Who 7 How 8 know 9 an 10 travel

Unit 2

1 1 supplier 2 supplies 3 delivers 4 deliveries 5 delivery
   6 orders
2 1 speaking 2 help 3 like 4 have 5 much 6 cost
   7 many
3 1 d 2 a 3 e 4 b 5 f 6 c
4 1 h 2 a 3 g 4 e 5 b 6 c 7 f 8 d
5 1 e 2 c 3 g 4 a 5 h 6 b 7 d 8 f

Unit 3

1 1 start/create 2 move 3 produce 4 launch 5 expand
   6 open 7 hire 8 create/start
2 1 To all staff 2 please do the following 3 We thank you for your help 4 Best wishes
3 1 Dear 2 follow 3 appreciate 4 Regards / Best wishes
4 1 How 2 well 3 had 4 happened 5 made 6 What
   7 didn't 8 change 9 improve
5 1 It 2 went 3 go 4 There 5 do

Unit 4

1 1 airport 2 delayed 3 passport 4 customs 5 bus
   6 rent 7 book 8 stay
2 1 connection 2 departures 3 cancelled 4 train
   5 stopped 6 taxi
3 1 departures 2 terminal 3 arrivals 4 baggage
4 1 arrivals 2 stay 3 platform 4 apartment 5 rent
   6 flight 7 book 8 connection
5A 1 you there 2 I'm here 3 see 4 working 5 it's working
   6 are 7 on mute 8 frozen 9 turning
5B 1 audio 2 repeat 3 connection 4 breaking 5 Hang
   6 back

Unit 5

1 1 meet 2 attend 3 launch 4 set 5 design 6 provide
2 1 badge 2 stand 3 centre 4 brochure 5 hall
3 1 can I help 2 not available 3 Can I take 4 It's about
   5 for me 6 It's about 7 you say that 8 I have your
   9 give her
4 1 a bit 2 like 3 agree 4 like 5 right 6 enjoy
5 1 c 2 b 3 a

Unit 6

1 1 energy 2 pollution 3 plastic 4 environment 5 recycle
   6 machines 7 electric 8 technology
2 1 help 2 problem 3 hear 4 number 5 sorry 6 address
3 1 It might take three days. 2 I'll talk to my manager.
   3 I understand this is important 4 help you with anything else 5 Thank you for your help.
4 1 g 2 e 3 b 4 d 5 l 6 c 7 f 8 h 9 a
5 1 afraid 2 discount 3 confirm 4 order 5 signature
   6 mistake

Unit 7

1 1 speed 2 experience 3 point 4 value 5 features
   6 design 7 life 8 weight
2 1 monthly 2 additional 3 cancellation 4 include
   5 booking 6 fixed 7 charge 8 administration
3 1 attending 2 aim 3 tell 4 explain 5 talk 6 question
   7 session
4 1 started 2 provider 3 based 4 offices 5 provide/offer
   6 provide/offer
5 1 d 2 b 3 c 4 e 5 a

Unit 8

1 1 communication 2 team-worker 3 organised
   4 language 5 analytical 6 IT 7 motivated
2 1 Advert(isement) 2 vacancy 3 Essential 4 Useful
   5 degree 6 choose 7 candidates
3 1 tell 2 work 3 started 4 became 5 qualification
   6 move
4 1 What are your main strengths? 2 helped to motivate your team 3 organised training sessions 4 had problems with difficult staff 5 want to work for our company
5 1 reputation 2 opportunity 3 qualifications 4 strengths
   5 analyse 6 candidates 7 communication 8 motivate
   9 experience

Videoscripts

1.1.1 N = Narrator LW = Liz Warnock
EJ = Ellen James MC = Muj Choudhury
N: What do you do at work? This is the working day of three people. They work for three different companies: an event management school, a pharmaceutical research company and a tech company.
LW: My name is Liz Warnock and I'm the Student Services Manager at the Event Academy. I usually start work at 8.30 and finish at five, but I sometimes finish work later. When I'm in the office, I check emails and answer the phone, and I have a meeting with my manager on Mondays. I sometimes go to meetings in London. I never teach students and I rarely travel abroad for work. I take a break around eleven and I have lunch around one.
EJ: My name is Ellen James. I work at Small Pharma, a pharmaceutical research company and I'm a Senior Research Manager. I don't drive to work. I always cycle to and from work. I usually start work at 9.30 and I finish at 5.30. On Mondays I don't come into the office – I always work at home on Mondays. On Tuesdays I finish work at 3.30 and I collect my daughter from school. At work, I analyse data. I email other researchers and I make phone calls. I sometimes go to conferences, but I never work in a lab. My manager and I work in the same office and we often have meetings. My manager arrives at work at ten and he leaves at six. I usually have lunch at one and I either eat at my desk or in the kitchen.
MC: My Name is Muj Choudhury and I'm the Chief Executive Officer of a tech company, Voice IQ. I usually start work at 7.30 in the morning and I finish at around eight in the evening. We have offices around the country and on Monday mornings I always speak to my team. I usually go to our Manchester office on Thursdays and Fridays. I often write reports and I never do company accounts. I sometimes travel for work. We have an office in Sri Lanka, so I sometimes go there and I occasionally go to California to meet with my investors. Sam is our Chief Marketing Officer. Sam starts work at 8.30 and he finishes at 8 o'clock. Sam sometimes visits Voice IQ customers.

1.4.1 MH = Max Hartmann IN = Izabela Nowak
MS = Maria Stavrou JM = Josie Marr
MH: Maria, this is Izabela. She's our Office Manager here in London. Izabela, this is Maria, from the Madrid office. Can you show her around, please?
IN: Of course, no problem. Nice to meet you, Maria.
MS: Nice to meet you, too, Izabela.
MH: See you later.
IN: Which department do you work in?
MS: The sales department.
IN: So, who's your manager?
MS: Monica Lopez. She's the Regional Sales Director for Southern Europe. And I'm a Sales Manager for Spain.
IN: Oh, yes, I know Monica. She often visits this office.
MS: Right.
IN: Do you travel for work a lot?
MS: Yes, I do. I visit clients and I work with the local sales teams.
IN: What are your plans for this visit to our office?
MS: We usually have a planning meeting with the other sales teams when we visit. I give a presentation about my work, and they give an update on their activities.
IN: Well, I hope the meetings go well. Shall we?
…
IN: Hi, Josie.
JM: Hi.
IN: Maria, Do you know Josie?
MS: No, I don´t.
IN: Josie, this is Maria.
MS: Nice to meet you, Josie.
JM: Good to meet you, Maria.
MS: What do you do, Josie?
JM: I'm an Admin Assistant.
MS: And which department do you work in?
JM: I work in office facilities, but I work with all the departments.
MS: Oh, OK. And who manages that team?
JM: Pietro Russo. Do you know Pietro?
MS: No, I don't.
JM: What about you, Maria? What do you do?
MS: I am a Sales Manager with the Madrid team. I do research, analyse sales data, write reports, visit clients …
JM: That's interesting. I also help the sales team here in London. I help the team process orders – and I make calls and write a lot of emails to the team!
MS: You're obviously very busy then! Nice to meet you.

2.1.1 N = Narrator JL = Jodie Lundie
MM = Maxwell McKenzie
N: Every day The Good Eating Company serves breakfast and lunch to lots of customers at this café in London. How much food do they use and who supplies it? The Good Eating Company talks about orders, deliveries and popular food at one of their cafés.
JL: My name is Jodie Lundie and I'm Operations Manager for The Good Eating Company. The Good Eating Company runs cafés and restaurants throughout London and Ireland. We run around twenty-eight cafés and restaurants.
MM: I'm Maxwell Mckenzie and I'm one of the development chefs here at Good Eating Company. Six people work at this café. We serve tea and coffee throughout the day. We also serve freshly prepared breakfast and lunch, as well as snacks.
N: How much coffee do you sell at this café each week?
MM: We sell five different types of coffee. We serve over 500 cups of coffee a week. And we use over eight kilos of coffee beans. We sell a lot of flat whites, but we don't sell many espressos.
N: Who supplies your food and drink?
JL: We order from many different suppliers that we contact directly. Some of our suppliers are from abroad and some are from the UK. Where possible, we like to use local suppliers. 'Please can I place an order for tomorrow?' We like to place our orders by telephone in order to build a relationship with our suppliers.
N: How many deliveries do you have for this café each week?
JL: We have about twenty-five deliveries every week. We have a lot of deliveries in the morning but we do not have many in the afternoon. The deliveries of our fresh produce normally arrive any time between 5 a.m. and 9 a.m.
N: How much produce do you use at this café each week?
MM: We use over twenty kilos of potatoes; we use over thirty kilos of carrots and ten kilos of lettuce. We use over 300 eggs per week. We use them to make omelettes or scrambled eggs.
N: What do customers buy for lunch?
MM: Some customers buy just a sandwich; some customers buy a salad and some fruit, and lots of customers buy just a hot dish.
N: What do you buy for lunch?

2.4.1 IN = Izabela Nowak RH = Robert Harris
IN: Please, take a seat. Would you like a tea or coffee?
RH: No, thank you. OK, let me just check … So, there's the reception area, one big office, two meeting rooms and the staff kitchen area on this floor. And then, upstairs there's another big office and four individual offices.
IN: Yes, that's right. And there are two staff toilets, one on each floor, and the stairs.
RH: Two staff toilets and the stairs. And… what do you want the cleaner to do, exactly?
IN: OK. Well, erm, clean the desks, empty the bins and clean the floors.
RH: And… clean the two staff toilets and the kitchen area?
IN: Yes, yes. Can the cleaner wash the coffee cups?
RH: Yes, of course. And the office windows? Do you want us to clean the windows?
IN: No. We have a specialist company to clean the windows.
RH: And… how many days do you need a cleaning service?
IN: Five days, Monday to Friday. How many cleaners are there?
RH: It's usually one cleaner for an office of this size. What time do you want the cleaner to come?
IN: We usually start at 8.30 in the morning. And people usually go home at 5.30 p.m. How about coming before we start work? Can the cleaner do that?
RH: Yes, that's fine. The cleaner can do that. Before … 8.30 in the morning.
IN: How much time does the cleaner need?
RH: About three hours a day. So, fifteen hours a week.
IN: And… how much is that for fifteen hours a week?
RH: £300.
IN: Can you provide the cleaning products?
RH: Yes, we can.
IN: Does the price include cleaning products?
RH: No, it doesn't. There's a small charge for those.
IN: How much is that?
RH: It's £10 a week. So, the total per week is £310. We send an invoice each month.
IN: OK, we can agree to that.
RH: Is there a place for the cleaning products?
IN: Yes, there is a cupboard in the kitchen. There is cleaning equipment in there. When can the cleaner start?
RH: How about… next Monday?
IN: That's fine.

3.1.1 N = Narrator LJS = Leona Janson-Smith
MD = Morgan Dudley JD = Julie Deane
MK = Max Karie
N: Postmark is a company based in London. It sells quality cards and gifts. The Cambridge Satchel Company makes and sells bags. These are their stories.
LJS: My name is Leona Janson-Smith and I am a director at Postmark.
N: Who started the business?
LJS: My husband, Mark, started the business in 2004. He wanted to sell really good quality cards at a great price. After two years, in 2006, the annual turnover was approximately £120,000. Last year it was approximately £1.3 million.
N: How many stores and how many employees do you have?
LJS: We now have four stores and employ twenty-four people.
N: Postmark hired Morgan Dudley as Head of Operations in 2015. Morgan has a lot of experience in sales. Leona thinks this was an important decision for the business. Morgan helped them to expand the business.
MD: My name's Morgan Dudley. I studied fashion design in South Africa from 2003 to 2006.
N: When did you arrive in the UK and what did you do?
MD: I arrived in the UK in 2008 and I started as a Sales Assistant.
N: When did you join Postmark?
MD: I joined Postmark in 2013. I started as a Sales Associate and then I managed a store; and then I moved on to Head of Operations. I love the small business environment. Leona and Mark really look after their team and you're allowed a lot of flexibility.
JD: My name is Julie Deane. I created The Cambridge Satchel Company. I started the company in 2008 with £600. Four years later the company was valued at £40 million. When I started Cambridge Satchel there were brown bags, dark brown bags and black bags. But we then moved into a range of different colours. I decided to start a factory in 2011. We have 155 employees. Now we have shops in Cambridge, London, Oxford, Brighton and Edinburgh.

Videoscripts

MK: My name is Max Karie and I am Head of Special Projects with Cambridge Satchel Company. Before I joined The Cambridge Satchel Company, I had my own shop. I joined The Cambridge Satchel Company in 2012 to manage the sales of bags and accessories to other shops.
N: Max's job changed when The Cambridge Satchel Company opened their first shop in London.
MK: I started to work on store design, which is the look and the feel of the shop. My new job was to design our first shop. What I most enjoy about The Cambridge Satchel Company is that I have the freedom to work on creative projects and that is a real joy.

3.4.1 WJ = William James HS = Haru Sakai
EM = Ellen Morgan
WJ: Congratulations, Ellen and Haru. I saw the winter collection in the shops! I talked to customers and they really like it. They made a lot of very positive comments.
HS: Thanks, William. Ellen's designs are great.
WJ: Yes, well done, Ellen.
EM: Thanks, I'm very happy!
WJ: As you know, I set this meeting up because I wanted to talk to you about the production process of the winter collection.
EM: Yes, of course.
WJ: So, let's begin with your views. How did it go, generally?
EM: I think it went well.
WJ: Haru?
HS: Yes. I think so, too.
WJ: OK, let's start with the positives. What went well, in particular? Ellen?
EM: Well, the teamwork was really good. It was difficult at first, but then I started to ask questions. Everyone helped me ... and answered my questions! I learnt a lot.
HS: Yes, we have a great team.
WJ: Great. That's important.
EM: And I'm very happy with the design of the jackets. And you said the shops like it, too. So, we created a good design, I think.
WJ: Yes, I can see that. I have to ask ... what didn't go well? Anything? Haru, what was your experience?
HS: Well. Yes, there were one or two problems with the jackets. We had some problems with the supplier. First, there was a problem with the quality of the material.
WJ: So, what did you do?
HS: We changed to a different supplier. We got the right quality material from them.
WJ: OK, I see.
HS: But then, we had a problem with the manufacturer.
WJ: What was the problem?
HS: They didn't meet the deadline, so we delivered the jackets to the shops a few days late.
WJ: Why did this happen?
HS: Well, we didn't communicate the new dates for delivery of material to the manufacturer.
WJ: So, what do we need to change?
HS: Communicate the dates to everyone. We need to have regular update meetings with both manufacturers and suppliers.
WJ: I see.
HS: It was OK in the end. And the jackets are in the shops.
WJ: Yes, great work. Everyone's really happy with them!

4.1.1 N = Narrator CD = Claire Derrick
MD = Michaela Drake
N: In some jobs, employees travel for work. There are lots of different reasons for visiting other countries on business – for example, to visit clients or customers, to see colleagues in a different location, or to go to a conference. Claire works at the Event Academy, an event management school, and she often travels for work.

CD: My name is Claire Derrick and I am the Principal for the Event Academy. I travel quite often around Europe for work and I often travel in the UK. My next trip is to Oxford. I'm travelling with my colleague.
N: How are you getting there?
CD: We're renting a car because it's quicker than going by train. It takes about two hours. We're travelling there and back in one day.
N: Where are you meeting your client?
CD: We're meeting our client at his office in central Oxford. After Oxford I'm going to Manchester for two days for a conference. I'm going by train to Manchester and I'm staying in a hotel for one night.
N: What are you planning to do in the evening?
CD: In the evening, I'm planning to meet some friends and go to a restaurant.
N: Michaela works at Shed Collective, a digital design company.
MD: My name's Michaela Drake and I am an Operations and Client Director for Shed Collective. I travel quite regularly, sometimes within the UK, often near London, but sometimes also travel internationally. I'm travelling to Hong Kong for two weeks in September. On this trip I'm travelling alone, but previously I went to Hong Kong with two colleagues.
N: How are you getting there?
MD: I'm travelling to Hong Kong by aeroplane from London Heathrow airport to Hong Kong airport. I booked my flight one month ago and I booked it online.
N: Where are you staying?
MD: I'm staying in a hotel in central Hong Kong.
N: Why are you going to Hong Kong?
MD: I'm working with my client at their offices in central Hong Kong. It's in a tall building and it's on the 35th floor. Our client is opening a sports stadium and we're building the website for the sports stadium.
N: What are you planning to do in the evening?
MD: Some evenings I'm planning to do some sightseeing in Hong Kong and some evenings the client is taking me to restaurants. And I'm planning to do a cable car trip up a mountain where you get a really good view across Hong Kong.

4.4.1
Conversation 1
HS = Haru Sakai   WJ = William James
HS: Hello?
WJ: Hi, Haru. How's it going!
HS: William! Hello? Can you hear me?
WJ: Yes, I can. But you can't hear me, can you?
HS: I can't hear you, William. Are you on mute? Try unmuting your microphone.
WJ: Oh! Yes, sorry, I am. How about now? Can you hear me?
HS: Yes, no problem! It's OK now.
WJ: OK, great. So, how's it going with the new jeans collection?
HS: I finally had a call from the material supplier. He's sending me some information later today.
WJ: That's good.
HS: I'll have a look, then I'll send it to you.
WJ: Fantastic. Now, what about ...

Conversation 2
WJ = HS = Haru Sakai   William James
HS: William, Hello?
WJ: Hi, Haru.
HS: Are you there? The screen is frozen.
WJ: Are you there? The connection isn't very good.
HS: The connection isn't very good. You're breaking up.
WJ: Sorry, my internet connection is slow.
HS: Try turning off your video.
WJ: Sorry, can you repeat that, please?
HS: I said, try turning off your video. Let's have an audio call.
WJ: Hello? Can you hear me?
HS: Yes, I'm here.
WJ: Ah, yes, that's much better.
HS: OK, good.
WJ: We need to talk about the new designs. The client wants to change some details.
HS: OK, Ellen has a few ideas. She's working on two more designs. I have some drawings to show you.
WJ: Oh, great! Tell me more about that ...

Conversation 3
WJ = William James   MS = Maria Stavrou
MH = Max Hartmann
WJ: Hi, Maria.
MS: Hi, William.
WJ: Where's Max?
MS: Just a second. I'm adding him now.
WJ: Sorry, what did you say?
MS: I'm adding Max to the call.
WJ: Oh, OK.
MS: Hello, Max.
MH: Hi, Maria. Hi, William.
WJ: Maria, I can't see Max.
MS: Max, we can't see you.
MH: Sorry. My camera isn't working.
MS: Oh, OK. No problem. You can stay on audio.
MH: OK.
MS: I'm sharing my screen now. Can you see it?
MH: Yes.
WJ: Not yet. My internet connection is slow. Oh, OK, there it is. I can see it now.
MS: So, let's discuss these sales figures.
WJ: You have all the data now?
MS: Yes, I do.
WJ: Great.
MS: You can see the sales so far this year ...

4.4.2 WJ = William James
MH = Max Hartmann
WJ: Hello Max.
MH: Hello, William.
WJ: I can't hear you. Try unmuting your microphone.
MH: Sorry.
WJ: That's better.
MH: The connection isn't very good. Now the screen is frozen. Try turning your video off.
WJ: Can you hear me?
MH: Can you repeat that, please?
WJ: You're breaking up!
MH: Hang up! I'll call you back!
WJ: OK. Max?
MH: Hi, William.
WJ: Ah, that's much better!

5.1.1 N = Narrator MR = Martyn Roberts
N: Graduate Fashion Week is a fashion exhibition. It takes place every year in London and shows the best work by fashion students from all over the world. It needs a lot of planning.
MR: I'm Martyn Roberts. I'm the Managing Director of Graduate Fashion Week. Graduate Fashion Week is the world's largest and leading event for fashion graduates. Our show is going to open next week and it's going to be our 28th year. Our event is going to run for four days and it runs from 2 June to 5 June.
N: How many visitors are going to attend?
MR: We're going to have 30,000 visitors during those four days. It's a big event and there are more and more visitors each year. So many visitors are going to be coming. We print thousands and thousands of badges, brochures and lanyards.
N: What services are you going to provide?
MR: For our visitors, we're going to have bars and cafes as well as lots of fun things to do on our exhibition stands.
N: Who is going to have stands at the exhibition?
MR: There are going to be thirty-eight stands from our UK universities as well as forty international universities.
N: Popular brands like Givenchy, Ralph Lauren and LVMH are going to have stands at the exhibition. The exhibition is going to be huge. The building is 10,000 square metres and the catwalk hall is going to have seats for over 400 people. There are going to be three floors with exhibitions, sponsor stands, as well as the catwalk. The international section is going to show work from some of the graduates – fashion, accessories and shoes.
N: What else is going to happen at the exhibition?

Videoscripts

MR: There are going to be talks from all different people from the industry as well as twenty-four catwalk shows. And on our final evening we're going to have our gala awards show.
N: Good luck! We hope the event is going to be a great success!

5.4.1 JA = Julia Anderson   MH = Max Hartmann
MS = Maria Stavrou
JA: Max?
MH: Julia! How lovely to see you. I heard you were here. How are you?
JA: Very well thanks, and you?
MH: Good, good. Shall we get a coffee?
JA: That would be great.
MH: When did you arrive?
JA: Well, I went to Paris yesterday. I had some business meetings there and I flew here this morning.
MH: That sounds like a busy schedule.
JA: It is, but now I'm here I can relax and enjoy the conference.
MH: Yes, the conference will be great. By the way, what are you doing for lunch? Would you like to join me and my colleagues? I'll introduce you to Maria Stavrou, our new Sales Manager for your region.
JA: Thanks, I'd love to join you.
MH: Great! We're going to meet here at 12.30 and go to the restaurant.
JA: Sounds good. I'll see you back here.
MH: Absolutely.
...
MH: Oh, by the way, Julia Anderson is going to join us for lunch. She works for Urban Fashion.
MS: That's an important client for us.
MH: That's right. It's a good opportunity for you to meet her.
MH: Ah. Hello, Julia. Thanks for joining us.
JA: Thank you for inviting me.
MH: Let me introduce you to Maria, our new Sales Manager for your region.
JA: Hello, Maria. Nice to meet you.
MS: It's a pleasure to meet you, too.
MH: That was William. He's going to be five minutes late. Sorry about that.
JA: That's OK.
MH: So, what do you think of the trade fair?
JA: I think there are some good presentations. And I like some of the exhibitors' stands.
MS: Yes, I agree. I saw a presentation about the impact of technology on our industry this morning. It was very good.
MH: Yes, that sounds interesting.
JA: Yes, it does. So, where are you staying?
MH: At the Mason Park Hotel.
JA: That's where I am. Do you like the hotel?
MH: Well, it's comfortable and it's near a park.
JA: Yes, but it isn't near the city centre.
MS: Yes, it's a bit boring there. I wanted to visit the old town. I hear it's beautiful.
MH: Well, how about getting a taxi and having dinner in the city centre tonight? We can walk through the old town first.
MS: I'd love to.
MH: Would you like to join us?
JA: I'm sorry, but I can't. I have plans for this evening.
MH: Of course. No problem. So …

6.1.1 N = Narrator   LJS = Leona Janson-Smith
SM = Steve Morris   KM = Kate Morton
LFA = Lisa Francesca Anand
N: Technology has a big impact on our lives. But how will it change products and services in the future?
LJS: My name is Leona Janson-Smith and I'm a Director at Postmark. I think shops will still exist in ten years. I think there will be more online shopping, but people will still want to look at the things they're buying and touch and feel them. I think that in the future there will be robot shop assistants. Cash will become less and less popular and we will pay for things with our phones, our watches and with contactless credit cards. Packaging will change in the future. There will be less packaging on all products bought in store to reduce waste.
SM: My name is Steve Morris and I'm the CEO of the Morgan Motor Company. In the next five to ten years, electric cars and motorbikes will become very popular. Many people will buy them because they are good for the environment and they reduce pollution in our cities. Many people will choose to share cars. I think there might be driverless cars on the streets within the next five to ten years. Over the next ten years, Morgan will think about developing electric and hybrid cars. We won't plan to develop driverless cars, but we will continue to make exciting sports cars.
KM: I'm Kate Morton. I'm Trading Director for Fashion and Retail Personnel. I think technology will have an impact on clothes and soon we might go into a store and find clothes that change colour. We'll shop online and we'll try on clothes via an app on our mobile phones. In the next five to ten years, manufacturers will use recycled materials to make clothes and this will be better for the environment. People won't buy as many clothes, but if we need a new shirt or dress, then we might rent instead.
LFA: I'm Lisa Francesca Anand and I'm a travel journalist. I think hotels will be different in many ways in the future. There won't be a reception desk because guests will check in online. And when they arrive at the hotel, they will go straight to their room and open their door using an app on their smartphone. Guests will order food and drink via an app, and robots might deliver this to their rooms. Smart technology will also help hotels to save energy and reduce waste.

6.4.1 ED = Eduardo Dias   MS = Maria Stavrou
ED: The T-shirt designs are really nice, and we're definitely interested. Could we talk about price now?
MS: Yes, of course. So, how many T-shirts do you want to order?
ED: For this first order, we'd like 1,000, please.
MS: Well, for 1,000 T-shirts, the price is two euros fifty per T-shirt.
ED: That's quite expensive for a new brand in our stores. Can you give us a lower price? How about two euros per T-shirt?
MS: I'm afraid I can't agree to that. Because we're an ethical company, we pay a fair price to our cotton suppliers. And our T-shirts are 100 percent organic cotton. So, the price is two euros fifty on all orders below 2,000.
ED: OK, so 1,000 T-shirts, that's … 2,500 euros in total.
MS: Yes, that's right.
ED: OK, but could we pay 25 percent on signature and 75 percent on delivery?
MS: I'm sorry, I'm afraid for new clients it's 50 percent on signature and 50 percent on delivery.
ED: I see, 50 percent on signature and 50 percent on delivery. OK. When can you deliver the order?
MS: It might be… at the end of March.
ED: The end of March? We'd really like the order sooner. Can you deliver them by the 17th of March?
MS: Sorry, that's not possible. How about the 25th of March?
ED: The 25th of March?
MS: Yes.
ED: Does delivery usually take four weeks?
MS: No, it usually takes two weeks. The problem is, we had so many orders for that T-shirt last week, we have to request more from manufacturing.
ED: Hmm. I really wanted them sooner. OK. Is there a discount?
MS: How about 5 percent? That's 125 euros.
ED: How about 10 percent? 250 euros? What do you think?
MS: Well, I'm … OK, I think that's OK. What sizes do you want?
ED: We'd like 250 small T-shirts, 500 medium and another 250 large, all in black.
MS: OK. That's 250 small, 500 medium and 250 large.
ED: Yes, that's right.
MS: All black?
ED: Yes, only black.
MS: Only black. That's fine. I think we can do that.
ED: Great! We'll pay by bank transfer. Thank you.

7.1.1 N = Narrator   TB = Toby Blythe
GC = Graham Chapman
N: The Morgan Motor Company is a British car manufacturer that produces sports cars.
TB: I'm Toby Blythe and I'm Marketing Manager for Morgan Motor Company.
GC: My name is Graham Chapman. My job title is Technology Director.
TB: We make five different models of sports car. The Morgan Plus 4 was launched in 1950 and it's our most popular sports car. The Morgan Plus Six is a newer model. We launched it in 2019.
GC: The Plus Six is a brilliant car. The Plus Six has a much larger and more powerful engine than our Plus 4 model. The Plus Six goes faster than the Plus 4. The top speed of the Plus Six is 270 km per hour. The top speed of the Plus 4 is 170 km per hour.
TB: The Plus Six is more spacious than the Plus 4, making it more comfortable for taller drivers. The space behind the seats is bigger in the Plus Six, so there's more room for luggage. The Plus Six is wider and longer than the Plus 4.
GC: The Plus Six is heavier than the Plus 4. The Plus Six is 1,050 kilos where the Plus 4 is 900 kilos. The wheels – there's a very big difference. The Plus Six has bigger wheels than the Plus 4. The Plus Six uses nineteen-inch wheels, the Plus 4 uses fifteen-inch wheels.
TB: The Morgan Plus 4 is cheaper than the Plus Six. The Plus 4 costs £45,000 and the Plus Six costs £78,000. Morgan also make a three-wheeled sports car. The first model was produced in 1909. And the new model was launched in 2011. The 3 Wheeler is smaller and lighter than the Plus 4, but the top speed is around the same. It costs £39,000. The 3 Wheeler is hugely exciting to drive. There is nothing else on the road quite like it!

7.4.1 JP = Jonathan Potts
MH = Max Hartmann
JP: So, good morning. I'm Jonathan Potts. I'm Sales Director at Web Trade Builder. Thank you for attending this presentation. The aim of today's presentation is to introduce our company and services. First, I'll tell you a bit more about the company's history. Then, I'll explain our products and services and how we can help you. Finally, we'll have a question and answer session at the end.
So, let's start with more information about the company. Web Trade Builder started in 2001, and we are the biggest provider of e-commerce services in Europe. We're based in Birmingham, in the UK, and have offices in Madrid and Frankfurt. We provide a range of products and services for e-commerce, including websites, payment systems and secure payment wallets. We currently have over 20,000 clients and can offer the fastest, most secure payment packages on the web.
So, let's move on to our products and services. First, let's look at our website solutions. If you have a website, you can add our online shop to it. If you don't have a website, we can build a complete website, including an online shop.
Now let's talk about our credit card system. We created a secure credit card payment system that can manage payments from every country in the world. We can design a system that allows your customers to pay faster, wherever they are in the world. We can also store their details on our payment database, which is the most secure system in the world.
First, I told you about our company, then I told you about our products, and finally, I talked about the services that we offer. OK. So that's the end of my presentation. Does anyone have any questions?
MH: Yes. I'd like to ask…

Videoscripts

8.1.1 N = Narrator JW = James Warwick PB = Polly Barnes DC = Dan Cullen-Shute

N: People need different skills and experience in their jobs.
JW: My name is James Warwick. I'm a Senior Content Developer for an education company.
PB: My name is Polly Barnes and I am the Client Services Director at Creature, which is an advertising agency. I manage a team of people who speak to our clients every day.
N: What skills and personal qualities are important in your job?
JW: For my job I need communication skills to talk to customers. I also need analytical skills to assess information, analyse data and solve problems.
PB: You need to be able to understand people and communicate very well and you have to be able to express ideas very clearly. When you're working with an international team, you need to be good at communicating, reliable, but also have a positive attitude and to be funny and friendly.
N: How many companies have you worked for?
JW: I've worked for five different companies in the past, as a teacher and an editor, and I've also managed my own company.
PB: I've worked for three different advertising agencies.
N: Have you ever lived and worked abroad?
JW: I've lived and worked in three different countries. I was an English teacher in Malta from 2012 to 2014. I ran my own business in Valencia in Spain for two years from 2014 to 2016. And then I moved to Singapore. I worked as an editor for nine months in 2017. I've never worked in the USA or in South America, but I'd really like to.
PB: I've worked in Amsterdam and Eindhoven and Germany, and in Paris. In Paris I spent three months working on a television project where we made television and radio ads in French.

N: To own or run a business also requires particular skills. Dan Cullen-Shute is Chief Executive Officer at Creature.
DC: My name's Dan Cullen-Shute and I'm the Chief Executive Officer here at Creature. We're an advertising agency that I set up eight years ago with some friends. I've worked for three large businesses before I started Creature, so Creature is my fourth job. I manage the business. I have to be organised and decisive 'cause I have to make the final decision on what we do and what we don't do. To talk fluently or write well about ideas, and understand those ideas, is important. The team at Creature are a group of very hard-working people. We all work very closely together, and I think that ability to work well with people as part of a team is hugely important.

8.4.1 MR = Matt Reece AD = Angela Davis

MR: So, Angela, can you tell me about your work experience?
AD: Yes. Well, I work as a team leader in customer services for a retail company. I started my working life as a Shop Assistant and then I moved into customer services. I have a lot of experience dealing with customers.
MR: And what are your main strengths?
AD: I have excellent communication skills, both speaking and writing, but I think the most important skill is listening, really listening to your staff and customers.
MR: Yes, that's an important skill for customer services.
AD: I think I also have good problem-solving skills, as that's part of my job every day. It's essential to listen to customers and my team and help to solve their problems.
MR: What other skills do you have?
AD: I have good IT skills, because we deal with customers via many digital channels these days. And I have good people skills; I'm good at motivating my team to do their job well. That's essential when you manage Customer Service Advisers.
MR: How have you helped to motivate staff?
AD: Well, there are lots of ways to do that. I've always set goals with staff and when they meet those goals, we celebrate, for example. It's important to have a good team spirit. The job can sometimes be stressful, when customers get angry.
MR: Yes, you're right. And, have you ever organised training sessions?
AD: Yes, I've done a lot of staff training and given presentations.
MR: What about staff? Have you ever had any problems with difficult people in your teams?
AD: Yes, there have sometimes been problems between team members. I usually ...
MR: Yes, that's true. Why do you want to work for our company, Angela?
AD: I want to progress in my career and your company has an excellent reputation for customer service.
MR: Why do you want to leave your current job?
AD: I enjoy my work and I've learnt a lot, but your organisation has more opportunities.
MR: Where do you see yourself in five years?
AD: I'd like to develop my skills and do more staff training.
MR: Do you have any questions for me?
AD: Yes, I do. What training opportunities are there with this job?
MR: Well, we have an excellent management training programme. We'll train you in all our products and processes. We'll also provide on-the-job training.
AD: Sounds great! Another question I want to ask is about ...

Audioscripts

1.01 S = Susan D = David
S: Hi, David.
D: Oh hi, Susan. How are things?
S: I'm fine, thanks, but we need to change the date of the new project planning meeting, sorry. Are you available on Friday the 29th, in the morning?
D: Sorry, no, I'm not. I have a presentation on Friday morning until eleven. Let me check my calendar after eleven. Er … then I have a phone call with the Berlin office at noon, for an hour. I'm available in the afternoon. How about Friday afternoon?
S: Sorry, I'm afraid I'm busy then. I meet clients on Friday afternoon from two o'clock. Er … wait. How about lunchtime on Friday?
D: Friday lunchtime is good. I'm available. Er … what time, exactly?
S: I usually have lunch at one o'clock. How about then?
D: Sounds good. Shall we meet in your office?
S: Yes, that's fine. Then we can go to lunch for about an hour.
D: OK, so new project planning meeting at one o'clock on Friday the 29th. See you then.
S: Thanks. See you then.

1.02
1 We need to change the date of the new project planning meeting.
2 Are you available on Friday 29th, in the morning?
3 How about Friday afternoon?
4 Sorry, I'm afraid I'm busy then.
5 Friday lunchtime is good. Shall we meet in your office?
6 I usually have lunch at 1 o'clock. How about then?
7 Yes, that's fine. Then we can go to lunch for about an hour.
8 See you then.

2.01 L = Laura I = Igor
L: Eco Boxes. Laura speaking. How can I help you?
I: Hello, my name is Igor Mazur. I'm calling from Polka Café.
L: Sorry, can you spell your surname for me, please?
I: Yes, it's M-A-Z-U-R. It's pronounced 'Mazur'.
L: And the name of the café?
I: It's Polka. That's P-O-L-K-A.
L: Thank you, Mr Mazur. Can I have your CRN?
I: Erm, what is my CRN?
L: It's your customer reference number.
I: Ah, yes, it's 19-00-01-36-78.
L: Thank you. How can I help you?
I: I'd like to order some of your new takeaway boxes but I can't see the prices in the online catalogue.
L: I see. Do you have the product reference numbers?
I: Yes, I have them here – TGB01, TGB02 and TGB03. How much are the three boxes?
L: The TGB01 costs £2.50 for twenty-five boxes. The TGB02 costs £3 for twenty boxes and the TGB03 costs £2 for ten.
I: So that's £2.50 for the small ones, £3 for medium and £2 for the large size.
L: Yes, that's right.
I: What are the two colours?
L: Natural and white.
I: And how much does delivery cost?
L: It's free delivery for orders over £100. How many boxes do you need?
I: 400 of the white TGB01 boxes and 500 of the natural TGB02 boxes. Can you deliver by Monday 26th?
L: I'm very sorry, we can't. We don't have any white boxes in stock. But we can send the natural ones by Monday.
I: OK, I'd like to order those now, please.
L: Certainly, I'll put your order on the system.
I: How much is that in total?
L: The total cost is £115 including tax. Delivery is free of charge for this order. Can I help you with anything else?
I: No, that's fine. Thank you for your help. Goodbye.
L: You're welcome. Goodbye.

2.02
1 Eco Boxes. Laura speaking. How can I help you?
2 I'd like to order some of your new takeaway boxes.
3 Do you have the product reference numbers?
4 How much are the three boxes?
5 How much does delivery cost?
6 How many boxes do you need?
7 Can you deliver by Monday 26th?
8 I'm very sorry, we can't. We don't have any in stock.
9 Certainly, I'll put your order on the system.
10 How much is that in total?

2.03
1
A: Is there any photocopy paper in the office?
B: Yes, there's some pink A4 paper. Here you are.
A: No, I need white paper. Is there any white paper?
B: Sorry! No, there isn't. I'll order some now.
2
C: Three new employees start work today. Are there any desks and computer chairs for them?
D: Yes, there's some new furniture in the warehouse.
C: Is there any office equipment for them?
D: No, there isn't. What exactly do they need?
C: Three phones, three computers and a printer.

3.01 A = Andrew C = Claudia
A: OK, Claudia. So, the first item on today's meeting agenda is the office move. Do you have the plans for the office move next Thursday?
C: Yes, I do. Finally!
A: Oh, that's great! The ten new employees we hired, well, they all start on Monday. And this office is really small. We definitely need new, bigger offices …
C: We do! And I think the new location is great for us. There are lots of good restaurants nearby, and the new office has much better facilities.
A: Oh, that's good to know as well! Anyway, I need to write to all staff before I leave work later. So, what's the plan?
C: OK. Well on Thursday, I need everyone in the office by 9.00 a.m.
A: OK, no problem.
C: They need to put all their desk items in boxes. And these boxes need to stay in the office on Thursday.
A: Right …
C: At 12.30, you can send staff home. We don't want any staff in the office after 12.30.
A: So, there's no work on Thursday afternoon?
C: No. There's no space. And no work on Friday morning either.
A: Really? OK. That's great for them!
C: Yes, it is! OK, so on Friday, please ask them to arrive at 1.00 p.m. When they arrive, they need to find a desk with their name on it and their personal desk items.
A: OK …
C: And these desks are permanent. Please tell staff that they can't change desks.
A: Of course, no problem.
C: So, the only thing after that is the office party to celebrate!
A: OK. So, what are the plans for that?
C: Well, I arranged for food and drinks to arrive at the new office for 6.00 p.m. The party can start then!
A: That sounds great! I'm looking forward to it.

4.01 B = Bea D = Dom
B: Dom, I booked a flight for your trip to Japan, on Japan Airlines.
D: Thanks, Bea. What about my hotel?
B: I need to book a hotel room for you tomorrow.
D: Am I going by plane from Osaka to Tokyo?
B: No, you aren't flying. You're going by train. It's only two-and-half hours by train – the trains are very fast in Japan.
D: Where am I staying? For a two-week visit, I usually rent an apartment.
B: Yes, that's what we're doing. It isn't big, but it's very comfortable. And it's near the office.
D: OK. Where am I meeting customers?
B: In the office. There's a meeting room there.

4.02 P = Pietro B = Barbara
P: When are you flying to Munich?
B: I'm flying on Monday.
P: Is Claudia meeting you at the airport on Monday?
B: No, she isn't. She's meeting me at the hotel on Tuesday morning. We're visiting the factory in the afternoon.
P: Are the area managers visiting the factory with you?
B: Yes, they are.
P: And when are you travelling to Augsburg?
B: On Wednesday morning. I'm going by train.

4.03
1
This is an announcement for passengers on flight AI663 to Rome. The flight is delayed due to technical problems. We currently expect a delay of about one hour. Passengers, please wait for more announcements.
2
This is a customer announcement for passengers on platform ten. We are sorry to announce that the 10.15 service to Paris is cancelled. This is due to bad weather. We apologise to all customers travelling on the 10.15 service to Paris.
3
We're sorry to announce that the 12.25 service to Leeds on platform seven is delayed by approximately thirty minutes due to a problem with the train. Please listen for more announcements. We are sorry for the delay to your journey.
4
We are sorry to announce that flight EY825 to New York JFK is cancelled tonight. All passengers please go to the customer service desk for more information. We apologise for the cancellation of flight EY825 to New York JFK.
5
This is a gate change announcement for passengers. Flight CA2424 to Abu Dhabi is now departing at gate ten. All passengers currently at gate seven for flight CA2424 to Abu Dhabi, please go to gate ten.
6
This is a platform change announcement. The 12.16 service to Brussels is now departing from platform nine. That's platform nine for the 12.16 service to Brussels.
7
Attention departing passengers. The airport is very busy today. Please allow forty-five minutes to go through security. Thank you.
8
All arriving passengers, please follow the signs for passport control. Passengers with connecting flights, please follow the signs for flight connections. For more information, visit the airline information desks.

4.04
1
Attention departing passengers. The airport is very busy today. Please allow forty-five minutes to go through security. Thank you.
2
This is a customer announcement for passengers on platform ten. We are sorry to announce that the 10.15 service to Paris is cancelled. This is due to bad weather. We apologise to all customers travelling on the 10.15 service to Paris.
3
We are sorry to announce that flight EY825 to New York JFK is cancelled tonight. All passengers please go to the customer service desk for more information. We apologise for the cancellation of flight EY825 to New York JFK.

Audioscripts

4
We're sorry to announce that the 12.25 service to Leeds on platform seven is delayed by approximately thirty minutes due to a problem with the train. Please listen for more announcements. We are sorry for the delay to your journey.

4.05
1
This is an announcement for passengers on flight AI663 to Rome. The flight is delayed due to technical problems. We currently expect a delay of about one hour. Passengers please wait for more announcements.
2
This is a gate change announcement for passengers. Flight CA2424 to Abu Dhabi is now departing at gate ten. All passengers currently at gate seven for flight CA2424 to Abu Dhabi, please go to gate ten.

4.06
We are sorry to announce that flight EX499 to Tokyo is cancelled tonight due to bad weather. All passengers please go to the customer service desk for more information. We apologise for the cancellation of flight EX499 to Tokyo.

4.07
We're very sorry about the cancellation. We're putting you on the next flight to Tokyo. You're arriving in Tokyo at 12 o'clock midday tomorrow – that's Tuesday. And we're booking a hotel room for you tonight.

4.08 A = Alex K = Karl
1
A: Hello? Karl? I can't hear you. Karl, are you there? I can't hear you. The connection isn't very good. OK, I'll try …
K: I don't think the connection is very good. But I can hear you.
A: I still can't hear you. Try …
2
K: Hello? Er … can you hear me?
A: Hi, Karl. Yes, I can. That's better. Can you hear me?
K: Yes, I can. But the screen's frozen. Now I can't see you!
A: Oh, no!
K: My internet connection is slow. Sorry.
A: OK, try …

5.01 F = Finley H = Hinata
F: Good morning, Wallace Hotel. This is Finlay speaking. How can I help you?
H: Hello, can I speak to Mary Duffy, the Conference Centre Manager?
F: I'm sorry, she's not available right now. She's in a meeting at the moment. Can I take a message?
H: Yes, can you tell her Hinata Nakamura phoned about our conference next month, on the 25th and 26th January?
F: Yes, certainly. Can you spell your name for me, please?
H: Sure, it's Hinata, that's H-I-N-A-T-A. And my surname is N-A-K-A-M-U-R-A.
F: Thank you, Ms Nakamura. And it's about the conference next month?
H: Yes, that's right.
F: And what's the company name?
H: It's Dallas Corporation Europe.
F: Sorry, could you say that again, please?
H: Dallas Corporation. That's D-A-L-L-A-S.
F: OK, thank you. And can I have your phone number?
H: Yes, my number is 0044 3584 751 059.
F: So, that's 0044 3584 751 059. I'll give her your message, Ms Nakamura.
H: Thank you very much.
F: Have a nice day!
H: You too. Goodbye.

5.02
1 How can I help you?
2 I'm sorry, she's not available right now.
3 Can I take a message?
4 Yes, can you tell her Hinata Nakamura phoned?
5 Can you spell your name for me, please?
6 And it's about the conference next month?
7 Sorry, could you say that again, please?
8 OK, thank you. And can I have your phone number?
9 So, that's 0044 3584 751 059.
10 I'll give her your message.

5.03 M = Mary H = Hinata
M: Hello, Ms Nakamura?
H: Yes.
M: This is Mary Duffy, the Conference Centre Manager at Wallace Hotel. I'm sorry, I was in a meeting when you called earlier today.
H: Hello, Mrs Duffy. Thank you for calling me back. I just wanted to talk about next month.
M: Yes, of course. The conference on the 25th and 26th January. Now, how many participants are there going to be?
H: About 120 to 130.
M: And how many guests are going to stay at the hotel on the nights of the 25th and 26th?
H: Between forty-eight and fifty-five. I don't have the exact number, but I will confirm on Friday.
M: Thank you. Can you send me the list of participants and the names of the hotel guests on Friday?
H: Certainly. I'll send all the details by email on Friday morning. Does the conference room have a data projector, screen and sound system?
M: Yes, all the equipment you need is in the room.
H: Are we going to have some help with the equipment?
M: Yes, there´ll be an assistant from our team in the room with you. Don't worry, I'm sure she'll help you.
H: Oh good. You see, it's the first time I'm organising this event and I want everything to be perfect.
M: I understand. We will do our very best for you. What time do you want to have the breaks and lunch?
H: Well, we're going to start at nine. So, let's see … I think we'll have a break at 11 for tea and coffee. Then the buffet lunch at 1 p.m. and then another break at about 3.30.
M: OK, now there´s going to be another big event at the conference centre that day. I'll just check that the break times are different … . Yes, that's fine.
H: Thank you! And I won't forget to send the list of names and final numbers on Friday morning.
M: Bye for now, Ms Nakamura. I look forward to hearing from you.

5.04
1 Would you like to join us for dinner?
2 Do you want to see the factory?
3 Thank you very much. That would be nice.
4 Thanks! I'd love to.
5 I would like to join you, but I have a meeting.
6 Thanks for the invitation, but I'm not free today.
7 I'm very sorry, but I'm not available today.
8 Do you want to join us for coffee?

6.01
1 Gas and electricity are two common types of energy.
2 The air in this city is full of pollution.
3 Many people are buying electric cars today.
4 The land, water and air that people, animals and plants live in is the environment.
5 All machines need to use power, usually electricity.
6 Digital technology is changing how we live and work.
7 We recycle paper in our office. It's good for the environment.
8 There is a lot of plastic in the sea and it's bad for marine life.

6.02 M = Marek C = Customer
M: Customer Service, Marek speaking. How can I help you?
C: Good morning. I'm calling from Patterson's Limited. There's a problem with the laptops you delivered yesterday. You sent the wrong model.
M: I'm sorry to hear that. Can I have your order number, please?
C: Yes, it's FT90087.
M: That's FT90087. I see you ordered fourteen of the CR673 laptops.
C: Yes, that's right, but we received the wrong model. These are the CR653 model.
M: I'm very sorry about the mistake. We'll change those for you. OK, can I just check your delivery address?
C: Yes, it's our office near Manchester airport. That's Patterson's Limited, 13 Northport Road, Manchester M19 5LH. When will you deliver them?
M: It might take three to four days.
C: Oh no! We need them as soon as possible. We have a lot of work here.
M: I understand this is important for you.
C: Is there anything you can do about it?
M: I don't know. I'll talk to my manager. One moment, please. OK. I can send them express delivery. They'll arrive within two days. You can return the other computers to the delivery driver.
C: Thank you!
M: Can I help you with anything else?
C: No, thank you for your help.
M: You're very welcome. Goodbye.

7.01 M = Misako K = Karim
M: What do you think of your new laptop, Karim?
K: I don't know. It's not as fast as I expected. It's got a larger memory than my old one, but it feels slower. It's got a really good battery, though, and it's really light. I can carry it anywhere.
M: I know. It's so light! But for me, the main thing is the battery – it lasts for a really long time. I know what you mean about the memory. It takes a long time to open some video files. I don't think it's that large.
K: You're right, Misako. And I don't know about the security software. Waiwex says it has more advanced security software and should be more secure than older models, but I got a virus in the first week of using it.
M: Really? I think it's much more secure than my old one. It was probably your fault, Karim.
K: Well, only two years until the company gives us new ones again!

7.02 E = Ellie T = Tom
E: Hi, Tom. Thanks for your email on the recruitment companies.
T: No problem. So which agency do we want to use? We're recruiting for two jobs at the Manchester office and one in London.
E: I'm not sure. All Recruit has a London office, and Jones doesn't. Is that a problem?
T: I don't think so, Jones is bigger. And they have offices near London.
E: Yes, that's true. But I can see that All Recruit offers a six-month guarantee on candidates.
T: Yes, that means, if the candidate leaves the company in the first six months, All Recruit will not charge us any fees. Jones only offers a three-month guarantee.
E: Right, and it says here All Recruit do background checks on candidates as well – does that mean a check on job history and their use of social media, that kind of thing?
T: That's correct, although Jones can also do that.
E: Ah, Yes, I can see that. But All Recruit also searches for candidates on professional networking sites …
T: … Yes, that would be useful.
E: … and then do candidate interviews with their expert consultants. So they will do everything for us and probably find the right people.
T: Yes, they will. The problem might be the cost.
E: Hmm. Good point. So, All Recruit charges a fee of 10–15 percent of the candidates first-year salary.

So, that's around 3,000 on a 30,000 salary. That could be expensive, you're right.
T: Well, the alternative is Jones. They charge a fixed fee of £399 for their standard service. It includes advertising and selection of CVs, but obviously no interview for that fee. They can do background checks for an additional fee.
E: OK. Maybe we just need the agency to advertise the job, check the candidate's background and then give us a list of ten candidates. We can do the interviews. I'd like to meet the candidates anyway.
T: Yes, exactly. But first, we need to know Jones' fee for background checks. I'll phone them now.
E: Great. If Jones are cheaper then All Recruit overall, let's use them.
T: OK, that sounds good. I'll let you know what they say.

8.01 E = Elsa D = Dan
D: Hello, Elsa. I'm just phoning about your email. How did the video interviews go?
E: Very well. A few technical problems at first with the video and sound quality as usual.
D: Yes, it's always the same.
E: The good news is, I have three excellent candidates for you to meet.
D: Sounds great! Tell me about them.
E: Well, first there's Vicki Grant. My impression of Vicki is she's very friendly and has good communication skills. She has all the essential skills, with three years' experience in sales and she manages a team of twelve staff.
D: Does she work in the chemical industry?
E: No, but she works in a related industry – pharmaceuticals. And she has a chemistry degree.
D: A chemistry degree! That's a useful qualification for the job.
E: Yes, I know. She doesn't speak German, but she's studied French and speaks it well and says she's happy to study German.
D: That's good to know.
E: Next there's Sam Gowan. My impression of Sam is he knows a lot about our company and products and he has good language skills. He also has three years' experience in sales and manages a team of eight staff.
D: Where does he work?
E: For a smaller company in our industry called, Centrin. Have you ever heard of them?
D: No, I haven't.
E: He has a business degree. He's worked in Germany and he says his German is excellent.
D: Ah, that's interesting. We work a lot with Germany.

E: And finally, the third candidate. His name's Isaac Lange. My impression is he's a good team worker and he has a friendly personality. He plays in a football team at weekends, so you have something in common.
D: Yes, we do!
E: He has more experience than Vicki and Sam – five years in sales – and he manages a bigger team of staff – twenty people. He works for a paint manufacturer, so it's a related industry. He's travelled a lot in Europe for work but says his German is basic. No university qualification.
D: That's no problem, it isn't essential for the job. The right experience and personality is more important to me.
E: Yes, I agree.
D: Well done, Elsa! It'll be difficult to choose the candidate. Can you contact them and arrange the interviews for next week? Tuesday morning is the best time for me.
E: Yes, OK. I'll do that, and I'll send you their full curriculums.
D: Thanks, I'd like to read them. And can you do the interviews with me? Two heads are better than one.
E: Certainly! I'll email you the details. Bye for now.
D: Cheers. Bye!

P1.05
/s/
assistants   makes   starts   tasks
/z/
answers   emails   phones   travels
/ɪz/
addresses   misses   spaces   watches

P2.09
1 I have cheese sandwiches for lunch.
2 This is the agenda for the March conference.
3 We have ten regional centres in China.
4 Each budget meeting is difficult.
5 Digital projects are never cheap.

P3.09
1 I have an urgent report to write for Thursday.
2 Complete a short survey about your last purchase.
3 I bought this purse from an online store.
4 She does research and calls clients every morning.
5 Do you prefer to walk to work?
6 Furniture is one of their most important exports.

P4.06
1 Things are going well and the business is growing.
2 I don't think the advertising is winning new clients.
3 They're emptying the bins and cleaning during the break.
4 There's no black ink in it so it's printing in blue and pink.
5 We're booking our spring holidays this evening.
6 The link isn't working because you're putting in the wrong PIN.

P5.10
1 We would both like to thank you for the invitation.
2 I have other plans for Thursday, the tenth.
3 Are there any delivery charges within the EU?
4 Because of the weather most flights are cancelled this morning.
5 We have more than three thousand customers in the north.
6 The Smith brothers opened that clothes shop in 1935.

P6.08
1 No chemicals are used to produce fruit here.
2 Our popular T-shirts always look cool on you.
3 This shampoo isn't sold through supermarkets.
4 The good news is that we'll move to a bigger room soon.
5 Ask the woman at the reception to make a booking for two nights.
6 We might lose sales in the future due to the distribution problems.

P7.04
1 Video files open slowly on this computer.
2 How long does the mobile site of the hotel take to load?
3 They sold the house at a discount of ten thousand pounds.
4 There's no progress without a good plan.
5 We chose new posters and brochures for the show.
6 The sound quality is so low that you can't understand announcements.

P8.06
1 She was very calm at the interview.
2 He knew a lot about our company.
3 Can we talk about your experience?
4 I didn't get the right answer.
5 You have the wrong information.
6 It took several hours to interview everyone.

Pearson Education Limited
KAO Two, KAO Park, Hockham way,
Harlow, Essex, CM17 9SR, England
and Associated Companies throughout the world

www.english.com/businesspartner

Business Partner A2 Teacher's Resource Book with MyEnglishLab
© Pearson Education Limited 2020

All rights reserved; no part of this publication may be reproduced, stored in a retrieval system, or transmitted in any form or by any means, electronic, mechanical, photocopying, recording, or otherwise without the prior written permission of the Publishers.

Photocopying: The Publisher grants permission for the photocopying of those pages marked 'photocopiable' according to the following conditions. Individual purchasers may make copies for their own use or for use by the classes they teach. Institutional purchasers may make copies for use by their staff and students, but this permission does not extend to additional institutions or branches. Under no circumstances may any part of this book be photocopied for resale.

First published 2020
Fifth impression 2023

ISBN: 978-1-292-23716-9
Set in Burlingame Pro
Printed by CPI Group (UK) Ltd, Croydon CR0 4YY

We are grateful to the following for permission to reproduce copyright material:

Illustrations
Ben Hasler (nb Illustration) 118, 120; Designers Collective all charts and graphs.

All other images © Pearson Education

Every effort has been made to trace the copyright holders and we apologise in advance for any unintentional omissions. We would be pleased to insert the appropriate acknowledgement in any subsequent edition of this publication.